The Boykin Spaniel

Boykin Spaniel, by wildlife artist Prescott "Sonny" Baines, painted in 1978 and released in 1981 as limited-edition print. By permission of Prescott S. Baines, Lexington, South Carolina

The
Boykin Spaniel

South Carolina's Dog

Revised edition

MIKE CREEL AND LYNN KELLEY

The University of South Carolina Press

First edition published by Summerhouse Press, 1997
Revised edition published by the University of South Carolina Press
Columbia, South Carolina 29208

www.sc.edu/uscpress

Manufactured in the United States of America

18 17 16 15 14 13 12 11 10 09
10 9 8 7 6 5 4 3 2 1

Library of Congress Cataloging-in-Publication Data
Creel, Mike.
 The Boykin Spaniel : South Carolina's dog / Mike Creel and Lynn Kelley. — Rev. ed.
  p. cm.
 First published: Columbia, SC : Summerhouse Press, c1997.
 Includes bibliographical references and index.
 ISBN 978-1-57003-860-0 (cloth : alk. paper) — ISBN 978-1-57003-861-7
 (pbk : alk. paper)
 1. Boykin spaniel. 2. Boykin spaniel—History--South Carolina. 3. State dogs—South
Carolina. I. Kelley, Lynn, 1943– II. Title.
 SF429.S7C74 2009
 636.752'4—dc22
                                        2009034437

Appendix 1: "The Boykin Spaniel Society Breed Standard." © 1996, 1997, 1998, 2004 the
Boykin Spaniel Society Board of Directors. Reprinted with permission
Appendix 2: "The Boykin Spaniel Society Code of Ethics." © the Boykin Spaniel Society
Board of Directors. Reprinted with permission
Appendix 3: "Grooming Your Boykin Spaniel: Boykin Spaniel Society Guidelines." © 1996,
1997, 1998, 2004 the Boykin Spaniel Society Board of Directors. Reprinted with permission
Appendix 4: "Choosing A Breeder: Boykin Spaniel Society Guidelines." © 1996, 1997, 1998,
2004 the Boykin Spaniel Society Board of Directors. Reprinted with permission

To Dena Crosby Creel and Barbara Spragens Kelley, our wives, who encouraged us and gave us the time to pursue this project, and to Sarah Creel, Allen Creel, Laura Smallwood Kelley, and Allison Kelley Croxton, the best of children and wonderful young adults, and to grandchildren, who bring joy to Poppa

Our love and thanks to them all

CONTENTS

ILLUSTRATIONS

PREFACE

This first University of South Carolina Press edition of *The Boykin Spaniel: South Carolina's Dog* is a revised and updated version of the book of the same name that was first published in 1997. The two authors came to writing about Boykin spaniels from different perspectives and very different sets of experiences.

Until his retirement Mike Creel, a native South Carolinian, devoted his career as a professional writer and photographer to focusing on the environment, hunting, fishing, and wildlife of South Carolina. A graduate of the University of South Carolina with a major in journalism, he began his career as an outdoor writer for the *Columbia Record* newspaper and later served on the staff of the South Carolina Department of Natural Resources. In 1974 he became fascinated with the slowly disappearing breed known as the Boykin spaniel and wrote a definitive article for *South Carolina Wildlife*—"The Spaniels of Boykin" (September–October 1975)—that helped to change the development of the breed. Before the second generation of Boykin spaniel breeders passed into history, as the first already had done, Mike set for himself the goal of documenting the Boykin spaniel's past. His search for understanding the breed's history led him and his family to become owners of two beloved Boykin spaniels.

On New Year's Day in 1975, newlyweds Mike and Dena Creel drove to a farm in Wedgefield, South Carolina, where they met and fell in love with the first of their two Boykin spaniels. Their newly adopted three-month-old pup, Booger, later became the great-great-grandsire of a champion Boykin spaniel, Dixie Blair.

Booger, a good problem solver and a fun dog, inspired Mike to travel all over South Carolina and to write or call every known Boykin spaniel owner in the continental United States while researching for a twenty-eight-page article about the breed's history, present, and—at the time shaky—future. A good watchdog, Booger expressed his love for the family in many ways. Even though it was against family rules, Booger sometimes crawled quietly into the Creels' bed on a cold night and stretched into a sausage shape. On being discovered, he adopted a faraway look that said, "You can't see me. I'm not here."

When Booger died, he was succeeded by Governor Riley—named after perhaps the most revered of modern South Carolina governors, Richard Riley. Riley, as the dog was normally called, had a short life ended by an automobile accident. But his life was packed with devotion to the family and exciting things such as learning to pick and eat rabbit-eye blueberries and scuppernong grapes. He loved the Creels' cats, often curling up beside a self-adopted black stray named Silky. Mike will never forget the big snow when the family sledded down a driveway on cafeteria trays. Once Riley tried it, sledding became a one-child, one-dog proposition.

In 1991 Lynn Kelley and his family, including a beloved Airedale named Benji, settled in South Carolina. Benji's unexpected death on Friday, December 13, of that year put the family in mourning. Their longing for another dog peaked just after New Year's Day, when Barbara Kelley spotted an ad for a Boykin spaniel. Curious, Lynn called the breeder and found that one puppy was left. When he asked what a Boykin spaniel was, the response from the breeder was, "Mister, you must not be from around these parts!"

After the breeder had extolled the breed to Kelley—including the fact that a Boykin would even ride on the back of a motorcycle—the entire family decided it was worth a ride to the Batesburg-Leesville countryside to see the puppy. On their arrival at the farm, they were greeted by the pup's parents and the puppy himself. The pup came directly to Lynn and looked up at him with big golden eyes that begged for attention. Lynn picked up the pup and looked at Barbara, who said with a smile, "I'm already writing the check." On the way home, the puppy went from lap to lap of the two Kelley daughters, licking fingers, curling up for a snooze, and being petted. By the time the family had arrived home, the newly named Lord Berkeley was surrounded by a court of obedient vassals.

The Kelleys' enjoyment of their new puppy led Lynn on a search for articles and books about the breed. One of his neighbors—a Camden native who was almost daily besieged with Boykin questions from Lynn—finally said, "Why don't you just write a book on Boykin spaniels if you can't find one?" Lynn laughed, but the seed had been sown. About four weeks later, during the spring arts festival in Columbia known as Artista Vista, Kelley's asking a local publisher if she had any books on the breed led her—after listening to him talk about the Boykin spaniel for several minutes—to offer him a contract to write a book on the breed. Beginning to research the topic with new interest, Kelley found a number of references to Mike Creel and got in touch with him. Their conversation about Boykin spaniels—as well as Mike's long years of involvement with the breed and Lynn's enthusiasm for it—led to their decision to coauthor the first edition of this book. Twelve years later, interest in this wonderful dog has remained high and has led to this revised and updated edition.

In this University of South Carolina edition of the book we have retained most of the information from the first edition while adding fresh, contemporary updates on what has occurred in the past twelve years. In that effort we have included new stories of hearth and hunt, new records of championships and honors, and new illustrations to try to communicate something of the inimitable manners and mysteries of this friendly and hardworking dog. Above all we have sought to celebrate the spirit of South Carolina's historical best, which this homegrown canine breed and the Boykin family itself have long exemplified.

The Boykin spaniel is possibly the only hunting dog that a mother's love cannot spoil. Beginning its career about one hundred years ago flushing wild turkeys from the Wateree Swamp, the Boykin continues to capture human hearts and the hunter's quarry today, not only in South Carolina but also in all other parts of the country. The Boykin spaniel is a dog for all seasons—a trick artist, a crackerjack retriever, and a family favorite—serving double duty in many homes as a Saturday afternoon retriever and a beloved family pet.

ACKNOWLEDGMENTS

Writing a book is rewarding, but it involves work and time that might well have been used for other, more pressing things. This edition of *The Boykin Spaniel: South Carolina's Dog* is no exception. The first edition of this book, published in 1997, was popular in the marketplace. The need for some changes in the book became clear shortly after that edition was published. A new edition became even more desirable after a decade of new developments.

This edition could not have come about without the cooperation and participation of many people. We extend our thanks for the help provided by so many thoughtful and kind members of the extended Boykin family, to many past members of the Boykin Spaniel Society board of directors, and to individual Boykin enthusiasts. In addition we thank the current board of the Boykin Spaniel Society, the current executive secretary of the society, Jane Sexton, and office assistant Phyllis Kelly for reviewing previous work and assembling new information to be included in the book.

A belated debt of gratitude is owed to those now past—Sarah Boykin Holmes, "Wrennie" Boykin Alexander, "Duck" Boykin, L. W. "Whit" Boykin II, and others—whose conversations more than thirty years ago provided a last link with those early hunting days. Two people who helped in special ways were the late J. Bernard Scott of Ponte Vedra Beach, Florida, whose father, a Baltimore banker, hunted with the Boykins on the Wateree, and the late Thomas A. Moore of Spartanburg, South Carolina, who hunted with Alec White, knew his grandson well, and corrected the much-circulated church story to the proper denomination.

To bring out a new edition of book takes a great coordination of efforts among parties. This is perhaps especially true when publishers change. For this reason we are particularly thankful to have had the advice of Director Curtis Clark, Assistant Director for Operations Linda Fogle, Project Editor Karen Rood, Assistant Director for Sales and Marketing Jonathan

Haupt, Design and Production Manager Pat Callahan, and Acquisitions Editor Alexander Moore at the University of South Carolina Press. We are also grateful to Debbie Bloom, local history manager at the Richland County Public Library, Susan Thoms, Spartanburg County Public Library, and Brad Steinecke, Spartanburg County Historical Society. Their patience and faith in this book as a history of an enduring part of South Carolina's cultural history and folk heritage sustained us through the process of text revision and helped us produce a work that reflects the spirit of the dog that is the chief reason for this book.

1

Origins and History

I have heard much discussion and read a great many books from people
who concern themselves with the art of civil courtesy. If they knew Camden,
they would know something not very far from the ideal exists.

William F. Buckley Jr. (1925–2008)

This book is about canines—the species *Canis lupus familiaris,* domestic
dog—and specifically about that breed now known as the Boykin spaniel.
The story of this little brown dog has been linked to humans since its
unexplained appearance outside a church in Spartanburg, South Carolina. From that point onward, people have recognized the little brown
spaniel's exceptional field ability, its problem-solving personality, and its
affection for people.

A Boykin spaniel is unmistakable, if a person knows what to look
for. It is a little dog with a spaniel's floppy ears and a liver-brown coat,
often with sun-bleached reddish fringes. The coat may vary from kinky to
straight, and eye color may range from dark brown to copper to bright
yellow. Docked tails are a breed standard. Even more distinctive is this
spaniel's master-winning personality. Adapting so well to the needs of
different family members, the Boykin spaniel becomes everybody's favorite pet.

In large part the history of this breed is a history of the human owners
and breeders who, since the dog's appearance among them, have realized
they have been graced with something special in their lives—a hunting dog
that the warmth of the home fires will not spoil, a hard-charging retriever
that curls up on the couch, and a trick artist that seems to teach itself.

"Boykin" is the surname of one of South Carolina's oldest and most
widespread families. It is also the name of a small settlement on a mill
pond between Camden and Sumter in the state's Midlands region. And
"Boykin" is the name given to an increasing number of aristocratic, but
spirited, little brown dogs that are gaining fame and growing in numbers

across America, far beyond the breed's original realm, where it has been "knighted" as the official dog of the state of South Carolina.

The Wateree Created a Reason for Boykin Spaniels

Throughout history water has played a central role in the stories of humankind and the animal kingdom in general. The great Wateree River, which flows through the Midlands of South Carolina, created a primeval environment lush with fish, game, and forests—a lure to hunters and a haven for the hunted. In the early 1900s sportsmen such as the extended Boykin family and their friends in the Camden area sought constantly to improve their access to the waterway, their hunting methods, and their hunting success. Dogs gave hunting parties a needed edge in hunting ducks and geese in this watery environment. These conditions set the stage for discovery of the Boykin spaniel's progenitor and spurred development of the breed.

Hunting parties with dogs grew out of Camden society as naturally as the cypress and tupelo trees had emerged from the surrounding swamps. Since colonial times the hunt has been an institution in South Carolina. Camden, the oldest interior city of the Carolina colony—and to many the most gracious—was and remains the heart of Carolina hunt country. The hunt was a noble way for some young gentlemen to supplement the family's fare; for others it was just pure sport.

Like all South Carolina, the Camden area experienced an economic catastrophe after the end of the Civil War, which continued until the coming of well-heeled Yankees as seasonal tourists. Eager for mild winters in a place where they could spend their newly earned industrial dollars, northerners came in increasing numbers from the 1870s through the 1940s. This winter migration ushered in an era of great Camden hotels, where whole families stayed for weeks at a time. While the women shopped and took care of the children, the husbands engaged in commercially arranged hunts along the Wateree. The local planter class included families with names such as Boykin, Cantey, and Chesnut, who established a mannerly ambience that charmed the northern vacationers, making them want to establish their winter homes in Camden. The Buckleys of New York were among this group of northern families who wintered in the Camden area.

In the early 1900s wagons and wooden boats—not the four-by-fours sportsmen use today—afforded hunters access to rugged river landings along the game-rich corridor of the Wateree River, a slow-moving stream with high banks that wends its way through the rich farmlands of Kershaw County and beyond. Boat travel limited what hunters could carry. Carrying the typical heavyweight retriever—primarily a Chesapeake then—was awkward in a craft loaded with men, guns, provisions, and other gear, particularly if that dog had to jump into the water and reboard the boat with a downed duck.

Hunters along the Wateree at that time sought an able dog that would not "rock the boat" and could handle all the work in the water as well as flushing turkeys and retrieving and tracking a variety of game on land. L. W. "Whit" Boykin, his kinsmen, and his friends were involved in that search for a dog that would be perfect for hunting on the Wateree.

The Forerunner of the Boykin Spaniel

The much-circulated story of where the first Boykin spaniel came from is simple. In the early 1900s a little stray dog—a spaniel of some type—was found along East Main Street in downtown Spartanburg, South Carolina, by Mr. A. L. White during a brief Sunday walk between his home and church. He took the dog home as a pet, and it apparently displayed some aptitude that he considered useful in hunting. Mr. White decided to send the dog by train to his good friend Whit Boykin, who lived near Camden. Boykin had long sought a smaller retriever to carry in a boat for duck hunting. As Boykin applied his training know-how, the little stray soon developed into a superb waterfowl retriever and turkey dog. This dog is said to have been a male and the forerunner of all Boykin spaniels in existence today.

Until Mike Creel began his research in 1974 for an article that appeared in the September–October 1975 issue of *South Carolina Wildlife* magazine, authentication of the Boykin spaniel foundation story and details about it were lacking. Creel sought to fill this void by uncovering every written record available. He studied the lives of the two men involved, interviewing their relatives, friends, and contemporaries. He was also able to locate and assemble related photographs from the period. In the process the story developed verifiable substance as a few people were able to remember the first dog's name and to establish the relationship between White and Boykin.

Whit Boykin and Alec White

Known to friends and kin as "Mr. Whit," Lemuel Whitaker Boykin, was the son of military hero Alexander Hamilton Boykin and Sarah Jones deSaussure. Grandson of the first Boykin to come to the Wateree River area, Whit farmed Pine Grove Plantation, which had been cut from the original land grant and had been tilled by Boykins since the 1700s. Born on November 26, 1861, at Plane Hill, ten miles from Camden, Whit came into his majority in the early 1880s and became a land appraiser and

Lemuel Whitaker "Whit" Boykin Sr., founder of the Boykin spaniel breed.
Photographic copy by James A. Monarch, courtesy of the Boykin family

farmer in Kershaw and Sumter counties. As many Camden families did during the time when Whit was growing up, the Boykins vacationed in cooler parts of the state during the sweltering summer months.

Whit Boykin's youngest daughter, Ellen Cantey "Wrennie" (Mrs. T. L. Alexander), said Alec White, whom she called "Uncle Knox," became a friend of her father's when both were young men courting the same girl, Lavolette McGowan (who later became Mrs. White). Miss McGowan and Whit Boykin had apparently known each other from the time they were teenagers because the Boykins and the Laurens County McGowans vacationed each summer at the same spot in the North Carolina mountains.

Born on March 11, 1860, Alexander Lawrence White had moved with his family in 1864 from his birthplace in Charleston to Spartanburg County. He was the son of John Thomas White and—according to *Men of the Time: Sketches of Living Notables* by J. C. Garlington (1902)—a great-grandson of one of the original settlers of South Carolina, John White. Alec, his sister, Sarah Carolyn "Carrie," and his two bachelor brothers, Thomas J. and Parker White, were raised in Spartanburg. His two brothers later resided at White's Mill, outside Spartanburg. Alec White, who entered the labor market as a railroad worker, eventually became president of Farmers and Merchants Bank at 117 Morgan Square in Spartanburg and secretary-treasurer of Peoples Building and Loan Association.

Records of the First Presbyterian Church of Spartanburg show the marriage of Alexander White to Miss Lavolette McGowan on May 20, 1885, by Rev. Thomas Hart Law. Also recorded there are the dates of the baptisms of sons Homer and Alexander in 1888 and 1890 respectively and the death of Mrs. White in June 1934.

A town about 130 miles from Camden by railroad, Spartanburg sits at the base of the Appalachian Mountains. The time it took to travel between Camden and Spartanburg was considerable in South Carolina's prehighway era. Yet, despite the physical distance between Whit Boykin and Alec White, their friendship persisted throughout their lives. In 1975 Whit Boykin's daughter Wrennie said that "Uncle Knox" and "Pappa Whit" wrote each other once a week and hunted together every time they got a chance. These two were united not only by friendship but also by a common commitment to preserving the game environment. Ahead of their time as hunters, they could be called game conservationists. In 1919

Alexander Lawrence "Alec" White. Photograph courtesy of
Mac White Jr., Wilmington, North Carolina

they were founders of the South Carolina Sportsmen's Association, which demanded daily limits on quail, bag limits on tom turkeys, and no shooting of hens.

Tom Moore, a Spartanburg native who had known and admired Alec White, stated in 1975 that "Mr. White was the grandest old Chesterfieldian gentleman I have ever known, a breed which has since passed from this earth. I was a teenager when I duck hunted with him in the 1930s. He always made a point of wearing his coat and tie. Even when hunting, he didn't neglect to wear one, at least a small black tie." The grandson of Alec White, Homer McGowan "Mac" White Jr., lived for a long time in Wilmington, North Carolina. Many years after his grandfather's death, Mac White remembered the first time he took his wife, Mary, to meet his grandfather: "My grandfather was sitting on the porch, but when he saw us coming, he immediately went back into the house. At first we couldn't quite figure out what happened. In a couple of minutes he was ready to greet us, of course in a clean shirt and tie."

Alec White died in 1942 at the age of eighty-two. Mac White remembered him as vital late in life: "At age eighty my grandfather could walk me into the ground when he took me hunting. He took me hunting regularly with his friends down in Boykin, and we rode the train making a

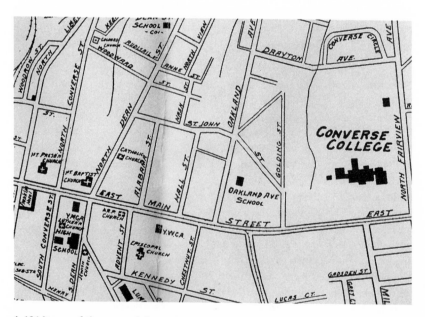

A 1914 map of the area of downtown Spartanburg where Alec White met the little brown dog he named Dumpy. Courtesy of Spartanburg County Public Library

couple of connections and taking a wagon ride before we got there. We had some outstanding goose and duck hunts in the drainage canals down there. My father, Homer, didn't go with us since he was strictly a quail hunter."

In 1997 Mac White described his grandfather's house in the center of Spartanburg; the big backyard held chicken coops for his game chickens, a glass greenhouse, and a dog pen for his Chesapeake Bay retrievers and other large dogs. The Whites and the Boykins were related distantly, recalled Mac White. "My great-aunt Rose, my grandmother's sister, married Boykin Cantey and another sister's son, Mac Holmes, married Sarah Boykin, Whit Boykin's next eldest daughter."

A Little Brown Dog

By 2008 the landmarks in downtown Spartanburg were very different from those A. L. White encountered the day he and a capable little brown dog met one another. In the early 1900s the fifteen-minute Sunday stroll along this route would have been a most pleasant outing for man or dog, as they would have been in an area of town dominated by large, white clapboard houses.*

At some point in his walk, White noticed he was being trailed by a little reddish-brown dog. He leaned over and petted the dog, which— according to some accounts—acknowledged this treatment by accompanying White all the way to the church doors. While it may seem improbable, some raconteurs would have it that the little dog waited until

---

*If someone today retraced Alec White's walk from his home to church, they would find entirely new landmarks. The walk begins on the sidewalk along the east wing of the AT&T Building at 461 East Main Street, just down from the College Inn motel at 491. In 1905 the A. L. White home place was at 459 East Main Street, but the number was changed to 481 after 1925. Converted into apartments in 1942, the Whites' Victorian home was razed in 1972. From here the walker proceeds downtown toward Morgan Square and crosses over to the north side of East Main, ending in front of Price's Store for Men at 196 North Main Street. In the period when Mr. White met the little brown dog, the third building occupied by the First Presbyterian Church of Spartanburg was located at 200 East Main Street. At the time the church was on a block of East Main by itself. Later that block was divided into three by two streets—East Dunbar and Commerce—and renumbered. The highly regarded Aug W. Smith Department Store was in business at the old church site from 1926 until 1981; today the church block is occupied by Price's Store for Men at 196 East Main Street and the Bishop Furniture Company at 174 East Main Street. The present-day First Presbyterian Church was built at 393 East Main Street in 1925.

White had entered the church and then bolted down the aisle toward him—only to be ejected by church ushers. White did enter the assembly, find his family, and take part in the church service. Whit Boykin's daughter Sarah Holmes, who exchanged visits with the Whites to see their daughter Mary and two sons, thought the walk on which the stray dog followed Alec White may have occurred in a summer between 1905 and 1910, certainly before Mrs. Holmes's mother died in 1912.

As is true of all oral histories, different spins are placed on stories by different storytellers. Where the dog went to church became over time a matter of which church the storyteller wanted him to attend. Published accounts offered several variations of the story. Even the Boykin Spaniel Society printed in an early brochure that the dog appeared at the First Methodist Church of Spartanburg. Such discrepant accounts led to considerable good-natured joshing between Methodists and Presbyterians about the dog's religious persuasion. Not to be outdone, Southern Baptists have also gotten involved in this debate. As one Southern Baptist wag put it, "Let the Methodists and the Presbyterians carry on all they want to about the religious preference of this dog, but I'm telling you that any dog in South Carolina who loves water as much as a Boykin spaniel *has* to be a Baptist."

When Alec White left the church service at First Presbyterian, he discovered the little dog was waiting for him outside, and it then proceeded to follow him home. It is thought that White may have left services a little early to get a head start home and to avoid the exiting crowd of worshippers. Maybe he also did so to check on the dog. The little brown dog became an instant favorite with his new owner, who dubbed him "Dumpy," because of his small size in relationship to the much larger Chesapeake Bay retrievers and bird dogs in White's kennel.

A Boykin on an Old Postcard?

In 2008 Mike Creel was shown a century-old photograph album that had belonged to Mrs. Reynolds Marvin Kirby-Smith from Sewanee, Tennessee, which included photographs of Spartanburg in the early 1900s. In the album was an early-twentieth-century postcard bearing a photograph of an unknown location that features a Boykin spaniel–like dog. Other photographs in the album are of traveling circuses somewhere in the South. Postcard photographs of traveling circuses appeared a lot in Spartanburg and other towns after 1907, when the technology of placing these local scenes on cards for mailing had become very popular. According to Brad Steinecke of the Spartanburg County Historical Society, Ringling Brothers Barnum and Bailey Circus appeared in Spartanburg four times

The third building of the First Presbyterian Church of Spartanburg, near which Alec White encountered Dumpy. Photograph courtesy of George D. Malone, First Presbyterian Church, Spartanburg

A Boykin spaniel–looking dog featured on vintage postcard, possibly from Spartanburg in early decades of the 1900s. Photograph courtesy of Mariah Kirby-Smith, great-granddaughter of Mrs. Reynolds Marvin Kirby-Smith

between 1908 and 1914; and Robinson's circus appeared three times from 1908 through 1910.

Although it is very unlikely that we will ever know for certain, it is entertaining to speculate that Dumpy was a circus-performing animal that wandered away from a circus parade in downtown Spartanburg—or was lured away by a female in heat—and was left to his own devices once the circus left town. Such a hypothesis might help explain why the dog eagerly sought out Mr. White's affections and why he was so easy to train. The Boykin's trainability and its tendency to be a trick artist might—just perhaps—all stem from an early relative who was a circus performer.

Dumpy's Trip to Camden

Though Alec White found Dumpy to be a quick study, willing and able to retrieve anything, he did not have the time to train him properly. While hunting with Chesapeake Bay retrievers, Dumpy so distinguished himself that Alec White decided to send the dog to "Mr. Whit" for master training. Dumpy seemed to be a good start toward the small retriever that Whit Boykin had been trying to develop for his style of boat hunting on the Wateree River. Besides, White figured that his friend would probably get more use out of this little dog than he would, since White already had several good retrievers in his kennel.

The dog was crated and placed on the train bound for Columbia, where Dumpy would have been switched to the Seaboard Line, which ran directly to Camden with a stop at the rural community of Boykin, just outside Camden. Ellen "Duck" Boykin—wife of Whit Boykin's son J. W. C. "Stew" Boykin and mother of Camden architect Henry D. Boykin—said in 1975 that Alec White sent Dumpy to Whit Boykin at the end of a duck-hunting season. She explained how White gave a train conductor explicit directions that this dog was to be delivered directly to Mr. Whit Boykin.

On Dumpy's arrival at Pine Grove Plantation in Boykin, Whit quickly began to share his Spartanburg friend's belief in the dog's extraordinary ability. Years later Whit's youngest daughter, Wrennie, recounted that Dumpy not only was viewed as a superior hunting trainee but was also the only dog in her father's kennel ever to gain house privileges.

The Search for Dumpy's Mate

The early 1900s were a time in the American sportsmanship tradition when a hunting dog's breed name was secondary to its hunting abilities as a flusher, tracker, and retriever. The critical question was not "What kind of a dog do you have?" but rather "Can that dog hunt?" Whit Boykin's delight in the dog's skill levels quite naturally led him to look for

A hunting party camped at Motley's Duck Roost on the Wateree River, February 1904, including breed founder Whit Boykin Sr. (second from left), friend and fellow hunter Edward Richardson "Toot" Sanders (center foreground), Baltimorean George Mordecai (second from right), and Baltimore banker J. Bernard "Legs" Scott (far right). Photographic copy by James A. Monarch, courtesy of the Boykin family

acceptable bitches with which Dumpy could be bred for producing even better hunting stock. Whit and his friends are said to have widely advertised for a suitable female through local church bulletins and a flier that was distributed among railroad workers. A porter found a small curly, reddish-brown dog in a small crate at the Camden railroad station and notified the Boykin family. This little bitch, whose owner apparently shipped her to Camden but never claimed her, was identified as a likely partner for Dumpy.

Whit gave her the name "Singo." This bitch and Dumpy produced at least one litter. All Boykin spaniels are said to have originated from Dumpy and Singo's first litter. Stories from Boykin family members and friends testify to the intensity of Whit's dedication to developing a line of hunting dogs from Dumpy and Singo's stock, breeding Dumpy and Singo's offspring to good hunting dogs from other breeds. Whit bred for several qualities, including small size, good temperament, strong swimming desire and ability, and a strong desire and ability to retrieve on land and in water.

Early Boykins

An April 29, 1997, letter from Donald H. Buhrmaster Jr. of Mount Pleasant offers some early evidence of the Boykin family's interest in turkey-hunting spaniels, probably no more than ten years after Dumpy's appearance in Spartanburg. Buhrmaster found a February 13, 1915, hunt record from Millbrook Plantation in Charleston County. According to this record Allen J. Boykin of Camden (an older brother of Whit Boykin) had brought his two water spaniels to trail turkeys on a hunt with J. Ross Hanahan Sr. and his two sons. Whether the dogs in this report were early Boykins cannot be confirmed, since no one is left who might confirm the tale—or the lack of tails.

In a November 11, 1975, letter, DeVore Andrews of Greenwood, South Carolina, recounted his 1918–20 prep-school days with Whit Boykin's son Stew. Andrews remembered going to Stew's family's home whenever possible to hunt and taking wagon trips to the river with "five, six or seven real pretty and smart dogs. They were not called Boykin spaniels then." Andrews described turkey drives, jump-shooting ducks, and pass-shooting geese on moonlit nights. There were also nocturnal raccoon hunts using these spaniels.

A Wateree Swamp hunting party in the mid-1920s: James Willis Cantey (with a Boykin spaniel at his feet), unidentified hunter, Bolivar D. Boykin, Deas Boykin, and Whit Boykin Sr. Photographic copy by James A. Monarch, courtesy of the Boykin family

McKee Boykin Sr. in the mid-1930s with an English setter and a bright-eyed Boykin spaniel. Photograph courtesy of McKee Boykin Jr.

Through a combination of chance and Whit Boykin's selective breeding, by the mid-1920s little brown retrievers are said to have begun showing up frequently in hunters' boats that traveled South Carolina's Wateree River. The fruits of a search for the perfect dog that began in the 1880s, the dogs were known just locally then and were called "Mr. Boykin's spaniels," "Boykin retrievers," or "those hunting spaniels from Boykin."

In a February 1975 interview, L. W. Boykin III of Yonges Island—Whit Boykin's grandson and son of Whit's eldest son, Buck—spoke of two dogs named Patty and Singo born right after World War I. In his father's opinion, he said, these two dogs were "the first with all the characteristics now considered Boykin." At least one photograph of a Boykin family hunting party during the 1920s era shows what appears to be at least one Boykin spaniel with members of the Boykin family after a hunt. In 1932, the year his grandfather Whit died, L. W. Boykin III remembered "quite a movement was made to get them registered and recognized as a dog breed." A photograph dating to the mid-1930s, shows McKee Boykin Sr. as a teenager with an English setter in his lap and a dark-haired, yellow-eyed spaniel waiting his turn to be petted on the same bench. By the early 1930s the term "Boykin spaniel" had become known well beyond South Carolina's borders, a recognition that has grown worldwide since the formation of the Boykin Spaniel Society in 1977.

A Boykin in Home Movies?

An old home movie may well contain the earliest motion-picture footage of a Boykin spaniel. Walter M. Dunlap III of Sumter, South Carolina, grandson of the dog's master, Walter Dunlap Sr., says the black-and-white film of a dog displaying a Boykin's typical crowd-pleasing antics, was taken at a 1939 family gathering by his father, Walter Dunlap Jr. The dog, named Mr. Jones, had been purchased for Walter Dunlap Sr. after his previous dog was killed by a train.

Walter Dunlap Sr. was a Rock Hill attorney who had served in the South Carolina Senate and House of Representatives. According to a July 2008 interview with his ninety-four-year-old daughter, Mrs. Dora Dunlap Gaston of Rock Hill, he carried his dog every day to his law office in a bank building in Rock Hill, South Carolina. The solid-brown spaniel was "really too large for a cocker, though we called it that."

Backtracking Boykins

Since the early 1930s Boykin enthusiasts have tried to reconstruct the little dog's origins back to that little stray mutt that Alec White befriended outside a church on Sunday morning in Spartanburg. Written records of the very earliest breeding do not exist. In fact Kitty Beard of the Boykin Spaniel Society found references to breedings going back only to the 1940s. The dog-by-dog specifics of the early era of Boykin breeding, while entertaining to explore, have been pursued many times before by people who were chronologically closer and had more resources at hand than are available today. There are, however, some interesting early histories of the Boykin spaniels, as the following stories suggest.

Early Breeding and Subsequent Myths

One look at early Boykin spaniel breeding is the result of a 1948 project by the late James L. Sweet, a former New Yorker who married a Camden woman and settled in Boykin to be a farmer for the remainder of his years. He named some dogs for dances, including Two-Step and Rhumba. (Matilda "Tillie" Sweet Boykin, the wife of Whit Boykin's grandson Baynard, is James Sweet's sister.) Through many interviews with dog owners, Sweet assembled notes on eight individual dogs going back for two to three generations. The earliest dogs in Sweet's lists were probably whelped in about 1940.

Sweet's notes were not as complete as he would have liked. His records did, however, reveal several interesting things about the dogs that were bred to early Boykin spaniels. Richard B. "Dixie" Boykin bred his dogs to a Springer spaniel owned by Mrs. Walton Furgerson. Bolivar D. Boykin owned a registered American water spaniel, which he bred to Boykin spaniels in the 1940s to counter the ill effects of too much close breeding. In at least two instances a "small, well-bred pointer bitch" became part of the Boykin spaniel family tree. The owner of this dog, however, is not recorded.

Most of those instrumental in working with Whit Boykin to assure compatible early breeding matches of the dog were gone by the time Sweet did his work. However, a few people such as Baynard Boykin recalled years later that his grandfather and father brought about a number of important crossbreedings to create the modern Boykin spaniel's genetic makeup.

Baynard remembered that his father, Deas (pronounced "Days"), took over the breeding of the Boykin spaniels to a great extent even before his grandfather Whit retired to Columbia in the mid-1920s. In Baynard's opinion at least eight breeds were selectively used to develop the Boykin spaniel. These included the American (hunting) cocker spaniel, the springer spaniel, the Brittany spaniel, the relatively rare English field spaniel, the Chesapeake Bay retriever, the English pointer, the English setter, and the American water spaniel.

Chesapeake Bay retriever blood was introduced into the lines before Boykin spaniels were ever referred to as such. The account of this cross has been passed down from generation to generation. The cross was said to have been for the purpose of enhancing the dogs' scenting and retrieving abilities and to give them stronger bone structure. Writers have often commented on the Boykin spaniel's noble head. Jeff Griffen described it in his *Hunting Dogs of America* (1964) as "spaniel-like but with something added." Many people think this trait is related to the putative Chesapeake Bay retriever crossing. The Boykin's amber eyes are ascribed by some to the Chesapeake and by others to the American water spaniel.

According to tradition, a white spot on the chest, which appears often at birth on the Boykin spaniel puppies (and can be a fault if it is too large) is probably the result of the crossbreeding with springers. Likewise white spots on puppies' feet—a breed fault not allowable for registration—are thought to result from the crosses with Brittany spaniels.

In the late 1980s, J. Marion Wooten of Orangeburg, South Carolina, completed a massive undertaking to trace the origins of the Boykin spaniel, compiling all known breeding records in chart form. While his effort was admirable, exact linkage of the earliest dogs to their breeding records has proved elusive. Some hope that somewhere there might exist a yet-to-be discovered cache of letters between Whit Boykin and Alec White that will shed light on the Boykin's early history. Boykin spaniel lore also includes reference to a "lost chart" of breeding parentage done by Mrs. George (Katherine) Herrick of Washington, D.C.

The American Water Spaniel Debate

Perhaps the most controversial issue to arise from the interest in Boykin spaniel breeding is the historical relationship between Boykin spaniels and the American water spaniel. The latter breed's recognition by the American Kennel Club (AKC) has heightened this issue's intensity and made comparisons between the two breeds more invidious. The developments

Rich Evans and his wife of New Palatine, Illinois, with their American water spaniel Sparky (left) and their Boykin spaniel Babe (right) at the April 1997 Boykin Spaniel Society field trial. Photograph by Mike Creel

of these two breeds show remarkable similarity. The Boykin spaniel's progenitor, Dumpy, may be traced through stories to around 1905–10. The American water spaniel is said "through stories" to have been used by Menominee Indians in the Fox River and other river valleys of Wisconsin during the 1840s. In fact the first known breeder of American water spaniels was Dr. F. J. Pfeifer of New London, Wisconsin, who in 1920 successfully demonstrated to an all-breed registry that these dogs were breeding true to type. In 1938 they were accepted as a breed by the Field Dog Stud Book, and in 1940 the AKC followed suit in recognizing them as an official breed.

The Internet home page for the American water spaniel characterizes the dog's temperament, coloration, and retrieving ability. Although in traits such as size and color (liver to dark chocolate) the American water spaniel appears similar to the Boykin spaniel, there are significant differences, especially in their personalities. Promoters of the American water spaniel call it a one-person dog that matures slowly, bores easily, and is not as eager to please as some other spaniel breeds. The Boykin spaniel makes many friends fast, starts young, and retrieves incessantly.

Though the two breeds may share some genetic history, over the years breeders have taken them in different directions. In the American water spaniel yellow eyes are a breed fault, but they are a breed standard in the Boykin spaniel. While the coat of the American water spaniel may be only curled closely or in a loose undulating pattern called a "marcel," Boykin spaniels may be curly, wavy or sleek. Least important for breeding, but noticeable for conformation, the Boykin's tail should be docked, whereas the water spaniel's is to be natural.

In 1988 Richard Wolters wrote an article on the Boykin spaniel's development for *Connoisseur* magazine. As a footnote to that article, he included a piece titled "The Real Origins of Boykin Spaniels." The story made him persona non grata among Boykin spaniel promoters, who felt it was unfair and poorly researched. Wolters pointed out that Boykin breeding records do not go back before the 1940s and then referred to a breeder of American water spaniels, who said that many yellow-eyed American water spaniels were shipped to the South in the 1940s, had their tails docked, and were redubbed "Boykin spaniels."

People close to the breeding of Boykin spaniels freely acknowledge that Boykin lines include American water spaniels some time back. In 1987, when Dave Duffey interviewed Whit Boykin II, a Boykin Spaniel Society founder, for an article in a 1993 issue of *Gun Dog* magazine, Whit acknowledged the role of the American water spaniel in the Boykin's past. Nevertheless Boykin spaniel aficionados take vigorous exception with

Wolters's conclusion that there is no such thing as a Boykin spaniel. In addition to the differences between the Boykin and the American water spaniel, the Boykin's defenders point to the variety of other breeds that are known to have been bred into the modern Boykin spaniel as evidence of distinctiveness.

The "real origins" or complete understanding of the Boykin spaniel's genetic heritage will remain shrouded in the mists of the past. Some believe that both Boykins and American water spaniels have a common ancestor in the rare English field spaniel. That Boykins and American water spaniels probably share some common past should not obscure the fact that the water spaniel was not a registered breed until the 1920s, after as many as fifteen years of breeding crosses in Boykin spaniels. It is conceivable Dr. Pfeifer and perhaps others were making additional crosses at that time, further distancing its lines from the Boykin. Even some of the faults in the Boykin breed—for example, the white spots on the body—do not seem to occur in the American water spaniel, suggesting again that considerable genetic differentiation has occurred between the two, regardless of some possible common ancestors. Whatever the backgrounds of these animals might have been, their distinctions have now been "frozen" on both sides through the establishment of breeding societies and distinct registries for both dogs.

It should be noted that the Boykin spaniel is the incontestable winner of number one "bragging rights" competition with its cousin, the American water spaniel. The Boykin became the state dog of South Carolina in 1985; it took the American water spaniel another year to achieve the same distinction in Wisconsin.

Decline in the 1930s

Bad economic times often signal the demise of much dog breeding. During the Depression of the 1930s, this did not occur with Boykin spaniels, in large measure because the wealthy northerners who visited Camden continued to hunt and the Boykin family was able to provide them with a good hunting dog. "If it hadn't been for these folks who continued to vacation and hunt in Camden during the winter and who wanted those little spaniels, the Boykin families might have been more hungry," remembered Baynard Boykin. "The sale of those dogs put a lot of food on Depression-era tables." He continued, "I expect there are lots of descendants of Dumpy and Singo and others all up the East Coast. We didn't have any difficulty, even during the Depression, selling those pups for ten dollars apiece, and that was big money in those days."

In that early period no effort was made to market the breed in any systematic manner through print advertising or to register the breed in a national association. As Whit Boykin aged and his health began to decline, he moved to Columbia, South Carolina, from his Camden farm and lost daily touch with farm work and dog breeding. Nevertheless he remained actively interested in the dogs that his son, Deas, the father of Baynard Boykin, continued to raise.

Deaths of Whit Boykin and Alec White

On June 4, 1932, Whit Boykin died at his retirement residence on 3208 Hunter Street (now 3208 Heyward Street) in Columbia, where he had lived with his second wife, Lulie Harvin, a Manning native. (His first wife, Ellen "Missy" Cantey, mother of their nine children, two of whom died in infancy, had died in 1912.) The day after his death, Whit was eulogized on the front page of the issue of the *State*.

The article described him as a conservationist, sportsman, farmer, and land appraiser. The list of pallbearers, including friends from the South Carolina Sportsmen's Association, read like a *Who's Who* of South Carolina for the day. "Few other men in South Carolina could boast as many genuine friends as did Whit Boykin," the obituary read. "Himself the most open hearted and generous and hospitable of men, he drew others to him and held them with his frank and charming nature. Anything that was his was also the property of his friends, or of anyone who might need it." No mention was made of the dogs that bore his name and today number in the thousands.

In a May 1975 interview with Mike Creel the legendary outdoor writer for the *State* newspaper, Harry R. E. Hampton, remembered Whit Boykin as a "hail and hardy fellow, always the life of any party, one who knew all the songs, skilled and ethical sportsman, and a man who could tell a hunting story better than Technicolor. He acted them out." Hampton said he went on his first hunt with the Boykins in 1909 at age twelve and from that time on "every Christmas and every summer" he revisited the Boykins in their great outdoors.

In 2009 two of Whit Boykin's granddaughters, Jeanie Holmes Martin and Ellen Holmes Wright, were living in Columbia. Born in 1924, Jeanie Martin was only eight when her grandfather Whit died. "Still, he is a vivid soul in my mind," she told Lynn Kelley. "For one thing he was our only living grandparent. We loved him and loved visiting him and his second wife on Heyward Street in Columbia. He'd sing us little songs, I remember." Mrs. Martin remembers visiting in Camden and at the Boykin settlement and even living there for a while as a child. Mrs. Martin also remembers that when she and her first husband married, they moved to 3119 Heyward Street. "I think it's so interesting—and special—that as a young, married woman I was living so close to where my grandfather lived his last years," she said.

A decade after Whit Boykin's death, Boykin's lifetime friend Alec White died on April 12, 1942, in Spartanburg, where he and his wife are buried in Oakwood Cemetery, not far from where he met Dumpy on East Main Street. In articles on April 12 and 13, 1942, he was eulogized in the *Spartanburg Herald* as a "pioneer Spartan." It was said that "he was associated with the Spartanburg, Union, and Columbia railroad during its construction, and until organization of the Merchants and Farmers bank here. He was president of the bank for more than 50 years and he was well known in this section." With both men gone and no significant written records of "their dog" having been kept, the first chapter closed in the history of the Boykin spaniel breed, leaving unsolved mysteries about the early years of this dog.

Boykins in the War Years

The Boykin spaniel began spreading in South Carolina from its Camden area home to a triangular area defined by Camden and Sumter at one point, Charleston at another, and Newberry at the third. There were also pockets of interest in Texas, Louisiana, New York, and other states. Although there are breeders in many areas of the state and beyond today, the rough triangle in the South Carolina Midlands has always been acknowledged as the Boykin spaniel breeding heartland.

A year after Alec White's death, the Boykin spaniel got its first taste of national attention in the press, when newspaperman Jack Foster, then editor of the *Columbia Record*, wrote a one-page article about the Boykin for the July 1943 issue of *Esquire* magazine. The article appeared in the middle of America's involvement in World War II, a time when hunting was confined largely to the very oldest Americans and to young boys because so many young men were at war. It was a time when bullets were being made for battle, not for sport.

According to the stories old-timers and insiders told to several authors, when World War II ended—for unknown reasons and despite earlier successes—the breed's popularity waned considerably. It is generally conceded that from the 1940s through the 1960s the Boykin spaniel went into a kind of eclipse. The breed was maintained to a great extent only through efforts of Boykin family members, relatives, and close friends, who bred Boykins for their own hunting purposes.

Boykins in the 1960s

This quiet period for the breed was interrupted by the publication of several articles about the Boykin and mention of it in two major books. The August 25, 1961, *New York World Telegram*'s "Breed of the Month" feature carried the headline "The Boykin Spaniel Great as a Retriever" and told the breed's history, using quotations from the 1956 edition of Henry P. Davis's *Modern Dog Encyclopedia*. Another Boykin book appearance was a three-page section in Jeff Griffen's *The Hunting Dogs of America* (1964). In the *State*'s November 1, 1964, "Woods and Waters" column, South Carolina writer Harry Hampton reported on a story about Northam Griggs's Boykin spaniel King that appeared in John McClain's October 31 "Man About Manhattan Column" in the *New York Journal American*. Hampton wrote at least two more columns on Boykins in the 1960s, and in 1969 Bud Seifert wrote an article about the Boykin spaniel as part of a *Spartanburg Journal* series on family pets. These articles sparked only slight flurries of interest.

Though the breed may have been experiencing a popularity slump in most of South Carolina during the 1960s, it certainly had a committed core of admirers, especially in the Camden area. Edmund "Beaver" Hardy, a Columbia insurance executive and great-grandson of Whit Boykin's brother Allen, recounts an incident around 1960, when, as a recent college graduate, he was invited to a garden party in Camden by another member of the extended Boykin family, who was entertaining a group of people from around the country. The hostess specifically asked Hardy to bring the litter of puppies that his Boykin spaniel had whelped several weeks before and that he was preparing to sell.

"I pulled up to this lovely homestead in my little Nash Rambler not expecting much of a party and thinking it would be kind of informal and low-keyed," Hardy said. "But the people there were all dressed to the nines and looking like New Yorkers out of *The Great Gatsby* or something. And there I was dressed in my jeans and an old, beat-up shirt. One of these New Yorker types wandered over shortly after I'd placed the puppies in the middle of the dining-room table and immediately spotted what to my mind was the prettiest, smartest, most willing to please of the puppies. In an instant he bought it for top dollar.

"But the hostess was a dog lover too, and she had other ideas about this dog's future," Hardy recalled. "She sized up the situation real fast and said to the New Yorker, 'Oh, what a cu-u-u-te little pup. Except for that fault with the nose and the undershot jaw, his head is almost perfect.

It'll probably be better when he gets older, just as the disproportionate length of the body and the crooked front legs will probably right themselves somewhat more. But, he sure is adorable—no wonder you chose him.' Then, she walked into the kitchen. Well, the new owner became instantly flustered, saw another pup he liked, and asked if he could trade. I allowed as how that was really no problem, and he walked away with a great big smile on his face to show his partying friends this great little pup. While I was watching all this with amusement, the hostess came up behind me and, pointing to the originally sold pup, whispered, 'Now *that one* is *my* dog. Get him out of here now and I'll pay you later. You can sell all the rest.' And I did. I sold every one of them that evening." A successful young Boykin salesman, Hardy later became a founding member of the Boykin Spaniel Society and served as its president for a term.

To the outside world things were temporarily quiet on the Boykin front, but the bloodlines of eager hunting spaniels were sustained among a scattered network of Boykin relatives and friends up and down the East Coast and in remote places such as Brownsville, Texas, all linked back to Camden. The subject of breed registration cropped up, but it was promptly silenced when Boykin owners failed to agree on a definition for the breed (known as the "breed standard"). However, calls and letters continued to connect Boykin spaniel masters with prospective breeding mates, and stories were passed along of outstanding hunts by particular dogs and the new tricks they had learned. But this was only the quiet before the storm of national interest that came in the 1970s.

2

A Boykin Spaniel Revival

Society, Standards, and Field Trials

Most of them are smarter than the man who gets them.

Nat Gist, speaking of the Boykin spaniel

By the 1970s at least thirty years had passed of quiet Boykin spaniel breeding, memorable hunting and home experiences, and simple word-of-mouth promotion among dedicated supporters in South Carolina. The breed had also become known and loved in areas of the North and West, where owners of Boykin spaniels had become residents. The time was ripe for a Boykin spaniel revival. Sparked by an article and photographs in a South Carolina magazine with nationwide readership, this revival gained momentum as wave after wave of families discovered this personable, compact retriever.

The "revival" began after Mike Creel became fascinated by Boykin spaniels in 1974. Creel was then a University of South Carolina journalism graduate working in state-government public affairs and freelancing for *South Carolina Wildlife* magazine. Having grown up in Hemingway, in the Pee Dee region of South Carolina, Creel had heard tales of Boykin retrievers all his life, but he had never seen one until 1974. Beginning to research the breed, he traveled the state and communicated across the nation by letter and telephone in search of the little spaniels and their masters.

Creel and his wife, Dena, had been married only two months when they became the owners of a Boykin puppy they named "Booger" on New Year's Day 1975. Earlier Creel had sent a query to *South Carolina Wildlife* magazine and made repeated calls proposing to write the "untold" story of the Boykin spaniel. Acceptance of this offer, however, was not forthcoming from the editor of the magazine, John Culler (who had become a Camden resident and the owner of a Boykin named "Lucky"), until a number of Boykin spaniel owners prevailed on him. Culler finally agreed to run the piece in the September–October 1975 edition of *South Carolina Wildlife*.

South Carolina Wildlife *Hits the Stands*

Culler's reservations about running the article had been centered on concerns that reader interest might be limited because the numbers of Boykin spaniels had declined and that there might not be enough new information for a story. Mike's article "The Spaniels of Boykin" turned out to be the longest on a single topic published in the magazine up to that time. When the article was printed, Culler's reservations vanished, and the reddish-brown issue with a Boykin retrieving on the cover was a runaway best seller. Copies of the September–October 1975 Boykin spaniel issue of the magazine have been collectors' items ever since. The original article was reprinted in full by *South Carolina Wildlife* in its 1978 hardcover book of hunting stories, *Carolina's Hunting Heritage*.

Many people acknowledge that the 1975 article in *South Carolina Wildlife* acted as a catalyst and rallying point for Boykin spaniel breeders, admirers, and owners because the story brought the dog's plight to the attention of people who cared. Mike listed the steps needed to preserve the Boykin's future: "There needs to be a widespread avid interest by Boykin spaniel enthusiasts in South Carolina and other states to, first of all, establish a reasonable breed standard for the Boykin spaniel and to maintain consistent breeding and breeding records. An organized club would probably serve as the most effective medium for bringing everybody together to work toward the same end. The maintenance of good breeding records is the key. The best plan would be to start with breeding of the present or immediate past and continue on to document breeding activity until adequate generations have been recorded and verified."

Boykin Demand Increases

Friends and members of the Boykin family, as well as a handful of other breeders, were encouraged by the outpouring of interest that the *South Carolina Wildlife* article had elicited. At the same time, the article created an unquenchable—and unrealistic—demand for Boykin spaniels.

As much as he admired Creel's *South Carolina Wildlife* article, Dr. Peter McKoy, a Camden veterinarian, was appalled by commercialization of Boykin spaniels that came in the story's wake. McKoy had cared for the animals of Camden's respected families for some years. He knew and admired the quality of breeding that he saw in the spaniels that Whit's son Deas and his children had raised. "After that article appeared in the

South Carolina Wildlife magazine," McKoy remembered, "I started getting phone calls at 2 and 3 A.M. virtually every morning from as far away as Alaska asking me where these dogs could be bought." For several years Creel was also deluged by "fan mail" from readers who were introduced to the breed by the article. Most just wrote: "I enjoyed your story. Where can I buy one of these dogs?"

Although the nuisance factor disrupted McKoy's sleep schedule, it was another aspect of the Boykin spaniel's sudden popularity that truly alarmed him. Twenty years later McKoy still remembered two jarring events that occurred in his clinic on the same day in 1977: "First, in one examining room, I saw the most deformed little creature called a Boykin spaniel that I'd ever seen in my work experience with the breed. We had to put it to sleep. It was simply the result of greed and indiscriminate breeding. I left there and went down the hall to another examining room, and there was a lady with her white poodle and two mixed breed puppies that I'd seen a couple of weeks before." That time the lady had brought in four puppies—two white and two chocolate poodle-mix puppies. "So I asked the lady, 'Where are the two chocolate pups?' and she answered me saying, 'Oh, those two? Why, I sold them last week as Boykin spaniels for $150 apiece.'"

Breeding Concerns

McKoy said this "double whammy" of experiences convinced him something had to be done fast on behalf of the breed. "I got on the telephone right then and called Baynard Boykin and said 'If your father and grandfather could see what I've seen today, they'd turn over in their graves.'" Baynard Boykin and his wife, Matilda "Tillie" Boykin, invited him to a social gathering at the Boykin Mill Pond with other "interested parties" to discuss protecting the breed and possibly forming an association.

The other guests included Whit II and Alice Boykin, Edmund "Beaver" Hardy, and Geoffrey and Christie Gordon-Creed. The Gordon-Creeds were Camden-area dog breeders whose dogs from several breeds had won national championships. Members of the extended Boykin family filled out the invitation list. Some who attended this gathering long remembered that there was something electric in the air that night. A new sense of commitment energized the group and consumed their time over the next several years in ways they might never have expected. A new phase of the Boykin spaniel's history had begun.

Many long-time Boykin owners look back to Dr. Peter McKoy as the person whose expertise in breeding and whose outrage at the genetic atrocities he had seen helped to drive home the need for an organization to control indiscriminate breeding of Boykins. "Peter knows his genetics," said one observer. "He is a very careful veterinarian with what you can honestly describe as a devout sense of his calling as a doctor *for* animals." McKoy galvanized opinion among Boykin family members by demonstrating that the demand for the Boykin spaniel and the lack of protection for creating quality in breeding had produced a crisis: an intersection of danger and opportunity.

Idea for a Society

The crisis in 1977, McKoy argued, presented a time either to act decisively to change the future of the Boykin spaniel for the better and actually improve on past accomplishments or to let the short-term market demand for the breed destroy what several generations of the Boykin family had worked to nurture and develop. Earlier attempts at forming a society had lacked the voice of a concerned expert, but in 1977 McKoy's pleas became a catalyst for action.

Shortly after the social gathering at the Boykin Mill Pond, Henry and Kitty Beard met with Peter McKoy, Tillie and Baynard Boykin, Geoffrey and Christie Gordon-Creed, and Alice and Whit Boykin at Millway, the home of Alice and Whit Boykin. Everyone present signed a letter dated July 5, 1977, and sent it with a questionnaire to Boykin spaniel owners and a few others who might be interested in the preservation of the breed. The letter was both clear and compelling:

Dear Friends:

A great many people are becoming concerned that over the past few years the Boykin spaniel, through indiscriminate breeding, is becoming endangered. To perpetuate the breed it will be necessary to compile records and establish better breeding opportunities.

Because of the tremendous interest already expressed, we are attempting to form a society which will then determine the constitution and bylaws. We hope because of your present and/or past interest in the Boykin spaniel you will give us your support in establishing THE BOYKIN SPANIEL SOCIETY.

Attached are the tentative objectives of the Society and a questionnaire. We would appreciate your considering the enclosed material, fill out the questionnaire and return it to the above address. The information will be compiled and all interested parties will be informed of future plans.

After the letter was mailed, the group met again on August 9, 1977, and called themselves the "Steering Committee for Organization of the Boykin

Boykin Spaniel Society founders in 1986: Edmund Hardy, Henry Beard, Kitty Beard, Baynard Boykin, Tillie Boykin, Alice Boykin, Whit Boykin, and Dr. Peter McKoy. Photograph courtesy of the Boykin Spaniel Society

Spaniel Society." Present at that meeting were Alice and Whit Boykin II, Tillie and Baynard Boykin, Kitty and Henry Beard, and Edmund "Beaver" Hardy. From then on this steering committee did the work to get the society underway.

Kitty Beard

One member of the founding group in particular, Katharine DuVal "Kitty" Beard, eventually took on the role of chief organizer and promoter. The job grew as she did one task after another. Eventually she acted as a one-person clearinghouse for information, director of traffic, and system maintainer. After the formation of the Boykin Spaniel Society, Mrs. Beard was always acknowledged as the one who had kept up the steady drumbeat for the first years, allowing the society to become a stable, functioning organization.

A lifelong Camden resident, Kitty Beard served for three decades as a school nurse in Kershaw County. As a tireless worker for civic causes, she was asked repeatedly to address civic groups about the health of schoolchildren. Shortly after she helped to establish the Boykin Spaniel Society, the Lugoff Rotary Club asked her to speak to them about the society. A week earlier she had given a talk at the Camden Rotary Club on sex education in Camden schools. When she appeared in Lugoff, a Rotarian who had heard her earlier talk asked her if she was going to be discussing sex education for young people again, to which she replied, "No, this time it's all about Boykin spaniels—I'm very versatile."

In the beginning no one knew exactly how to reach others interested in saving the Boykin spaniel. "I remember putting the mailing lists together to try to get the society underway after the first couple of organizational meetings," Mrs. Beard said. "The first list was from the old Boykin-Cantey family reunion, and it just grew from there. I asked for ten-dollar donations from each respondent, and before I realized it, we already had three thousand dollars in the treasury."

Mrs. Beard's interest in this work went back to a childhood filled with rich, pleasant memories of growing up with Boykin spaniels. "I had always loved those little dogs from the time I was a child myself, and I just couldn't bear the thoughts that they'd be messed up by becoming too popular." She also felt that preserving the breed was important: "I guess we all have a need to leave a legacy in the world with something good that we have done. Maybe because I didn't have children and was married to one of Whit Boykin's great-grandsons, the organization of the society in a way became 'my baby.'" Mrs. Beard has always denied that she made a great sacrifice in doing the volunteer work she undertook for the society. As she remembers it, she was just one busy person among many trying to help bring about a goal: "That time period was fun and although it kept my husband, Henry, and me very busy; I would do it all over again. We started doing all the work in our home. I was the writer, editor, mailer, typist. Then, we finally got some paid support and moved the society's work first to Henry's office in downtown Camden before the society got its own location."

Proposed Objectives

Tentative objectives of the Boykin Spaniel Society were "to encourage and promote the breeding of pure-bred Boykin spaniels and to do all possible to bring their natural qualities to perfection; to urge members and breeders to help establish standards by which the Boykin spaniel can be judged; to do all in its power to protect and advance the interests of the breed by encouraging sportsmanlike competition in field trials; and to maintain records on all Boykin spaniels in order to form a Boykin spaniel registry." A proposed bylaw stated that "the club shall not be conducted or operated for profit, and no part of the profits or remainder or residue from dues or donations to the club shall inure to the benefit of any member or individual."

The organizational questionnaire sought to measure interest in "the perpetuation of the Boykin spaniel as a breed; individuals' willingness to pay a ten-dollar membership; present and past ownership of Boykins; dogs currently being bred and the names and addresses of any others who would be interested in this effort."

On July 17, 1977, survey respondent Dana T. Crosland of Bennettsville wrote:

> I am glad this movement is taking place and look forward to being a part of it. The trick is going to be taking a good thing—the dogs— and making them better and still keep everyone happy enough to still work together. There is going to be variation in the looks of dogs, and as I see it the standard should not be set on a 'forever' basis but have in mind amending it as conformity becomes easier to come by. I want it always to be a hunting breed; looks should always yield to that ability. Whatever is needed, men with purpose and good will can bring it about. To you people who are initiating this project, your parents, grandparents, and kinsmen gave this state and this country a very special and unique dog. In trying to perpetuate it you are doing the right thing and all people who love the Boykin spaniel want to help.

Ms. Crosland raised an issue that is not unique to Boykins. Form should always follow function. From the start of the society, the idea of keeping keen hunting instincts alive in the Boykin spaniel, a true working dog, has been considered paramount to the breed's long-term success. Members such as Peter McKoy, however, have taken the position that breed competitions should be maintained at a level of proficiency, instead of increasing the level of difficulty as some breeding groups have done. By encouraging a "proficiency standard" as the norm for the breed's competitions, Boykin Spaniel Society leaders who hold this view hope to preserve the Boykin's hunting instincts and the traits that make this dog a good-natured family companion.

Barely before people had time to return the first questionnaire, a second mailing was sent out to prospective spaniel supporters. The first official *Boykin Spaniel Society Newsletter,* dated August 18, 1977, conveyed a buoyant message to its readers: "The response from the July 5th letter has been overwhelmingly enthusiastic, and it is apparent that it will be well worthwhile to continue with our efforts." The newsletter outlined the meeting of the organizational committee on August 9 and provided detailed coverage of the events and promising outcomes on a number of fronts.

The Boykin Spaniel Society made an almost immediate impact. The March–April 1978 issue of *South Carolina Wildlife* featured a letter from Dr. McKoy, in which he stated: "As a result of the tremendous interest shown in the article on the Boykin spaniel by Mike Creel, the Boykin Spaniel Society was formed last summer. We presently have 250 members in 20 states who are interested in promoting the breed. On behalf of the society, I would like to thank Mike Creel and the staff of *South Carolina Wildlife* for their part in promoting the perpetuation of this hunting dog, which is a favorite of many South Carolinians."

The Need for a Breed Standard

The heady enthusiasm during the first few months of the Boykin Spaniel Society's operation had to carry it through some trying days ahead, for it was one thing to elicit excitement in an initial bout of organizational hoopla. It was yet another to define the breed's standards closely enough to meet concerns of conformationists and geneticists while also including enough diplomacy to soothe the feelings of proud owners of Boykins that might not meet the standards as defined.

While researching his 1975 *South Carolina Wildlife* article, Creel had asked the *American Field,* a Chicago-based sporting-dog and field-trial journal that registers bird dogs through its Field Dog Stud Book (FDSB), and the New York–based American Kennel Club (AKC), which maintains the largest registry of purebred dogs in the United States, what it would take to register the Boykin spaniel. William F. Brown, then editor of the *American Field,* responded on April 15, 1975, explaining: "A breed standard must be written and three generations of the breed depicted in photographs. . . . Three generations of pedigrees must be authenticated for individual dogs, with photos of each, and at least fifty FDSB applications for registration must be submitted." Brown went on to suggest that Boykin owners should form a breed club, so that its officers could "do whatever needs to be done to comply with the requirements," and he explained that "there must be sufficient interest in a breed, which breeds true to type, to have approximately one hundred dogs registered annually."

An AKC official said in a 1975 telephone interview that, even though the AKC had no hard-and-fast regulations on the matter, there were several necessary prerequisites that must be fulfilled before the AKC would consider a breed for official AKC recognition: "A club must be organized specifically for the advancement of the dog breed in question and that club's primary function must be to maintain a stud book or breeding register. There must be several generations of the breed which have been breeding true to type over a period of eight to ten years. Specimens of the breed must be distributed all over the country and number well into the hundreds. These dogs must be owned by a good many different people in various parts of the country. The dog owners and members of the promoting club must be interested in breeding and exhibiting at AKC sanctioned shows."

Establishing a Breed Standard

Essentially these responses set the goals of the new Boykin Spaniel Society board of directors. While the main work of the society was to register dogs considered to be Boykin spaniels, doing so was impossible until the breed standard had been developed. After receiving about one hundred descriptive and pedigree forms and looking at most of the eligible dogs under consideration for inclusion as foundation stock, the board of directors agreed on a statement of the breed standard in mid-1978.

Tillie Boykin was an important member of the steering committee for the organization of the Boykin Spaniel Society, chairing the working group that was charged with the task of developing a proposal for the breed standard. On July 19, 1978, she wrote to Creel about a lengthy meeting held the night before for "establishing the characteristics of the typical or true Boykin spaniel." According to Mrs. Boykin, "The meeting finally broke up about 10:30 P.M. without our completing our analysis (of a dozen dogs in attendance and detailed information on thirty-five males and forty-nine females sent in by Boykin spaniel owners)." Thus they met again on July 24 "to try to work out further details."

Clearly it was not an easy process to arrive at the breed standard. The group Tillie Boykin chaired realized its report would have to be accepted by the new board of directors, whose members held a very wide spectrum of opinions about what the breed standard should be. As the editor of the *Boykin Spaniel Society Newsletter* wrote on the group's ongoing efforts: "To give you an example of how much negotiating and compromising took place, it took four hours for the committee to agree on the height and weight of the Boykin dog and bitch."

The final agreement on the proposed breed standard was based on two bedrock assumptions: "First, and most important, was the need to establish these standards to guarantee a distinct, recognizable breed of quality in the future. Second, just because a particular dog did not meet all elements of the standard, it should not mean that the dog could not be registered." The standard was meant as a benchmark toward which breeders should strive. When Tillie Boykin's committee finished its work, the board of directors made a few additional changes, and then the proposal was ready to be submitted to the general membership of the Boykin Spaniel Society.

The November 3, 1978, *Boykin Spaniel Society Newsletter,* included a ballot for the membership to vote on the breed standard. At the end of the proposed standard was an admonition: "Remember, very few of the members' dogs will meet all of the categories of the standard, so do not vote with your dog in mind. The future of the Boykin spaniel depends on this." The membership accepted the breed standard by an overwhelming margin, and it went into effect almost immediately as the basis for including dogs in the Boykin Spaniel Registry. The current Boykin spaniel breed standard is published as appendix 1 in this book.

Beginning the Registration Process

With the standard defined and formally accepted by the society, the registrations of dogs to be included as Boykin spaniel foundation stock began in earnest. The June 20, 1980, issue of the *Boykin Spaniel Society Newsletter* reported that sixty-four dogs were already approved as foundation stock. The board of directors had decided that all dogs accepted to the registry within an initial time period would be labeled as "Foundation Stock" or "FS" for future reference. Even if they had no outcrossing with other breeds, dogs and their descendants that had not been accepted for the register as foundation stock by August 1, 1980, could not in the future be officially identified as Boykin spaniels. The board hoped that at least 250–300 dogs would qualify as foundation stock and was exceedingly pleased when more than 667 finally achieved the mark. These dogs provided a sufficiently diversified gene pool to allow for breeding toward the ideal that the executive committee had sought in promoting the breed standard.

By January 1, 1979, the Boykin Spaniel Society had three hundred members from twenty-two states and the District of Columbia. In just a year and a half of hard work, much had already been accomplished. A constitution and bylaws for a legally incorporated Boykin Spaniel Society had been established by democratic process. The breed standard was operative; the registry was underway; and a newsletter was being published. The newsletter was invaluable for keeping information flowing to members outside Camden.

A National Hunting Test for Boykin Spaniels Only

The *Boykin Spaniel Society Newsletter* of March 12, 1980, announced that a "mini" field trial would be held for dogs to "show off" during the annual meeting and barbecue on May 24 at Edmund Hardy's Rice Pond, near Elgin. Plans included one water retrieve and one land retrieve for each dog entered. By then some eighty-four dogs were listed as foundation stock in the Boykin Spaniel Registry.

The June 20, 1980, newsletter judged both the third annual meeting and first national field trial a "tremendous success." Attendance was double what it had been at the previous annual meeting. Sixty-one dogs were entered in the first-ever national field trial, and "it was most exciting to realize how many well trained Boykin spaniels there are." John Chappell, Eddie Durant, and Edmund "Beaver" Hardy made up the field-trial committee. First place winners in this first trial were

Puppy Dove (land retrieve): Bo, owned by Alton Yeargin of Simpsonville, South Carolina
Puppy Dove-Duck (land and water retrieve): Bo again
Open Dove-Duck: Cricket (the over-all winner), owned by Nat Gist of Sumter, South Carolina
Open Dove: Rusty Triever, owned by Allan Fallaw of Batesburg, South Carolina

The second Boykin Spaniel Society field trial was held on May 9, 1981, at Mill Creek Park near Pinewood, South Carolina. The event began at 10 A.M. and lasted all day with puppy (twelve months or under) and open (all ages) classes, including two tests for each dog entered. Puppy class included retrieving on land for dove and on open water for duck. Open dog had retrieving on open field and wooded land for doves and in water, through decoys, for ducks. White canvas dummies with applied dove scent were used for the bait throws, and a blank pistol was shot.

The 1982 event was called the "National Boykin Spaniel Retriever Trials." Fifty-four dogs were entered in the open-land series, forty-nine in open water, thirty in puppy land, and thirty in puppy water. Bull Island Beau, owned and handled by Mark Shields of Mount Pleasant was named open champion. Nat Gist's Dixie Two of Sumter won the puppy championship. The event began at 9:00 A.M., and lasted until the winners were announced at 7 P.M. Sixteen states and Ontario province were represented.

In 1990 the Boykin Spaniel Society board of directors substituted the words "hunting test" for "field trial" in the name of their annual event to represent more accurately the objectives of the society and the event itself. The 1990 Boykin Spaniel Society national field trial was held on May 19 at Wateree Correctional Institution, outside Camden. Some three hundred people attended and competition included twenty dogs in open, twenty-four in intermediate, thirty-nine in novice, and twenty-five in puppy.

The overall open 1990 champion title was captured for the third year in a row by Pocotaligo's Coffee, handled and owned by Kim S. Parkman of Sumter. Dixie Blair, handled and owned by Bubba Pope of Columbia, was overall champion in the intermediate class, and the novice class overall champion was Casey Jones, owned and handled by Olin Lee of Cheraw, South Carolina. Overall puppy champion was Lynch's Comin' To Daddy, owned and handled by William Lynch of Moncks Corner, South Carolina.

Since that time the annual national Boykin spaniel hunting tests have aimed to reflect realistic hunting conditions and have attracted both experienced and novice trainers from nearly every state. Boykin owners are a diverse group. The event attracts families, young couples, retirees, and singles. It has provided an opportunity for Boykin enthusiasts to compare breeding successes and to compete in the trials. It has also been a great way to establish friendships and even courtships leading to marriage.

The Carolina Boykin Spaniel Retriever Club

A companion, cooperating group to the Boykin Spaniel Society was founded in 1982 as the Carolina Boykin Spaniel Retriever Club. Its purpose in the promote the breed through holding hunt tests and to encourage the use of trained Boykins in hunting. Its first gun-dog trial was held on August 15, 1982, at Eugene C. and Ann Griffith's home on Lake Murray, near Columbia. Participants gathered from all across South Carolina, and one came from Georgia. Then secretary-treasurer of the club Janice Caulder reported in the October 1982 issue of the *Boykin Spaniel Society Newsletter* that a total of twenty-nine dogs were entered. Watching from under tall oaks, everyone enjoyed the fine performance in the field. Ned Beard's dog Banjo placed first in the open class, and Russell Fox's Maggie won the puppy event. Boykin spaniels now compete regularly in the sanctioned field tests of the National Hunting Retriever Club, an affiliate of the United Kennel Club (UKC). Since 1986 the UKC has recognized the Boykin spaniel as a separate dog breed and has permitted its participation in all the UKC events. Appendix 9 lists all Boykin spaniels that have earned placements in the Hunting Retriever Club (HRC) licensed test from 1998 through 2007.

Anyone with a Boykin spaniel may participate in Boykin Spaniel Retriever Club trials, but in order to accumulate points toward the club's Dog of the Year Award, the owner and handler of the dog must be members of the Carolina Boykin Spaniel Retriever Club. In club field trials, five stakes are offered. There are two for puppies: junior puppy for ages up to six months and senior puppy for ages six months to one year. The three stakes for any age dog are divided by difficulty: novice, requiring single retrieves on land and water; intermediate, requiring double retrieves on land and water, blind retrieves, and walk-ups; and gun dog, requiring multiple marked retrieves, blind retrieves, walk-ups, and diversions may

Young hunters in training: Ryan Jordan of Florence, South Carolina, and Ryan's Swamp Fox during a 1986 Carolina Boykin Retriever Club trial near Andrews, South Carolina. Photograph by Mike Creel

be included. Different skills are involved in different events. In a "walk-up," for example, the dog must remain steady as the shot is fired and the bird falls, moving only after its handler releases it to retrieve the bird. In a "blind retrieve," the dog does not see the bird fall, and the handler uses hand signals to guide the dog to the bird. Appendix 8 has a complete list of winners from the first trial and a list of the club's year-end awards from 1983 through 2008.

The 2008 Carolina Boykin Spaniel Retriever Club officers were president: Blake Waggoner of Durham, North Carolina; vice president: Chris Maurer of Valdosta, Georgia; and secretary-treasurer, Dawn Crites of Blythewood, South Carolina. Also serving on the board of directors for 2008 were Gary Edmonds, of Columbia; Scott Kinder of Sumter; Jamie Newman of Lawrenceville, Georgia; Dan Caton of Henderson, North Carolina; and Marie Hodge of Sumter, South Carolina.

Controversy over AKC Acceptance of the Breed

The Boykin Spaniel Society has consistently not sought to have the breed recognized by the American Kennel Club because the society's central commitment is to maintaining the dog's hunting abilities and to keep it from becoming a bench dog, or "show dog." Although the society's board of directors has repeatedly endorsed this view, the Boykin Spaniel Club and Breeders Association of America (BSCBAA), a group that incorporated in South Carolina during the 1990s, has made AKC acceptance of the breed its chief effort. In 1997 BSCBAA received approval from the AKC to enter the Boykin spaniel in the AKC Foundation Stock Service, a category in which a breed being sponsored for inclusion in the AKC Stud Book is placed as a "candidate member" until the AKC's board of directors accords a breed regular status.

According to the group's Web site, the AKC named the BSCBAA the "parent club" for the Boykin spaniel in July 2005. On January 1, 2006, the Boykin spaniel became eligible to compete in AKC-sponsored spaniel events. In February 2006 the first Boykin AKC spaniel title was awarded. On July 1, 2006, the Boykin became eligible to compete in AKC Companion Dog Events, which include obedience, rally, and agility trials, among other things. Boykins were awarded titles in that category the same month. In January 2008 the BSCBAA announced on its Web site that as of January 1, the AKC had approved the Boykin spaniel in the Miscellaneous Group, another step that the BSCBAA sees as leading toward full AKC acceptance of the breed.

The vast majority of Boykin spaniel owners are committed to having the Boykin Spaniel Society represent their canine interests. The actions of the BSCBAA have elicited legal responses from the Boykin Spaniel Society over the effort to promote AKC acceptance of the breed, including a decision to copyright the Boykin spaniel breed standard established by the Boykin Spaniel Society. This action would prevent use of the Boykin Spaniel Society's version of the breed standard unless the society grants its permission. This controversy between the Boykin Spaniel Society and the BSCBAA demonstrates the strong opinions humans can have regarding how a Boykin spaniel should look and what roles it should be bred to fill. What the dog is today and what it should become in the future are being questioned and challenged.

The Boykin Spaniel Society Today

In May 2008 the Boykin Spaniel Society reported more than 2,728 current members from all fifty states and Canada. Since 1977 the society has registered more than 22,800 dogs and 7,055 litters, including the 667 dogs designated as foundation stock. Increasing numbers of litter registrations are received each year. The *Boykin Spaniel Society Newsletter* is published quarterly and mailed to all members. The fifteen members of the

Two Boykin spaniels—smooth and curly—obediently watching a field trial. Fewer of the smooth-haired Boykin spaniels are seen in the early twenty-first century. Photograph by Mike Creel

board of directors serve three-year rotating terms, so that five board members are elected each spring by the society's membership.

The society's 2008 board of directors included chairman: James Latimer of St. Matthews, South Carolina; vice chairman: Bill Crites of Blythewood, South Carolina; secretary: Dock Skipper of Eufala, Alabama; treasurer: David Alford of Henderson, Texas; Elaine Baker of Waco, Georgia; James Braswell of Pendleton, South Carolina; Wayne Frederickson of Bozeman, Montana; John Huddleston of Birmingham, Alabama; John Inabinet of Elgin, South Carolina; Millie Latimer of St. Matthews; Skip Nelson of Madison, Mississippi; Pete Peerson of Leeds, Alabama; Carson Quarles of Roanoke, Virginia; Frank Register of Sewanee, Tennessee; and Russell Scott of Lincolnton, Georgia. Jane C. Sexton of Camden, is the society's executive secretary, and Phyllis Kelly of Elgin is office assistant.

The Boykin Spaniel Society celebrated its thirtieth anniversary in 2007 and extended its gratitude to the eight founders who saw the need to save the breed and share this wonderful animal with the world: Edmund H. Hardy of Columbia, Dr. Peter McKoy of Camden, Kitty and Henry Beard III of Camden, Alice and the late Whit Boykin (who died in 1989) of Boykin, and Tillie and Baynard Boykin of Rembert.

Each year the Boykin Spaniel Society hosts two major field events with participants from all across the United States. The society's National Field Trial, started in 1980, is held in March or April. Its Upland National Field Trial, started in 2002, is held in January. In 1996 the society formed the Boykin Spaniel Foundation in order to maintain the Boykin breed and rid it of genetic disorders. The Boykin Spaniel Foundation sponsors heart clinics and free Canine Eye Registration Foundation (CERF) clinics at the Boykin Spaniel Society National Field Trial for participating Boykin Spaniel Society members. The foundation also continues with efforts to improve the breeding stock by identifying genetic hip issues. A portion of the proceeds paid to the Boykin Spaniel Society to register each Boykin spaniel litter goes to support the Boykin Spaniel Rescue Foundation. Professional articles addressing dog health concerns are regularly published in the *Boykin Spaniel Society Newsletter.* Because of all these efforts, the breed has already dramatically improved in the past ten years.

Litter registration applications are available on the Boykin Spaniel Society Web site or by contacting the Boykin Spaniel Society office (see appendix 6). Once a litter application has been filed with the society, the litter owner is sent a packet with an individual registration paper, known as the "blue paper," for each pup. The new owner of a puppy then completes the individual registration form and returns it to the Boykin Spaniel Society office. The society enters each dog's information into its registry, issues a registration number for each dog, records the dog's ownership information, and sends an official registration certificate to the owner.

Prospective dog owners who contact the Boykin Spaniel Society are provided information on litters that have been registered in their area and directed to health information on the society Web site. They are cautioned to see as many litters as possible and to do their homework before buying a puppy or an adult dog. Another option is adopting a Boykin spaniel through the Boykin Spaniel Rescue. Dogs found through the rescue are usually adults.

Boykins, Boykins Everywhere

The world of Boykin spaniels underwent tremendous change during the 1970s and early 1980s with the increasing geographical spread of the little brown dynamos across the country and the creation of a national organization that united Boykin spaniel owners. A single new Boykin in a neighborhood would often ignite an explosion of interest from neighbors, friends, local media, and even casual passersby wanting to know "what kind of dog is that?" Many who took the time to meet that new dog became sold on Boykins and wanted one of their own.

Inevitably more dogs and more masters brought new challenges. The Boykin Spaniel Society began to lead its members toward wise breeding practices designed to improve each generation of dogs. Researchers spent countless hours looking at the Boykin's past in efforts to learn more about the dog's origins and early breeding practices. Newfound health considerations brought about an alliance of experts on veterinary health, Boykin spaniel owners, and Boykin Spaniel Society directors to focus on healthier and happier dogs.

3

Good Breeding, Health, and Training

Recollect that the Almighty, who gave the dog to be
companion of our pleasures and our toils, invested him
with a nature noble and incapable of deceit.

Sir Walter Scott

A first contact with South Carolina's little brown wonder dog often brings
a reaction such as "where have you been all my life?" Whether hunting
enthusiasts, nature lovers, or simply pet lovers, young or old human con-
verts to this special breed share a contagious affection for Boykin
spaniels. For Boykin owners one of these dogs may not be enough. Some
folks want a house full of them.

Growth in the breed has been steady and spreading nationwide since
the 1970s, when Boykin masters formed local groups and made plans
through Boykin Spaniel Society registration lists to locate unrelated males
and females that would strengthen their own dogs' bloodlines. The best
advice for Boykin owners who want to breed their dogs is to avoid trying
to reconstruct the earliest years of the breed, to concentrate on the breeding records that start with the Boykin Spaniel Society's foundation stock
and breed registry, and to focus on a well-planned breeding program that
will produce outstanding dogs in the future. Breeding practices designed
to protect the future of the breed have led to successively healthier generations of Boykin spaniels by limiting inherited disabilities while maintaining
the Boykin's hunting abilities, mental aptitudes, and unique personality.

The need to establish and nurture the bond between humans and dogs
is nowhere more important than between Boykin spaniels and their masters. For these dogs to achieve their fullest potential as hunters and pets,
they must live close to human contact. If kennel raising is the only option
available to an owner, a breed other than a Boykin should be selected.

Tillie Boykin playing with a healthy litter of pups at
her home in Rembert, South Carolina, January 1975.
Photograph by Mike Creel

These dogs will not "shine" as pets or develop to their fullest hunting
potential without regular daily human association. The indulgence of regular human contact will enhance, rather than ruin, a well-trained dog's
hunting abilities.

Through the interaction of Boykin owners and the Boykin Spaniel
Society with experts on veterinary health, new information is surfacing
regularly about proper health care and nutrition. When owners follow the
recommendations that flow from scientific research studies conducted by
veterinary experts, the lives of dogs improve. When owners apply research
to well-planned breeding, future generations of Boykin spaniels will be
the beneficiaries.

The training of Boykin spaniels is different from that of other retrievers. As many long-time owners have learned, finesse and well-timed coaxing will work better than some of the more severe methods sometimes used with large retrievers and other hunting dogs. Methods for training Boykins became better defined as some professional trainers chose to specialize in Boykins. This significant shift from a time when virtually all Boykins were trained by amateurs demonstrates the growing need for Boykin training specialists to assure that these dogs do well in their triple-duty roles as field-trial competitors, hunting companions, and family dogs. Owners and trainers alike must take care not to ask too much of their dogs. They must place a priority on each dog's health and well-being—which, in the final analysis, are more important than award ribbons.

Hereditary Health Issues

Each breed of domestic dogs inherits certain strengths through selective efforts to assure the continuation of desired qualities. As more becomes known about DNA, the building block of genetics, it will become more

Boykin spaniel Booger, offspring of Sweetie Pie and Turk, returning a training dummy to his owner Dena Creel at Wood Creek Lake, near Pontiac, South Carolina. 1975 Photograph by Mike Creel

and more possible to breed selectively for the elimination (or great reduction) of genetic traits regarded as weaknesses.

The Boykin Spaniel Society has been active in promoting ways to reduce the breed's weaknesses and to assure the continuation of the breed's many strengths. Several genetic issues have been recognized by the society and others as important to address in Boykin spaniel breeding. The one receiving the most attention is canine hip dysplasia (CHD).

Canine Hip Dysplasia

First identified in the 1930s, CHD is relatively common in a number of breeds. According to the Orthopedic Foundation for Animals (OFA), there is a high incidence of CHD among the small number of Boykin spaniels that OFA has tested. Dogs with severe cases of this hereditary condition may lose the use of their hindquarters entirely and have to be euthanized. Boykins with CHD should be spayed or neutered, so they can lead fulfilling lives as family pets without passing on this hereditary condition to future generations of dogs.

Since the mid-1990s the Boykin Spaniel Society has had a committee to evaluate CHD in the breed. The committee works closely with the OFA at the University of Missouri in Columbia, Missouri. Dr. Greg Keller, OFA's in-house board-certified veterinary radiologist and chief of veterinary services, has come to the Boykin Nationals and conducted a seminar on the Boykin spaniel hips and evaluations.

X-rays for Canine Hip Dysplasia (CHD)

The Boykin Spaniel Society actively encourages owners to have their Boykin spaniels X-rayed and evaluated for the presence of hip dysplasia before breeding the animals. X-rays can be evaluated on a preliminary basis when dogs are six months old although the OFA will not certify dogs with a rating—of Excellent, Good, Fair, or Poor—until the animal is at least two years of age when the bone structure is sufficiently mature. X-rays for the OFA evaluation can be taken by any veterinarian with the equipment; they are then sent to OFA in Missouri for evaluation. The evaluation is available for modest cost. According to some authorities, even when owners use the OFA evaluation as a guide for whether to breed, there is still a 20–25 percent chance of producing puppies with CHD.

The University of Pennsylvania School of Veterinary Medicine has developed another diagnostic tool known as "PennHip," which has also been valuable for detecting the CHP condition in Boykins and other dogs. Like the OFA, the PennHip protocol also relies on X-ray technology. Unlike the OFA, the PennHip protocol has a requirement that only veterinarians trained in its techniques may take the X-rays and that all dogs submitted to the protocol must be anesthetized. The company that markets the PennHip evaluation protocol and manages the database makes no recommendation of which dogs to breed after a PennHip evaluation. Neither is there any guarantee that dogs bred after a very affirming PennHip evaluation will be free of CHD. However, the company does recommend that only those dogs that score in the upper 50 percent of the PennHip index for tightest hips in a particular dog breed should be bred.

Perhaps the most poignant story to date of a Boykin spaniel owner's decision not to breed a dog because of hip dysplasia came in 1996. At the conclusion of the national field trials that year, Richard Coe, the owner of Hubba Bubba (the 1996 Boykin Spaniel Society's field dog champion), decided that the dog would not be available for stud and would not compete in future field trials because his OFA test had shown that he had dysplasia. Since then, other Boykin spaniel breeders have also pulled their dogs from the gene pool because of health issues including hip, heart, and eye problems.

Common Heritable Diseases

The breeding guidelines established by the Boykin Spaniel Society take explicit note of the need to assure good hips, eyes, and heart in litters of Boykins. Those guidelines further state that other disorders "which may have a genetic component" should also be examined by breeders—and, by extension, by prospective puppy buyers in the general public. Breeders of Boykin spaniels, such as Pam Kadlec, place important information on their Web sites, guiding people interested in puppy health to ask the right questions about the parents' health and health certifications. As the society's guidelines for breeders put it, the inherited disorders to be considered for potential breeding stock are ones "including, but not limited to, epilepsy, hypothyroidism, skin disorders (allergies), and orthopedic disorders such as elbow dysplasia and patellar luxation."

Some inherited diseases that have been identified as occurring with some regularity in some lines of Boykin spaniels include:

Pulmonic stenosis: A condition that thickens the right ventricle and, depending on its severity, causes a lack of energy, avoidance of exercise, difficulty breathing, and (without surgery in more extreme cases) death.
Juvenile cataracts: Cataract formation early in the life of a dog, even puppyhood. The resulting difficulty of seeing and the problems of mobility make the condition particularly important to avoid in hunting breeds.

Archondroplasia of the limbs: A condition that severely hampers the conversion of cartilage to bone and associated in some cases with dwarfism. Its manifestation in leg bones is exceedingly detrimental to working dogs. **Patellar luxations:** A condition in which the ligament of the kneecap (patella) "locks," causing considerable lack of mobility.

Through its Boykin Spaniel Foundation, the Boykin Spaniel Society has begun to provide educational programs and screening to discourage breeding of animals that have these or other known heritable diseases. The efforts of the foundation are done in support of two national foundations, the Canine Eye Registration Foundation (CERF) and the Orthopedic Foundation for Animals (OFA). These foundations work with the veterinary community to establish an understanding of what screening is needed to certify that potential breeding stock is free of these diseases. Another eye issue, known as collie-eye anomaly, can be detected by DNA testing after the age of five to seven weeks, according to long-time trainer and breeder Pam Kadlec, of Edgefield, South Carolina. The Boykin Spaniel Foundation recommends an annual CERF evaluation for any dog, male or female, being considered for breeding, to assure that puppies have the best chance for good eye health. Likewise, it is recommended that OFA and/or PennHip testing take place for screening for CHD and other inheritable diseases of the bones. A good veterinarian who is skilled in heart issues can detect pulmonic stenosis.

While it is important to know that parents of puppies were screened for inheritable diseases, it is equally important to point out that it is impossible to assure completely that puppies will be free of these diseases. The screenings of parents raises the probability that the puppies will be healthy, but thus far, there are neither enough sophisticated tests nor enough DNA samples from enough generations and individual Boykins to develop the markers for most heritable diseases.

Skin Problems

Skin problems also appear with some Boykin spaniels. "I get a lot of calls from around the country about skin problems among Boykins," said Dr. Peter McKoy. In his opinion high-energy dogs tend to have more skin problems than others. "It may not be any higher incidence than with other spaniels. But, fleas on a Boykin spaniel cause more problems than they do on a laid-back bloodhound." Applications of modern once-a-month topical medications during flea season can in many cases nearly eliminate the discomforts that Boykins suffered in the past from fleas.

Baynard Boykin of Rembert, South Carolina, getting the attention of his well-trained Boykin spaniel. Photograph by Mike Creel

Successful Breeding

On the whole the Boykin spaniel breed is probably as sound as most dog breeds in its basic health. In searching for a puppy, it is wise to consult reliable breeders. In the January 1, 1983, issue of the *Boykin Spaniel Society Newsletter,* Dr. McKoy admonished breeders not to breed for the sake of producing increased numbers of puppies. Before even considering the breeding of a bitch, it should be determined that she is free of diseases, external and internal parasites, and serious genetic problems. McKoy also stressed the desirability of not breeding a bitch in her first heat cycle if it occurs (as it frequently does) before she is twelve months old. While Boykin bitches may be bred two cycles in a row, the second breeding should only occur if the bitch is in good condition following the first litter and has been kept in a good state of nutrition. After a second breeding in a row, however, it is best to skip breeding during her next season.

According to McKoy, when a bitch comes in heat, she normally stays in season for three weeks. Most bitches will ovulate between the eleventh and fourteenth days of heat, and, this period is therefore the optimal time for breeding. Her willingness to stand for the stud is the best indicator of her fecundity. Once bred, she should be kept away from all other male dogs to prevent a mixed litter. She should be bred to the selected stud daily if she has a history of a short season—or every other day if she has a long season—until she is no longer receptive to the stud. If a bitch that refuses to stand for the male, the dogs may need some help from an experienced breeder, or the bitch may have to be bred artificially.

Between the twenty-first and twenty-fifth day after the bitch has been bred, she should be examined to determine if pregnancy has occurred. Nutritional needs should be given special attention during pregnancy, and vitamin supplementation may be desirable. The pregnancy period for Boykins is between fifty-nine and sixty-three days. Exercise for the pregnant dog is important, but during the last trimester it should not be forced.

Whelping Puppies

McKoy recommends that, after the puppies are whelped, they and their mother dog should immediately be placed in a whelping box with a heat lamp over the box. One area of the whelping box should be kept at eighty-five degrees Fahrenheit so that pups can move to this area to keep warm. Since puppies have no shivering reflex during their first few weeks of life, they are subject to chilling if the environmental temperature is below eighty-five degrees. Chilling is the leading cause of death in pups during their first few weeks. Chilled puppies become ineffectual nursers, causing the mother dog to push them away.

An owner of a mother dog and new puppies should make sure that the pups nurse the first twenty-four hours after whelping to ensure that the pups get an adequate amount of colostrum, the milklike substance that is initially produced by the mother. This substance is rich in antibodies and therefore a great assistance in providing the puppies with immunities against diseases during their first weeks of life.

The first day after delivery, both mother and puppies should be examined by a veterinarian. Dr. McKoy advised that the mother be given oxytocin (a hormone that stimulates lactation) and antibiotics at this time to help prevent "fading puppy syndrome," in which pups become very weak in the first week of life owing to their mother's poor health.

Once the health of mother and puppies is assured, between three and seven days after whelping, the puppies' tails should be docked. The breed standard recommends that a third of the tail should be left.

Reliable breeders follow the prescriptions McKoy recommended. The Boykin Spaniel Society cooperates with such Boykin breeders in several ways, and assists puppy buyers with publications such as "Choosing a Breeder," available on the society Web site and in appendix 4. Ultimately, however, breeders' reputations are established by the quality of their puppies. Names of reputable breeders are available through advertisements in the *Boykin Spaniel Society Newsletter.*

Finding the Right Boykin Puppy

Dr. McKoy has consistently recommended that the best time to adopt a Boykin puppy is around the seventh week of its life, not much earlier or later. Since dogs are pack animals, they need to be adopted by humans while they are still bonding. Owners will want the puppy to bond with them rather than with other dogs. Before purchasing a pup, prospective buyers are wise to observe both its parents to see if they are trainable and have been trained. Puppy purchasers are also advised to get a written three-day guarantee, so that the pup may be taken to a vet to be examined for obvious problems. Like all Boykin enthusiasts, Dr. McKoy admits to having certain individual preferences for puppies, recognizing that "beauty is in the eye of the beholder." A short muzzle on a Boykin, a fairly stocky body, and "four legs on the ground" are traits McKoy prefers.

Kennel shyness (also known as kennel-dog syndrome) is a condition that may be found in older pups that have not been socialized with sufficient human contact by the age of twelve weeks. In an article for the "Pet Pointers" page of *Family Circle* magazine for September 18, 1979, Mike Creel wrote about discovering and treating this condition in his family's four-month old puppy. According to veterinary researchers, kennel shyness is a fear reaction that develops from the lack of sufficient human attention during the fifth through twelfth weeks after a puppy is whelped, a critical period for socialization. A dog with this problem can appear quite friendly to other canines but exhibit an obvious "don't touch me" reaction to humans. Kennel shyness does not mean that a dog was mistreated by a former owner. The condition is found among all breeds, and it is relatively uncommon among Boykin spaniels.

In a thoughtful piece published in the October 1, 1995, issue of the *Boykin Spaniel Society Newsletter,* Elizabeth Collins, a public-school teacher and Boykin spaniel owner from Florence, South Carolina, specifies a number of questions that prospective Boykin spaniel owners need to ask

An alert Boykin spaniel awaiting his master's command
in a dove field. Photograph by Mike Creel

themselves and breeders about puppies they are considering purchasing. Ms. Collins did not state a preference for commercial breeders, but she pointed out that their experience is of great value for helping to determine a dog's potential for well being. Buyers should ask breeders to provide proof that the sire and dam have been tested for hip dysplasia and juvenile cataracts. "Structure, movement, and brains are important," Ms. Collins writes, "but good health and temperament are vital. Anyone looking for a long-term pet can live with a dog that doesn't have a proper coat or correct ear set, but a dog that is crippled at six months or that 'eats kids for breakfast' is another story."

Prospective buyers should be ready for a good breeder to interview them too. Good breeders are thoughtful people who want to assure the safety and well being of the puppies they have cared for and to assure a proper fit between buyer and puppy. Ms. Collins points out that buyers who work with selective breeders should be prepared to be put on a waiting list because good breeders do not overbreed their bitches just to satisfy a bubble of demand. They may even refer interested parties to other breeders if it appears the waiting time period for one of their own puppies might be excessive.

There are some interesting stories about how Boykin lovers "know" they have found the right dog. Dr. McKoy stressed avoiding dogs—especially older ones—that have any tendency to be fear biters. Because of his long-term commitment to the Boykin spaniel as a hunting dog, he recommended a fairly bold, aggressive pup with an interest in retrieving. Yet people seeking a family pet will be inclined toward lively and mild-tempered Boykins. Boykins are lovable dogs that will want to work for their owners and make them happy.

By the late 1990s, Mary Kinnear of Greenwich, Connecticut, and her family had had five Boykin spaniels over a period of thirty years. In a 1997 telephone conversation with Mike Creel, Mrs. Kinnear advised that a person interested in purchasing a good pup should start with a reliable breeder and know both the sire and the dam. But, as a veteran Boykin-puppy buyer, she was clear that in the final analysis the best method for choosing the right pup is to get into the puppy pen with the litter and lie down with them. "They all come to you, if they are going to be a good dog for you. I haven't been wrong so far. It's just sort of instinct," Mrs. Kinnear said.

The Boykin Spaniel Rescue

In an ideal world, every dog would find a proper home and human family on the very first try and live there "happily ever after." But, a perfect first home for man's best friend is not always possible. The all-volunteer Boykin Spaniel Rescue (BSR) finds new homes for Boykins whose owners

Logo of the Boykin Spaniel Rescue.
Courtesy of the Boykin Spaniel Rescue

have become unable to care for them, providing proper foster care until new masters are located.

BSR does not have an office facility or a permanent location. Its staff is composed entirely of volunteers who work to relocate, care for, and find new loving homes for Boykin spaniels in need. Boykin spaniels in the BSR system may be dogs from local shelters, strays, pets abandoned in veterinarians' offices, or dogs surrendered by their owners for many reasons. Once in the BSR network, any Boykin without a medical history is taken to a veterinarian for vaccinations and any necessary medical treatment. All rescue Boykins are spayed or neutered before they are placed in permanent homes. They also spend at least a week in foster homes, where they are evaluated before becoming eligible for adoption.

To adopt a Boykin spaniel from BSR, a prospective owner must complete an adoption application, which can be requested through the BSR Web site or by e-mail (see appendix 6). Once approved to adopt a Boykin, the candidate will be given information on dogs currently available. BSR strives to match dogs to particular home situations. If the right dog is not immediately available, the application will be held until the appropriate dog enters the BSR system.

The Boykin Spaniel Rescue is a tax-exempt charitable organization and welcomes tax deductible donations to aid Boykin spaniels in need. Donations help to cover medical expenses, transportation, and incidentals for the dogs. The mission of the rescue can also be supported by the purchase of BSR merchandise through the group's Web site.

Tracking Lost Boykins

All dog owners should consider getting their dogs tattooed or microchipped. These markings should then be registered so that animal shelters can trace a dog turned in to them.

Tattooing should be done in the hairless area on the inside of one of a dog's back legs. In South Carolina the Department of Natural Resources issues registration numbers for a modest fee for individual dogs and for kennels. Application forms may be obtained by writing to the Dog/Kennel Registry (see appendix 6) at DNR.

Microchips under the skin between the dog's shoulders have become relatively popular for reuniting lost dogs with owners. Information on the pet's owner and a toll-free telephone number are recorded on a microchip about the size of a kernel of rice that can be read with an electronic wand. BSR requires that its rescue dogs be microchipped and for the chip to be registered. Their registry of choice is the American Kennel Club Companion Animal Recovery (AKC CAR), which has only a one-time registration fee per owner per pet and registers all brands of chips. The registry does charge a small transfer fee when the ownership changes.

DNA profiling identifies a dog without a doubt, but it is primarily used for breeding purposes, according to Kim Parkman, a Boykin trainer and breeder from Sumter, South Carolina. DNA profiling is easy, requiring only that a veterinarian swab the inside of a dog's cheek and send it to AKC or UKC, both of which record dogs' DNA. AKC requires that any stud dog that sires three litters in a calendar year or seven litters in a life-time should be DNA profiled. Unless a dog's DNA has been registered with AKC or UKC, however, it is of little use in tracking a lost dog. There is no way a vet or a shelter can know if a dog's DNA is on record. A DNA profile cannot be found by scanning, and there is nothing visible like a tat-too for anyone to find. However, if a dog that has been DNA profiled is lost and the owner is alerted to one that appears to be a good match, DNA may be used as proof of ownership.

Housebreaking and Crate Training

Pam Kadlec of Just Ducky Kennel, now located in Edgefield, South Caro-lina, has put together some effective guidelines for starting to train young Boykin puppies:

> Give the pup time to explore its new world but also start teaching it right from wrong. If your pup starts chewing on something he's not supposed to (like your favorite hunting boots), tell him "no" firmly and give the pup something else to chew on. If the youngster piddles on the floor, and you catch him in the act, firmly say "no, outside," and take the pup out.
>
> If you don't catch your pup in the act, he won't know what he is being punished for. If you want the pup to relieve himself in the same area take him there and say "stool" or "potty" or whatever command you prefer. Realize that a young pup doesn't have much bladder con-trol, so don't fly off the handle and smack the pup hard for some-thing she doesn't understand or can't control yet.

A puppy should be taken outside often, especially whenever it wakes up from a nap. Kadlec also recommends walking it half an hour after it finishes eating, taking away its food and water bowls by six in the evening, and walking it again just before your own bedtime. "Don't expect pups to hold their bladder for 7–8 hours," she warns. "Pups can't, and it's not healthy for their kidneys or bladder."

Dog crates are useful tools for housebreaking. Most dogs do not want to soil the place where they sleep, but don't leave them in the crate for too

Boykin spaniel Brant, owned by Vic and Debbie Harlee of Winston-Salem, North Carolina, "kenneling up" in his crate at a field trial. Photograph by Mike Creel

long without an outside potty break. When a pup continually cries, take it outside for relief. Whenever the pup goes in an appropriate spot, heap lots of praise on it.

To protect your puppy from harm and to prevent it from chewing up your belongings, keep the pup in a crate when you are not home or when you are in bed at night. Place the crate in a readily accessible area, and teach your pup to go into in the crate when you say "kennel." Leave the youngster in the crate for a little while at a time with a bone or chew toy to keep them occupied. According to Kadlec, you should "expect a pup to cry at first, but if it gets excessive, say 'quiet' or 'no noise.'" Kadlec says it's good to take the pup outside quickly to make sure the dog does not need to relieve itself, but she cautions not to do this when the dog is actually whining: "If you do, you'll be sorry. The pup will be training you to let him out whenever he cries." Kadlec also encourages owner to cut back on crate use as a dog matures and can be trusted more. The dog will then see the crate as a safe place while it serves as necessary convenience for the owner.

According to experienced trainer Joni Bishop, an owner should spend as much time as possible with a pup. Nevertheless, if a puppy cannot be supervised in the home for a long period, it is better in Bishop's view to

Trainer and breeder Pam Kadlec with a Boykin puppy. Photograph by Millie Latimer, courtesy of Pam Kadlec

A young Boykin displaying natural curiosity. Photograph by Mike Creel

kennel him. It is to neither party's benefit to have the owner come home to find that a puppy has eaten furniture, chewed cabinets, and ingested toxic or potentially fatal objects. While the temporarily controlled, if sterile, kennel environment is not the ideal, it is better than risks posed to the puppy's health and good reputation in the family. But, when the puppy is out of the kennel, he should be centering his attention on the owner as much as the owner should be centering his attention on the pup.

Kadlec suggests a couple of old tricks calming an unhappy crated puppy at night. The ticking of a wind-up clock placed near the puppy simulates a heartbeat. Another trick is to put a piece of clothing that bears your scent in the puppy's crate. Either of these tricks may soothe a pup. If the puppy needs to relieve itself during the night, take it out, praise it when it goes, and put it back in the crate. "Don't play with the pup at this time," warns Kadlec; "just say 'kennel,' and I use 'bedtime' so they learn that it's time to sleep. Eventually your pup will come to accept the crate as its home and safe place and will even go into it voluntarily during the day to rest."

Training the Boykin Spaniel Pup

Since the founding of the Boykin Spaniel Society, the only major issue that has risen in regard to training for the breed is one of degree not kind. Some Boykin enthusiasts believe that hunting tests (and training for them) should be maintained at a level of basic proficiency. Others, however, are more or less of the opinion that Boykins should be trained for challenging, tougher hunting tests. No matter what an owner's training philosophy, there is no doubt that some disciplined training protocol for Boykin spaniels is essential to ensure that dogs bred for hunting are able to fulfill their destiny.

Chris Bishop of Goose Pond Kennel in Gresham, South Carolina, began training dogs in the 1980s. Although he has trained Labrador retrievers, golden retrievers, Chesapeake Bay retrievers, and occasional pointers, he developed an interested expertise in training Boykin spaniels. According to Bishop, Boykin spaniels mature at a slower rate than Labrador retrievers. New owners should not inflict a lot of stressful obedience training on a young Boykin, he says: "Overemphasis on obedience can break a dog's spirit, so necessary both for ownership of a pet and for a good hunting partner." Bishop's wife, Joni, also a trainer, says a Boykin should be trained to retrieve during the early months of its life, but she cautions that the pup should perceive this early training as a game rather than work. "The emphasis on training should be always to develop the natural retrieving instincts which are built into the Boykin spaniel's lineage without using harsh discipline," Chris Bishop states. "Owners should be consistent in their training without expecting wonders from a young pup, since pups learn from repetition of lessons."

"It's not good to try to train a puppy when it is clearly being distracted by children, interesting scents, other dogs and so on," Joni Bishop explains. "Run away from the puppy if necessary to get him to come back to you. Never allow him to run around and play with a training dummy. After a lesson, he should go back in his kennel to give him time to think about what he has just been through."

Getting Started with Training

According to Chris Bishop a puppy should always have a training rope. A long training rope, or check cord, should be used to teach the puppy to come when you call him, an important component of all subsequent retriever training. The check cord should be used to establish good habits, not to reprimand the dog. Although many Boykin spaniel owners think their dogs are born understanding English, Bishop assures us that they are not. "Dogs' minds do not work like ours," he says, "so to teach your dog to come to you, get down on your knees, give them lots of praise, and maybe (sometimes) a treat." He explains that "it will take some patience and understanding, but they will begin to understand what your command means."

Dena Creel using a check cord to work with her Boykin spaniel Booger.
Photograph by Mike Creel

A handler giving her Boykin a retrieving mark during a field trial.
Photograph by Mike Creel

Owners should keep their commands simple, he continues. "Commands should be limited to one word, if possible. Just as with humans, if you find a task is too hard for your Boykin spaniel, try to simplify it. When teaching a dog to stay, an owner should start by being two or three feet away, not twenty. Then, in gradual steps, back up further and further. It is easy to expect too much, too soon from a dog. People sometimes put a dog in a position where it is bound to fail. Don't make the dog *not* want to work for you," he cautions.

Both the Bishops recommend that training lessons should start out short and gradually get a bit longer. They also emphasize that a young puppy should "learn to use his eyes before using his nose." Don't start retriever training by throwing dummies into cover. Throw a dummy where the puppy can see it. Later, when eye coordination is better developed, you can throw the dummy into cover. "What a puppy learns in its early months will form a basis—good or bad—for his later training," according to the Bishops.

The Bishop's Boykin spaniel Clark was featured on the dust jacket for the 1997 edition of this book. Clark also appeared on the cover of the 1996–97 South Carolina hunting and fishing regulations, published in an edition of 450,000 copies. Clark's sire was Nancy Updegrave's dog Pooshee's Superman, also called "Clark" (as in Clark Kent). As their house dog Boykin, their hunter, and their photogenic model, Clark showed the

Boykin spaniel Booger Creel heading for shore with a training dummy on Wood Creek Lake, 1975. Photograph by Mike Creel

Bishops and others that it is possible to have a career as a well-trained superdog, a family pet, and a media celebrity.

A well-bred Boykin spaniel that is well fed and sufficiently trained, can be enjoyed at home or on the hunt, afield or afloat, doing tricks for visiting cousins, playing with the kids, or quietly making friends with grandma. If he's a well-balanced Boykin, he can fill every role with style. Because of their versatility in role playing, Boykin spaniels have been the subjects of many tales from the hunt and the hearth ever since Alec White was "discovered" by Dumpy.

4

Tales of the Hunt

For nearly a hundred years, men and women have gone into fields and waterways with Boykin spaniels to pursue wild turkeys, ducks, doves, geese, deer, and even raccoons. A vast archive of the adventures of long-gone dogs and hunters has been amassed as stories have been retold from one generation to another. The earliest accounts focus more on people and places than on individual dogs, but the more recent tales call these amazing canines by their given names.

Every Boykin master has a favorite hunting story. For this chapter we have chosen to repeat some that exhibit the breed's many attributes. Some tales come from hunters who were there with dogs who are still living. Other accounts were preserved in well-worn letters and hunting journals or told secondhand by people who knew the hunters and their dogs well. This collection of Boykin spaniel "tales of the hunt" begins with the two earliest, which came to light again only in the late 1990s.

Spaniel Hunts at Hanahan

We may never know if the spaniels hunting turkeys on February 13, 1915, at Millbrook Plantation in Charleston County, South Carolina, were what we would now recognize as Boykins. We do know that Whit Boykin's brother Allen Jones Boykin (1854–1937), one of the state's earliest professional hunting guides and dog trainers, brought "his two water spaniels to trail and call turkeys" from Camden for that occasion and that the dogs were skilled turkey dogs. This information comes from the hunt records kept by J. Ross Hanahan Sr. and was cited in a April 29, 1997, letter to Mike Creel from Donald H. Buhrmaster Jr., a Camden native who lived in Mount Pleasant, South Carolina, for more than twenty-five years.

In the 1915 account Hanahan, owner of Millbrook since 1911, described a Saturday morning hunt that started at 4:30 A.M. Four hunters—Allen Boykin, Hanahan, and his sons Ross and William—were placed in two

"Camp at Black Oak Island" is written on the back of this old photograph of Toot Sanders, Legs Scott, and Whit Boykin Sr. with the results of a "good day's sport" on the river. Photographic copy by James A. Monarch, courtesy of the Boykin family

blinds at a spot where bait had been put out. By 9:00 A.M. "no turkeys had come to either place," but Hanahan and his son William ran into a drove, killing one turkey that flew back over them and missing another. According to Hanahan, "Driver Henry Washington ran into a drove and one flew over Mr. Boykin who had a poor shot and missed." After that the hunters scattered, Hanahan wrote, "and Mr. Boykin called for two hours and had two come to his call, one he shot and another that made off. He called for one and half hours again, but none came. We went then to where JRH [Hanahan Sr.] had killed his bird and called. In about an hour a big gobbler ran by JRH about fifty-five yards, who shot and winged him but failed to get. We did not trail much with the dogs, but they surely could trail turkeys, and Mr. Boykin certainly knew how to call them."

Earliest Boykin Hunts

Memories of the earliest hunts that definitely included Boykin spaniels may be found in a November 11, 1975, letter that Devore Andrews, a heating contractor from Greenwood, South Carolina, wrote to Creel in response to Creel's *South Carolina Wildlife* article on Boykins that had been published one month earlier. Andrews wrote to "corroborate" many of the facts in the Boykin story, explaining that he and Stew Boykin, had been roommates at Bailey Military Academy in Greenwood in 1918, 1919, and 1920. "I would go home with 'Stew' every possible chance to go hunting," he remembered.

"We would all leave the house in a two-horse wagon pulled by two mules along with two servants and a tent and bed clothes and food to be gone almost a week at a time and pitched our tent of the bank of the Wateree," Andrews wrote. "We also carried in the wagon five, six, or seven real pretty and smart dogs. . . . They were not called Boykin spaniels then but that is a very fine name for them in honor primarily of Mr. Whit, Buck and Deas Boykin."

Andrews remembered, "On moonlit nights one of the Boykin boys, Buck or Deas, would be listening for the honk of geese flying down the river. When these sounds were heard way up the river they would alert everybody, and we would all get in the boats with the dogs and paddle out to the middle to shoot the geese as they flew over. I don't recall if anybody ever killed a goose." He said the spaniels were also used to trail and tree raccoons at night. "We kept coon stew in the larder all the time—I had never tasted it before—and the Boykins insisted that the coon's tail be cooked in the stew or it was no good."

Bred for Turkey Drives

Since Dumpy's day the hunting tales told about these little dogs have grown progressively longer. The masters of Boykin spaniels are a special breed, possibly because they spend so much time in the company of this most atypical canine. The stories passed on about Boykins and their feats may seem incredible, but these spaniels can do it all.

While it is illegal to hunt wild turkeys with a dog anywhere in South Carolina today, turkey hunting was the major impetus in the development of the Boykin spaniel. When turkeys were plentiful in the Wateree Swamp during the early 1900s, these dogs were used for flushing turkeys and trailing the wounded birds. Hunters from a blind would attempt to use turkey calls to attract birds that a dog had flushed or use the dogs in a "turkey drive."

Baynard Boykin, grandson of Whit Boykin Sr., has explained the turkey drive: "The hunters would travel downriver by boat until they came to a likely area for turkeys, usually where a flock was known to feed. Hunters, or standers, would be deployed on one side of the hunt area, and they would spread out in a line through the woods, concealing themselves behind a bush or tree. Drivers and several Boykin spaniels would then enter the woods, usually at a point downstream from the standers, and work back toward the waiting line of hunters." When the little Boykins hit hot turkey trails they went into high gear, frantically sniffing out turkeys on the run and making them reach skyward for escape. The spaniels barked as they flushed a flock of the big birds. It must have sounded like thunder from a quick summer storm, and to the anxious standers it meant action. Turkeys were everywhere, doing their best to outdistance their little brown pursuers. The hunters and their scatterguns took their toll on the turkeys, but the spaniels' work was not over, for next they were pursuing wounded birds.

Hunting on the Wateree River about the turn of the century demanded a small, rugged dog with many special talents. He had to be the right size for boat travel, good at retrieving, swimming, and close hunting, and fast enough to trail and flush wild turkeys without scattering them too far. The Boykin spaniel was that dog.

Certainly many a campfire bull session at river's edge must have included complaints about the problems with taking a typical heavyweight dog on a hunting trip down river. It was probably not unusual for hunters to tell about their boats tipping over as one of the big dogs fidgeted to a more comfortable position or tried to get back on board with a fresh-killed mallard.

When the Boykin spaniel arrived on the scene, he was called on to do many jobs and he did them all well. "My ancestors used him as a combination turkey and duck dog," Baynard Boykin recounted. "While paddling their boats downstream or just floating with the current, they would shoot ducks that flushed from the willows near the bank. The little spaniel could jump out to retrieve any duck they killed and get back in without disturbing the boat. He took up little room in the boat and so could easily be carried along on overnight trips that required more provisions."

Another way to get a turkey was known as "still hunting." It required one man and one Boykin spaniel. As the hunter walked through a likely patch of cover with his dog, the spaniel located the birds and flushed them while the hunter was busily constructing a blind close to the spot where the turkeys got up. Man and dog then got comfortable inside the blind and began the tedious process of making turkey music on a hand-carved call with the hope that a big gobbler would answer. The still-hunting technique was also used to call in turkeys that escaped with all their feathers from an earlier turkey drive.

"My Dad and I would build a blind close to the area where the turkeys had been," said Baynard Boykin. "If the turkeys had been scattered later in the afternoon, we'd erect a blind and come back sometime before first light in the morning to have a try at calling a turkey in. If they had been flushed in the morning, we'd start calling them that afternoon." While sitting in the blind "you weren't allowed to make a sound, particularly when a turkey was answering a call and on his way in." Boykin remembered. "In the blind with my Dad once, I was just on the verge of breaking that hallowed silence with a cough. Dad looked at me and made a motion that said, 'Here boy, eat this match stick.' Needless to say, that cough never happened."

Turkey hunting is the reason that the little Boykin spaniel has a docked tail, which is now a breed standard. Boykin spaniels are born with long tails, which had definite drawbacks in the turkey blind. While turkey hunters called a gobbler into shooting range, they made the dog remain absolutely still, but they could not stop that excited tail wagging. The blind was too small for a long, enthusiastic tail that rustled every twig and leaf it touched, so some smart hunter cut his dog's tail short. Even with that modification, it became a regular practice for hunters to clear a place on the floor of the blind to give the Boykin a little room for his ever-wiggling stub of a tail.

Just as turkey and duck hunting on the Wateree River required a special dog, a boat the hunters used was also unique, and the small Boykin was just the right size for it. Whit Boykin and his relatives often used a take-apart "section boat." Held together by bolts to form one large craft, the three sections with seats removed could be "nested" like cups to fit into a wagon or train baggage car. Once they had reached their destination downstream, hunters used sections as one-man boats, or waterproof duck blinds, just large enough for one person and a compact retriever. What is very possibly the last section boat was found in the late 1970s under a farm building owned by the family of the boat's maker—millwright Edward Richardson "Toot" Sanders (1845–1922)—and placed in the Sumter County Museum.

With no outboard motors or trailers in those days, hunters needed help taking their boats to rough river landings and then back upstream after a long float. Hunters could easily carry their section boat and gear to the river by wagon for an afternoon hunt, and a wagon could meet them downstream to carry their boat, dogs, and gear back home.

In 1976 another grandson of Whit Boykin, L. W. "Whit" Boykin II, from the settlement of Boykin, just south of Camden, stated in an interview: "In the old days the train was used only for return trips after long campouts. Travelers would go downriver to where the Southern railroad crosses the Wateree River at Eastover and return by train—men, boats, dogs, and all. These hunting trips would often last several days or a couple of weeks. On long trips the hunters might leave from here [Boykin]

The last known section boat open (*facing*), showing its rope handles, and nested (*above*) for easy transport. Photographs by Mike Creel

and take out at Trezevant's Landing [also known as Sawdust Pile Landing] well downstream on the Santee River."

The Adaptable Boykin

While its superior field abilities were developed by hunting turkeys and ducks during the 1920s in the Wateree Swamp, the Boykin spaniel continues to prove his versatility by adapting to a variety of game and conditions from the Atlantic to Pacific. Dove retrieving may be the Boykin's number one job, but hunters testify that this little dog excels at hunting ducks, quail, pheasant, grouse, deer, or whatever else hunters choose to pursue.

The Boykin's small size, willingness to retrieve, and love of water have many plusses. Edmund "Beaver" Hardy of Columbia remembers that "I was all set to go duck hunting a number of years back on the Little Lake Hunting Club, which is about seventy miles outside New Orleans, and decided at the last minute to carry Pat, my Boykin spaniel along. After I got there, it sure gave the fellows a big laugh when they discovered that I had

Toot Sanders (right), inventor of the section boat, and his nephew Julian Sanders Sr. (left). Photograph courtesy of R. M. "Bob" Moore of Horatio, South Carolina, and the family of Julian Sanders Jr., of Rembert, South Carolina

shipped a little fuzzy brown dog in a crate on the plane all the way out to Louisiana," but "before the end of the hunt, Pat had made Christians out of those gentlemen." Not only did she prove that she was an "outstanding" retriever but she "easily adapted" to their pirogues, "long narrow dugout boats similar to a canoe and are real easy to tip over," the sort of duck-hunting boat "that a larger retriever could not have worked from or even fit into."

A Boykin Overachiever

Many Boykin hunting tales are passed along to subsequent generations well after masters and dogs have gone to the Happy Hunting Grounds. One of the best of these is recorded in a September 14, 1943, letter from Jack Baum of Lake Forest, Illinois, and Palm Beach, Florida, to George N. Orr in Nokomis, Florida.

Jack wrote that he and his Boykin spaniel Little George were "all steamed up getting ready to shove off once again for Saskatchewan and Manitoba to lay in the winter's meat." He explained that Little George had helped "fill the freezer" last season with "wheat-fed Canada mallards, prairie chickens, and Hungarian partridges." The previous year some Canadians with big Labrador retrievers had made fun of his Little George before a prairie-chicken hunt because they were sure "that dog is too little to pick up and carry a full-grown prairie chicken by himself."

Little George proved them wrong. The group downed four birds from the first covey of prairie chickens. Little George had already taken the first bird back to his master on a dead run, and "just as their big lunk of a Labrador was about to pick up his first bird George came in from behind and almost snatched the bird out of the dog's mouth, then dashed back with it," Jack said. "While their dog got the next bird, George was back for the last one. Score: Boykin 3, Lab 1—not bad for a little bit of a dog."

Turkeys à la Boykin Today

By 1997 Joe Spears, proprietor of Adventure Game Calls and Guide Service in Spencer, New York, had guided turkey hunts over the United States for ten years, During that time he had become very enthusiastic about Boykins for fall turkey hunting in New York State. "Chuck Warner, a Pennsylvania dairy farmer, and his Boykin, Cutter, got me started," Spears said. "Cutter once ran a hen turkey right into my arms, and I grabbed it. They're the perfect turkey dog, a good family dog, a house dog, and the best hunting companion you could ask for." During fall turkey hunts he uses Boykins "to scatter the flock and track wounded birds."

Spears said that his Boykin Kee Kee "is so intelligent she knows the difference when I tell her to get in the truck or onto my four-wheeler." He added that after Kee Kee flushed all the birds, she would return, sit in a camouflage netting bag between his legs, and go to sleep. Sometimes, he said, she would stay still two or three hours, waiting for a gun to go off. "My Kee Kee's lightning fast and really surprises the birds, sometimes getting right up to them before they fly," Spears said. "I think the turkeys can't see these dogs coming at 'em because they're small. Often she gets right up to a bird-nipping range. She goes with hand signals and comes to my turkey call. I can stop her dead on a run by just clucking a call and she will go toward the sound of a turkey unless I stop her. In the fall of 1996 I was guiding a party of Pittsburgh Steelers players and retirees when we killed seventeen longbeards in three days with my Boykin."

South Carolinians wanting to relive the old days of turkey hunting with a Boykin spaniel must now venture out of state. The use of dogs for turkey hunting has not been allowed in South Carolina in recent history. Well before World War II, the state's wild-turkey population had become so reduced that years of closed seasons and restocking were needed for restoration. South Carolina now has a month-long statewide spring gobbler season with a five-bird limit and respectable harvests. There is, however, no fall season. A trial fall season was tested several years ago, but dogs were not permitted. The American Wild Turkey Hunting Dog Association (AWTHDA), founded in Wisconsin in 2004, reported in 2007 that of the forty-four states with fall or winter turkey seasons, twenty-nine allow the use of dogs. States allowing dog-assisted fall or winter turkey hunting include California, Colorado, Hawaii, Iowa, Idaho, Kansas, Kentucky, Maryland, Maine, Michigan, Mississippi, Montana, North Carolina, North Dakota, Nebraska, New Hampshire, New Jersey, Nevada, New York, Ohio, Oregon, Pennsylvania, Tennessee, Texas, Vermont, Virginia, West Virginia, Wisconsin, and Wyoming.

The fall method of wild turkey hunting—in states with a fall season—is for the hunter to scatter a flock and then call individual birds toward what they believe is their flock. Birds of either sex may be harvested during a fall season. Most birds bagged in fall are tasty young turkeys hatched that year, half of which would not survive their first winter with natural losses. Fall hunting demands greater calling skill by the hunter, since breeding season hormones do not come into play for attracting gobblers. During fall hunts the dog has multiple roles—to locate a flock, to flush the birds, to sit quietly while turkeys are called in, and finally to recover all dead and wounded birds.

During the spring turkey-hunting season, a hunter imitates the calls of a hen turkey, to lure a legal gobbler into effective range for shotgun or bow. Spring season bag is strictly gobblers only because hens are mating and about to begin nesting. Usually dog-assisted hunting is not allowed for spring seasons. Only Tennessee and Utah currently permit dogs in spring seasons. The turkey dog's role in spring hunting would be just to sit quietly while a gobbler is being called and then to locate the dead or wounded bird. The AWTHDA encourages states to allow the use of dogs during spring to reduce the reportedly high percentage of birds shot and not recovered. "Anyone with enough confidence in their well-trained dog to hold tight in the spring should certainly be allowed their company," the AWTHDA states.

The Boykin spaniel is quite popular with members of the AWTHDA, which features many stories of Boykins on the "Tales" page of their Web site (see appendix 6). In 2009 the page included articles such as "Turkey Hunting with Boykin Spaniels" by Dave Henderson, "Training Boykin Spaniel Pups for Turkey Hunting" by Chuck Warner, and "Boykin Spaniels Get Their Turkeys" by C. Scott Sampson.

Boykins as Deer Trackers

By the late 1990s, An McQuaig of St. Augustine, Florida, partner in a restaurant chain, had hunted deer for about twenty years, along with dove, duck, quail, and turkey. Having owned Boykins since about 1984, she found them to be great companions and able hunters, even for trailing or driving white-tailed deer. She had killed three almost perfect ten-point bucks in her years afield. In the late 1990s she had a squad of Boykin spaniel "recruits" with the names Florida Sandspur, Florida Annie Rooney, Florida Swamp Boogie, and Florida's Brown Sugar. McQuaig was justly proud of the exploits of her late dog McEe:

> I rattled up an eight-point buck once when hunting alone. I took the shot and downed the deer, I thought for keeps, but he got up under me. I ran to the truck, got McEe and he eagerly followed the trail right to the buck, where it took some coaxing to move him out of the way for a finishing shot. Later in the season after a period of trophy buck still hunting at my deer club near Ridgeland, S.C., we often use Boykins for driving. Four or five Boykins will run a deer with less pressure than the usual hounds, they'll stay on the drive and they'll come back.

Boykins in the West

Boykin spaniels Annie, Betsy, and Chip belonged to Wayne Frederickson, a Bozeman, Montana, dealer in recreational vehicles. His friend John Rucker from Tennessee introduced him to Boykins when Wayne sold John a vehicle in 1991. At that time Rucker's Boykin spaniel Jeb Stuart was still hunting at ten years of age.

In one year alone, Frederickson's Boykins "found, flushed, and retrieved more than six hundred birds . . . —dove, quail, duck, rooster pheasant, sage hen, sharptail grouse, Hungarian partridge, Gamble and Scaled quail, and pheasant, mostly in Montana and Arizona." What's more, he exclaimed, "they are hell on pheasant, even at twenty and twenty-five degrees below zero they handle it fine. Their feet hold up better because they have tough dark pads that don't grind down."

During that season his Boykins failed to find only 6 of 164 pheasant, Frederickson said, explaining that "normally you lose 30 percent of your bag with pheasant. It takes an outstanding dog to pin a rooster pheasant down. Late season birds are most difficult to flush. They'd rather run than fly, and it seems they know 'If you fly, you die.' Boykins really shine in the uplands—it's probably their best sport—consistently trailing crippled birds a hundred yards and more."

According to Frederickson, "Boykins can also handle five-and-a-half-pound sage hens with no problem." His thirty-three-pound Annie, once retrieved a seventeen-pound goose from Montana waters. But for

Frederickson the Boykin proved its mastery of the hunting game by its superior abilities with rooster pheasants, which "are without a doubt the most challenging game out there, smart, tough, and can take a shot like nothing else and still get away." His Betsy, which came from Keith Cain in South Carolina, won the 1997 Wyoming pheasant championship, competing with sixteen dogs—including English springers, labs, Chessies, pointers, and German shorthairs. The dogs and handlers were given only thirty minutes and twelve shells to find six birds, flush them, and retrieve them to hand.

Frederickson expressed great praise for his Boykins' long-term hunting memories. "You can put them up in the winter and take them out in the fall, and all the ability is still there, unlike many hunting dogs. They're special, we need to keep breeding for their hunting ability and their desire, more so than just conformation," he cautioned. Today Wayne and Trina Frederickson breed both Boykins and braque francais (French) pointers. Wayne continues to use Boykins in several types of hunting, preferring now to pick his shots with a double-barreled .410 shotgun. Frederickson says the Boykins' strongest value is in their retrieving crippled birds: "A wounded bird almost never gets away with a Boykin hot on the trail."

Boykins Down in the Bayou

In a 1979 telephone conversation, Boykin spaniel owner William L. "Bill" Quinlen III of Memphis described his waterfowl-hunting exploits of the late 1970s with his Boykin spaniel Frank: "You can put one of these dogs anywhere. When my Frank was retrieving I could hoist him into the boat with one hand, duck and all. While wading for ducks once I could find no solid ground for my dog, so I just perched him on a floating boat cushion and tied it to a snag."

"We hunted each year on the Bayou de View in Arkansas' Cache River Basin," Quinlen continued. "It's a ribbon of swamp running right down the middle of agricultural land and rough as hell hunting. We'd tried big retrievers there, but they were always swamping the boat. This rough country demands a small, rugged dog like the Boykin."

Quinlen remembered "a good flock of geese" in 1978, when "Frank brought in two or three of the big honkers through the icy water. He would get the birds to the edge of the ice and I'd lift them in." This is no tall tale. Quinlen took a photograph of little Frank pushing one of those big geese through the water.

Some time ago, on the opening day of duck season, Quinlen remembered that his party met at a cotton gin to hunt an oxbow lake off the Mississippi River. "As we pulled up I noticed a fellow there with a monstrous

Bill Quinlen's Frank bringing in a fifteen-pound Canada goose during
a 1978 hunt on the Bayou de View in Cache River Basin, Arkansas.
Photograph by William L. "Bill" Quinlen III, Memphis, Tennessee

Lab charging up and down. He cautioned me not to let my little dog out
of the truck right then because his dog might eat mine up. The joker then
asked whether I just carried that dog along in my truck as an ornament
or did I actually hunt with him. I was about to get ticked off." As it
turned out, Quinlen had the last laugh:

> We sent Frank out after one particular duck that was just wounded.
> The chase was on with the duck bobbing up and down and my
> Boykin in pursuit. The duck dove to escape, and Frank disappeared
> beneath the water. I was about to get worried when up he popped
> huffing and puffing like a locomotive but with the duck in his mouth.
> This really made our day, twenty gadwalls and one spectacular under-
> water retrieve. After the hunt I found out that the big talking fellow
> I had met earlier had lost—as in lost and found—his Lab during the
> first volley of shooting. He wasn't saying much now.

Lone Star Boykins

In 1979, the now-deceased Bill G. Hale, a drilling-equipment dealer and a
devoted Boykin enthusiast from Wichita Falls, Texas, said of his five Boykin spaniels, "They're just a different type of hunting dog—small, lovable,

Amos waiting in the truck for owner Wayne Childress of High Point, North Carolina, at a 1995 national hunt test. Photograph by Mike Creel

affectionate, hellacious hunters, and their stamina is just out of this world." He offered without apology his assessment that they were the greatest hunting dog ever. "My first dog, Beck, was six months old the first time I took her dove hunting," Hale said. "I had been working her some with a training dummy, but she had never seen a dove before this opening day." The hunt was rained out after Hale shot eight birds, "but my little Boykin spaniel brought the first six to my hand and, because of the rain, dropped the last two at my feet."

Beck, short for Indian Becky, went to work with Hale and stayed in his office eight hours a day. "She is small and rides in the front seat of the car with me or wherever I put her and just doesn't give me any trouble at all, whereas I couldn't get a Lab in there," he said. "She's a part of my office; everybody there knows her."

A Connecticut Boykin in Wyoming

In 1979, after nearly thirty years of hunting with Boykin spaniels, James W. "Jim" Kinnear of Greenwich, Connecticut, a retired Texaco executive, remembered one retrieve where he believed his dog used formal logic. While hunting pheasant in Wyoming, he shot a bird that fell into a stream with extremely heavy cover along the banks. The pheasant was wounded and swam up under the bank beneath an overhang: "I sent my dog to get the bird, but he couldn't get to the water because the cover was so dense. He just barked because he knew that the bird was under the bank. With no further instructions from me, he went about ten yards downstream where he could get into the water. He jumped in and swam back upstream under the bank. He got the bird and brought it back out the same way. You don't usually see a dog use his head like that to figure out a situation."

Kinnear also recalled hunting "grouse in very heavily wooded cover where you never get what you might call a good shot. The real secret of a Boykin on grouse is to keep him close and move real slowly through the woods. We also have a good flight of woodcock through here the third week in October and my dogs have no trouble in flushing and retrieving them."

"Boykins are especially suited for released bird shooting," Kinnear said. "A lot of pen-raised game birds such as quail, chukar, and pheasant don't really fly that well but prefer to run. So I think for this preserve-type hunting a flushing dog is a far better choice because they will put the birds in the air. Either you have to kick them up with a pointer or these birds will run and drive the pointer crazy. But with a Boykin you don't encounter that problem. When the birds get into the hedgerows and what not, by gosh, these little dogs put them into the air or the birds lose their tail feathers."

A Boykin Gets a Goose

Frank Register, a Boykin breeder and trainer in Mosheim, Tennessee, wrote in a 1997 *Boykin Spaniel Society Newsletter* about a hunt with his dog, Nip. While hunting a flooded grainfield in East Tennessee on January 3, 1997, Register called a group of three geese to his blind and decoy set. He killed one bird; Nip swam to the goose, circled it twice, and finally fetched the goose to land at his master's insistence. Surprisingly it was an uncommon specklebelly goose, which is seldom seen in that area. Little Nip also added a golden goose to his collection during that outing. For any dog, but particularly one not quite two years of age, to achieve such feats puts pride in the owner—and the dog.

A Winner off the Record

Well-known hunting-dog author Dave Duffey wrote in the August–September 1993 issue of *Gun Dog* magazine that, while Boykin spaniels are

Dr. Joe Lesesne (left), his Boykin spaniel, Woody, and three hunting pals at the annual Laurens-Clinton-Greenwood dove shoot and barbecue, September 1996. Photograph courtesy of Wofford College

not recognized as a breed by the American Kennel Club, a Boykin female named Dixie (owned and handled by Ham Rowen, retired head of AKC field trials) scored the highest of any dog competing in the very first AKC-sanctioned hunting-spaniel test, held about 1983. No official record remains of that test since the Boykin was not in the AKC's book. By 1993 Duffey had owned at least four Boykins and was a member of the Boykin Spaniel Society.

Over the years hunters from state after state recount experiences afield with Boykin spaniels that seem to exceed prevarication. Boykins undoubtedly have natural abilities that are refined with training, but it is hard to explain their sixth sense, which seems to allow them to read their masters' minds. Such rugged tenacity often makes a Boykin stick with a task that just seems too much. But the Boykins' special abilities do not end after a morning in the duck marsh or an afternoon on the dove field. These dogs just get rejuvenated and become the family wonder dog.

5

Tales of Hearth and Heart

The great pleasure of a dog is that you may make a fool
of yourself with him and not only will he not scold you,
but he will make a fool of himself, too.

Samuel Butler in his notebooks

Some say that the true test of whether a Boykin spaniel is going to be a good working dog is determined by how much he wants to play with his owner. Play is a form of training and socialization through which the pup develops problem-solving capacity, learns to look forward to the rewards given for hard work, and demonstrates his built-in desire to please others. If there is a place beyond the hunting fields where the Boykin spaniel's ability and sensitivity excel, it is in the home—around the hearth and in the hearts of family members.

Kirby Tupper and Balls of Fire

One legendary Boykin playmate was Balls of Fire, owned for many years by Kirby Tupper and his wife, Clara, of Camden. During the 1950s Tupper, a local businessman, was also the long-time manager of Mulberry plantation on the outskirts of Camden. His niece, Molly Sheorn Evans, who grew up in Camden and has lived in Columbia for many years, remembers that "Uncle Kirby knew and greeted everyone in Camden with the same degree of dignity. Rich or poor, everyone in town knew him and Aunt Clara and loved them both, and they all knew and loved his Boykin spaniel, Balls of Fire. The animal had such wonderful form and bountiful enthusiasm about everything he did. There is no doubt that he was Uncle Kirby's dog, because anything Uncle Kirby asked him to do, he would try to do. It was like the two of them were joined at the hip."

In 1996 Mrs. Evans's husband, Vic, also reflected on his association with Balls of Fire: "That animal was the most powerful little guy you can imagine. Kirby had a pond close by his home. He would literally take a brick, show it to Balls of Fire, throw it out into the water as far as it would carry and watch it sink. All the while, Balls of Fire was sitting there watching, churning with expectant energy. Then, Kirby would turn to Balls of Fire and say, 'Okay, Balls of Fire, go fetch!' Would that animal take off! He'd swim out as swiftly as you can imagine to where he'd seen the brick go under. Then he would dive again and again until he had found the brick, somehow secure it in his teeth and once back on land, he'd drop it at Kirby's feet."

In 1975 Kirby Tupper himself related that half his bird dogs never knew what a dead quail looked like because "a Boykin spaniel always beat 'em to it." Tupper was convinced "You can teach a Boykin to do almost anything," and his training methods were based on love. He remembered that Balls of Fire "had a special knack for locating quail. He'd start making game, I'd tell him to sit until I got there, and then I'd walk the birds up. How did I train my dogs? Well the first thing to do in training a dog is to get him to love you. That means doing a lot of things with him like letting him ride around with you in the car. If you let a Boykin spaniel stay in a kennel all the time, you can't teach him a thing."

Little George's Ins and Outs

Good Boykin spaniel stories get passed around. A 1943 letter from Jack Baum of Illinois to his old Princeton classmate George Orr in Florida was preserved after Orr sent a copy to his Camden cousin, Ruth (Mrs. Ralph Chase), who passed it on to Kirby Tupper, who in turn gave a copy to Mike Creel.

Baum had named his Boykin spaniel "Little George" in honor of his Princeton chum and was "somewhat" proud of his pet's exploits on the hunt and at home, especially when Little George learned to let himself back into the house: "It was easy enough for any dog to go out simply by pushing the door open, but to come in, opening the door toward him was something else again." Baum's yardman stapled a short piece of rope to the lower part of the door on the outside and then showed Little George a couple of times how to take the rope in his mouth and pull it. "Little George got on to that trick in no time and slipping in from the outside became old stuff. He went in and out fifty times a day and didn't bother anybody to open it for him."

Little George's new ability so intrigued Baum that he decided to find out if his dog could handle more sophisticated analysis. He placed the dog's favorite tennis ball outside the door and gave the command to fetch from inside. The little dog bumped the door and went outside for the ball without hesitation. On the outside with the ball in his mouth, he realized that he could not pull the rope with the ball in his mouth. Six times he tried and six times he failed to bring the ball back to his master. Then, wrote Baum, "he carefully laid the ball down so it wouldn't roll away from the door, took the rope in his teeth and instead of pulling the door open only enough to slip in, he opened it as far as it would go, only slowly and carefully while keeping an eye locked on that ball. When he got the door opened wide, he suddenly dropped the rope, grabbed the ball, and jumped inside before the door could swing shut. Now this is an old stunt and he performs it any time I want to show off to the proletariat."

A Boykin at the Store

Boykin spaniel owners frequently remark on their dogs' affability and protectiveness toward children. An old Camden tradition of giving first-time parents a Boykin pup to rear with their baby shows the faith that many have in these dogs' reverence for little tots.

In 1996 Colonel Gene Foxworth, who was a Charleston businessman and former state legislator, told about his Boykin spaniel's trustworthiness at his store. "That dog must have greeted thousands of children and never growled or complained no matter how indelicate the kids might have been. I have no doubt though that he was also a wonderful watchdog for the store. If anyone new or strange came in the dog would get up and then place himself between the newcomer to the store and the children, always making sure he was closer to the children than the newcomer."

Buster of the Bookstore

Until its closing in October 2008, the Happy Bookseller in Columbia had long been that city's largest independent bookstore. Founded and managed for many years by Rhett and Betty Jackson, the store was later owned by Andy and Carrie Graves. In the spring of 1998, at a book signing for the first edition of this book, Rhett Jackson expressed interest in the breed. Within a few weeks he had contacted the Boykin Spaniel Rescue and made an appointment to see a dog he had learned about.

As Rhett Jackson recalled in 2008, "When I arrived at the rescue, the dog was sitting outside. I'd had the window down on the driver's side when I stopped the car. I got out and spoke to the dog who had been eyeing the car as I drove up. Then, before going inside to talk to the person in charge, I petted the dog a little while. I knew I liked the dog, so I finished the paperwork for adoption and came outside to get him. But when I got outside, I looked all around—but couldn't find him, until I looked up and saw Buster already in the driver's seat behind the wheel, as if to say, 'C'mon man! What kept you so long? I'm ready to go—where're we goin' to?'" As soon as he was adopted, Buster began to accompany Rhett to work. Day after day Buster would lie beside Rhett's desk, "guarding" him from people entering the office.

Betty Jackson liked Buster, but was not enamored of him—something Buster sensed. "The staff at the bookstore realized this and we'd tease Betty that she and Buster were crazy about the same guy," said Carrie Graves. "So one day, I found a publisher's poster advertising a new children's book entitled *Buster*, about a fictional dog. We hung the poster in Rhett's office and had a good time laughing about it. Then I read the book and found that the nemesis of the fictional Buster was a cat named 'Betty.' You can imagine how much humor we got from that."

Buster was about seven years old at the time of his adoption. From June 24, 1998 until July 22, 2003, he was a constant companion at the store and at the Jacksons' home. In the final months of his life, his health had begun seriously to deteriorate. Rhett Jackson remembered that "the night before he died, he came to my side of the bed and nuzzled my hand. When I turned on the light, I looked into his eyes and I could feel him communicating to me, as if he were saying, 'I hurt too much. I can't go on.' So, that morning I took him to be put down, knowing that's what he

Rhett Jackson with Buster. Photograph courtesy of Rhett Jackson

wanted me to do." Until the closing of the Happy Bookseller in 2008, Rhett and Betty continued to fill in at the store. "It's been five years since Buster died, but people still come into the store and want to talk about him. Remembering him continues to give us a lot of joy," Rhett added wistfully.

Another Boykin Rescue Dog Story—from California to North Carolina

Lynn Morris Khan and her husband, Mahmood Khan, residents of Old Fort, North Carolina, were introduced to Boykin spaniels through a Camden friend who was never far from those great South Carolina traditions of duck hunting, barbecue, and polo—in all of which he took part in the company of a beautiful Boykin spaniel whose wiliness, energy, and prowess in the field captured the hearts of all around him. Eventually the Khans adopted three Boykin spaniels within three months of each other through the Boykin Spaniel Rescue.

"Our latest addition is the regal and enthusiastic 'Mr. Tubbs,'" Lynn Khan wrote in an e-mail to the Boykin Spaniel Rescue in May 2008. "He was owned by an older gentleman whose health demanded that he move in with his children. Unfortunately there was no place for Mr. Tubbs." When Mr. Tubbs arrived at the Charlotte, North Carolina, airport, his kennel was pristine after a fifteen-hour trip from California. He had a bad haircut, and he was recovering from hip surgery, but he quickly settled into the household routines on the Khans' farm.

According to Lynn Khan, Mr. Tubbs knows field commands and loves the openness of the farm. "He flushes wild turkey and then eagerly looks over his shoulder to see if one of us is smart enough to be carrying a gun. Mr. Tubbs is a wonderful field companion, ever vigilant, a noble friend." When Mr. Tubbs was advertised for adoption, he was characterized as being a "prince among Boykins," but Ms. Khan says, "This is not true. He has proved himself a king."

Boykin Chocolates

In 1978 then state senator Arnold Goodstein was the first lawmaker to propose making the Boykin spaniel the state dog. He had been introduced to Boykin spaniels at a tender age by his mother, a Camden native. In adulthood he had a favorite Boykin named Russell for Russell Stover candies because of his chocolate color. "Russell went everywhere with me— to the barbershop, grocery shopping, you name it," Goodstein said. "He even had a chair in my law office where he would sit. He was a great dove-hunting dog above all else. If I would shoot at a dove and miss it, Russell would become so annoyed he would bark at me."

Goodstein remembered one hunting incident in particular: "Toward the end of Russell's life, he and I went dove hunting with a good friend who was the manager at the Piggly Wiggly in Summerville," Goodstein said. "This fellow shot a dove, and Russell bounded out to retrieve it, but uncharacteristically, he ate it instead of bringing it back! He hadn't done such a thing since he was a puppy. But, I covered my embarrassment by telling my friend that since he was my grocer, Russell thought he was his grocer too, and so Russell thought he was supposed to eat whatever he received from the grocer."

Boykins on Campus

For more than twenty years, from the 1970s to the 1990s, Joab "Joe" Lesesne and his wife Ruth were the "first couple" of Wofford College in Spartanburg. In 1989 Ruth decided that she would get a Boykin spaniel as a Christmas gift for her husband, an avid bird hunter and dog lover. Ruth had studied the breed's history and was delighted to learn of Dumpy's origins in Spartanburg. On Christmas Day at the president's home, she remembered, "that little guy, wearing a red bow, came bolting in just like he owned the place, running at full tilt into the living room."

The Lesesnes named the dog "Dr. Henry Woodward," after the first English physician in the Carolina colony. "Woody," as he was known, did hunt with Dr. Lesesne, but Woody's legendary status on the campus had nothing to do with his hunting exploits. For years Woody belonged to the campus community as much as to the Lesesnes. "Woody thinks the students and faculty belong to him, not the other way around," said one

Joe and Ruth Lesesne with their Boykin spaniel Woody in 1997 at the President's House, Wofford College, Spartanburg, South Carolina. Photograph by Allison Croxton

student in 1996. Woody fathered several dogs that were adopted by college faculty and staff, and he also became a talisman. If students could see Woody before a big test or important athletic event or (better yet, but not probable) could get him to sit while they petted him, it was considered great good luck.

While Woody was everywhere on campus for years, he was not particularly known for following voice commands from students or faculty, perhaps because so many called him from opposite directions at the same time. But he did follow the voices and the strides of Dr. Lesesne and Dr. Dan Maultsby, then dean of the college. Woody stories became common on the Wofford campus, where one was used in a convocational faculty meeting. As the tale was related that day, two professors were ambling along the main campus walk when they spied Dr. Lesesne and Woody coming their way. One commented, "Have you ever noticed how much Joe Lesesne and Woody are starting even to look alike?" The other responded under his breath, "You better be careful. He might hear you and might not like that comparison." The first replied, "Oh, I don't really think Woody would mind that much, do you?"

When the Lesesnes retired from Wofford, Dr. Bernard "Bernie" Dunlap and his wife, Anne, became the new first couple at Wofford. Although the Dunlaps did not have a Boykin spaniel, Mrs. Dunlap's family lineage is centered on Camden and includes Boykins, and the Dunlaps' daughter's baptismal name is "Boykin." Speaking of his wife, Bernie Dunlap observed, "I've lived with my Boykin for over thirty-five years and find her to be wonderful."

Joe Lesesne and his brother, W. W. Lesesne, have shared two lifelong loves: higher education and Boykin spaniels. Like his brother, W. W. Lesesne made his career in higher education, retiring after a long tenure as vice president for student services and athletics at Erskine College in Due West, South Carolina. To help him fill his time productively after retirement, W. W. Lesesne decided to breed hunting dogs—Boykin spaniels of course.

The president of the College of Charleston from 1985 to 1992 was Dr. Harry Lightsey Jr. Dr. Lightsey, who had previously been a veterinarian and later became dean of the School of Law at the University of South Carolina, grew up in a family who had owned Boykins over many years at their residence in Columbia and their farm in Allendale. Dr. Lightsey's parents had a favorite Boykin spaniel named "Bonnie" for many years. When Beaver Hardy offered a puppy from a recent litter to Dr. Lightsey and his wife, Kathleen, they were naturally interested in seeing the puppies. "Harry was always a dog lover," Mrs. Lightsey said in 2009. "We went

The Lightseys' grandsons Daniel and David Ortiz with their Boykin spaniel Drake, June 2008. Photograph courtesy of Kathleen Lightsey

to Beaver's home; the puppy came right up to Harry and begged to be held, and he reached down, picked her up with a smile on his face and said to me, 'Well, Kathleen, I guess we have our own little Bonnie.' And from that time forward those two were inseparable, whether they were playing, hunting or just sitting around reading."

Mrs. Lightsey remembers how closely Bonnie watched over and cared for the Lightsey children, who returned Bonnie's love. "We had a cabin in the mountains at Crystal Lake. The children would go swimming, and Bonnie would bark and bark to let me know she could see them. I credit her love of them with the fact that today two of our children have Boykins. Even though our daughter, Kathleen, lives in Potomac, Maryland, and the Harry III is in Atlanta, both of them see the Boykin spaniel as a wonderful link to their own childhoods and share that feeling with their own children."

When Dr. and Mrs. Lightsey went to the College of Charleston, their Bonnie was already more than ten years of age. "But Bonnie made the transition to Charleston well, and she loved living on the campus and in the president's home," recalls Mrs. Lightsey. During her husband's six-year presidency, Mrs. Lightsey was renowned on the campus as a hostess and a gardener, so that even today a garden by Randolph Hall, the historic administration building, is known as the Kathleen Lightsey Garden. Bonnie was something of a gardener too, as a Boykin who loved to dig in the earth. "When she died, it seemed right for us to keep her remains close to the president's home. So, she was laid to rest in the garden there." While the Lightseys were at the College of Charleston, the Lesesnes began their tenure at Wofford College. "We of course knew each other because of the fact that Harry and Joe were presidents of two of the state's liberal arts institutions. We always found them to be such compatible people. I guess," Mrs. Lightsey says with a smile, "that you could say we Boykin spaniel admirers stick together."

After a distinguished career in the U.S. Army, General James A. "Alec" Grimsley returned as president to his alma mater, the Citadel, another public institution of higher education in Charleston. "The Citadel, too, has had a Boykin spaniel connection," the general observed in a 1997 interview. "They are wonderful animals and I hunted with them for many years. But, it took my thoughtful granddaughter to bring them into the family. She is a veterinarian in Beaufort and has two of the best-looking, most intelligent, Boykin spaniels you have ever seen," he said, speaking like a proud great-grandfather.

Boykins go with their owners to new places. So, in the 1990s, when a professor of Spanish at Furman University in Greenville, South Carolina, took a new faculty position at Centre College in Danville, Kentucky, her two Boykin spaniels went with her. She soon realized that her living circumstances did not allow her to maintain two dogs. Reluctantly she offered one of the dogs to Dr. Eric Mount and his wife, Truly, then Centre College faculty members and now retired. "Mattie" became an instant favorite of the couple's four adult children, their spouses, and grandchildren. She also became a special dog to the Centre College students to whom she was introduced at the Mounts' home. "Mattie had a real fan club among those students," said Eric. "In fact one of them would Mattie-sit when we would be out of town and became so attached to her that he and his fiancée even considered having her in their wedding party." In 2008 Mattie was twelve years old, and Truly Mount says that "she has become something of a celebrity in Danville." About ten years earlier, Mrs. Mount added, "I was playing Frisbee in the front yard with Mattie when a cameraman pulled up and took a shot of us. The next thing we knew both Mattie and I were on the front page of the *Danville Advocate-Messenger.*" After the photograph appeared in the newspaper, they began to get telephone calls from all over the Danville area, from both other Boykin owners and people who simply admired the breed.

In the mid-1990s, David Spragens, a resident of Nashville, Tennessee, was looking for a good dog for his children when he heard that a pick of the litter Boykin puppy was available in Columbia, South Carolina. He and his children, Liz and John, drove to South Carolina, looked over the litter, and decided on the pup for them. With the help of Liz and John's grandfather, Thomas Spragens Sr., they named the good-natured, chocolate-colored female "Sweet Carolina Hershey." When David Spragens joined the development staff at the University of the South in Sewanee, Tennessee, Sweet Carolina Hershey went with him. After life as a very spirited pup, for several years she enjoyed a more studious, reflective life as a Boykin coed on campus.

Muffin: Good Dog, Good Friend

Boykin spaniels pluck the heartstrings of people in all walks of life. Thomas F. Hartnett, former congressman from Charleston and Republican party challenger to Senator Fritz Hollings in the 1992 U.S. Senate election, wrote a moving tribute about his deceased Boykin spaniel, Muffin, in the July–August 1993 issue of *Quail Unlimited*. "It has been said you can love a dog too much and in so doing ruin it as a hunter: the old 'you can't hunt 'em and love 'em theory,'" he wrote. "Well, theories are made to be disproved. Muffin thrived on love and dove hunting."

Having received Muffin from his congressional office staff in 1982, Hartnett and his family had the joy of her presence for ten years. During the South Carolina dove-hunting seasons, Muffin accompanied Hartnett and his young son. At Charleston-area beaches she chased sand crabs with as much pleasure as she retrieved doves. A ubiquitous presence at the family home, Muffin buried tennis balls in the garden, where today her grave can be seen by the back fence when one looks out the kitchen window. Above the grave is a small wooden marker: "Muffin: Good Dog, Good Friend."

The Lazarus Boykin

Deas Boykin gave a Boykin spaniel named Patty to the family of Kitty Beard when she was a child in Camden. Although Patty was much loved by the entire family, a case of the mange made her fearsome looking to newcomers and terribly ill. Kitty's mother took the beloved family pet to the veterinarian one last time and was told there was no hope of recovery. Before weeping children, she reluctantly agreed with the vet to have Patty put down to end her suffering.

"The family left the vet's office in shock and tears," remembered Kitty Beard. "Two weeks later, however, Mother received a phone call from the vet himself. He told her that after we'd left he just couldn't bring himself to put poor Patty to sleep, so he just kept treating her—and she had recovered. I tell you, that was one sweet day in our household. Such laughter and happiness we all swam in on that day!"

A Boykin Lifesaver

Devotion to their masters among canines can sometimes translate into deeds of daring and even heroism. In the January 1985 *Boykin Spaniel Society Newsletter,* Laura Brown of Charleston, praised her dog, Little Raleigh, for a "heroic deed" that saved her life.

"In the early morning hours of August 20 suddenly my bedroom was ablaze," Brown wrote. "An electrical outlet had shorted out and ignited the dust ruffle on my bed. My smoke alarm had been activated, but being such a sound sleeper, I did not hear it. Raleigh pulled at me, persistently yelping and barking until I awoke. When I leapt from the bed, I saw that it too was in flames. Had it not been for Raleigh's diligent efforts, I would not have the great fortune of recounting this incident."

A Mountaintop Experience

Geoff Groat, who grew up with Boykin spaniels in the South Carolina Midlands, traveled several years ago to Colorado's ski resort area to deliver a couple of horses from Camden to new homes. When he pulled into the parking lot of the development where he was to stay, the horses began to put up a ruckus. It was about 2 A.M., and their neighing and stomping in the horse trailer awoke one of the neighbors, who was anything but pleased.

The angry neighbor had begun to state his displeasure when a little brown dog flew out of his house and ran toward Jeff. "Hey!" exclaimed Groat, "That's a Boykin spaniel!" The man rudely asked, "How do *you* know about Boykin spaniels?" to which Groat replied, "Because I'm from Boykin, South Carolina, and I own Boykin spaniels!" The conversation took a sharp turn toward civility, and the two men established a new friendship. The moral of this story seems to be that Boykin spaniels make great ambassadors in a mountaintop experience.

A Real New Yorker

Boykin spaniel stories also come from New York. During the 1980s a Pittsford, New York, newspaper reported that the three Rochow sisters there had become Boykin owners. Their family had opened a jewelry store in

Hilton Head, South Carolina, where one of the sisters, Debbie, decided that a Boykin spaniel was for her.

No one more enjoys stories about how Yankees are sometimes perceived in the South than Yankees themselves. So the fact that Debbie, a born-again southerner, had trained her dog, Banjo, to respond to a regional question must have gotten a few good hearty laughs in the Empire State even from frozen New Yorkers during a January blizzard. When Debbie asked Banjo, "Would you rather be a damn Yankee or a dead dog?" Banjo immediately fell over as if he had just been shot.

A Boykin/Airedale/Gator/Pit-Bull Cross?

Some Boykin tales sound like fiction; this one really is. Camdenite and former editor of *Outdoor Life* and *South Carolina Wildlife* magazines, John Culler wrote "The Retriever from Hell" (1995), the story of Lucky, a macho little Boykin spaniel. (Culler did have a Boykin named Lucky, a foundation stock dog.)

Former editor of *South Carolina Wildlife* and founding editor of *Sporting Classics*, John Culler of Camden, at a 1981 field trial where his Boykin Lucky placed first in Open Duck. Photograph by Mike Creel

Ernestine Player's Boykin spaniel Lizzie leaping into water for a retrieve.
Photograph by William Aston of Latta, South Carolina

Nine-week-old Boykin spaniel Dixie wondering what to think about two mounted
wood ducks. Photograph by David P. Smith of Blythewood, South Carolina

Boykin spaniel Governor Riley enjoying puppyhood at Mike Creel's home in the Redbank community near Lexington, South Carolina. Photograph by Mike Creel

Boykin puppy Booger wearing a too-large collar at his new home in Wood Creek Lake near Pontiac, South Carolina, 1974. Photograph by Mike Creel

Ned Beard and his Boykin Banjo taking a walk along a pond dam during the 1986 field trial. Photograph by Mike Creel

Richard Coe taking a break with champion Hubba Bubba at the 1995 national hunt test. Photograph by Mike Creel

Chris Bishop's Malcolm sitting at rest in broom sedge as his master asked him to do. Photograph by Mike Creel

The noble quality of a Boykin spaniel's head in profile is seen in this close-up of Lord Berkeley, father of Sweet Carolina Hershey. Photograph by Allison Croxton

Bubba Pope giving a soft command to Dixie Blair at the 1995 national hunt test. Photograph by Mike Creel

Professional dog trainer Pam Kadlec at the 1997 national hunt test with Curlee Gurlee, who became a multiple champion. Photograph by Mike Creel

Mary T. Dial and Katy, who tied for first-place puppy at the 1995 national hunt test. Photograph by Mike Creel

Tripp, owned by Zane Rollings, posing in a red Land Cruiser after the 1995 national hunt test. Photograph by Mike Creel

Chris Bishop's Clark posing in a boat at Goose Pond Kennels, near Gresham, South Carolina. Photograph by Mike Creel

Baynard Boykin and his dog Chip hunting doves in Sumter County, South Carolina, 1995. Photograph by Mike Creel

Paul and Marsha Sumner's Molly Brown, a beautiful example of a smooth Boykin and an able retriever. Photograph by Mike Creel

Mule retrieving. Owned by Chris Meurett and Pam Kadlec, Mule (Just Ducky's Justforkicks) is the first Boykin spaniel to earn the Grand Hunting Retriever Champion title from the Hunting Retriever Club and is the only dog from any spaniel breed to date to belong to HRC 2000 Point Club. Photograph by Pam Kadlec

A Boykin spaniel making a water retrieve during a 1986 Carolina Boykin Spaniel Club field trial at Indian Hut, near Andrews, South Carolina. Photograph by Mike Creel

Mike and Dena Creel's Booger readying himself for another toss of the retrieving dummy at Wood Creek Lake, 1975. Photograph by Mike Creel

Cover for the first children's book about the origins of the Boykin spaniel. Courtesy of Lynn Kelley

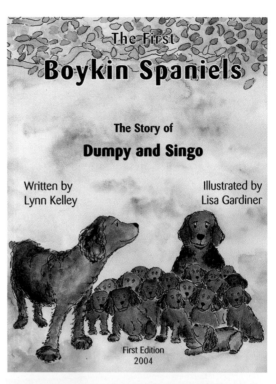

Sweet Carolina Hershey—daughter of Lord Berkeley, pick of her litter, and narrator of *The First Boykin Spaniels*—taking a nap at her summer home at Crystal Lake, Michigan. Photograph courtesy of Liz Spragens

Boykin Spaniel, by John Carroll Doyle, released as a limited-edition print in 1981. By permission of John Carroll Doyle, Charleston, South Carolina

South Carolina's Own, the Boykin Spaniel, by Burton E. Moore Jr., a limited-edition print that was a successful fund-raiser in 1984 for the Harry Hampton Memorial Wildlife Fund and Ducks Unlimited of South Carolina. By permission of Burton E. Moore Jr., Mount Pleasant, South Carolina

Boykin Spaniel, painted in 1994 by Matilda "Tillie" Sweet Boykin, a founding member of the Boykin Spaniel Society and wife of Dr. W. Baynard Boykin, grandson of breed founder Whit Boykin. By permission of Tillie Boykin, Rembert, South Carolina

Jim Killen's design for the 1988–89 South Carolina Migratory Waterfowl Stamp. By permission of Jim Killen, Owatonna, Minnesota

Pride and Joy, by Jim Killen, a 1996 limited-edition print showing a curious Boykin puppy watching a Carolina wren. By permission of Jim Killen, Owatonna, Minnesota

Dove Dreams, by Randy McGovern, a limited-edition print released in 1993. By permission of Randy McGovern, Acton, Georgia

Trio, by George T. "Griff" Griffith, a limited-edition print released in 1987. By permission of George T. Griffith, Lexington, South Carolina

Jigger, painted in 1981–82 by Jeni Quayle, then a resident of Waxhaw, North Carolina. By permission of Jeni Quayle, Waybyond, New Zealand

Generations, five generations of female Boykin spaniels in the bed of a restored antique yellow pickup truck: Harlequin of Pocotaligo "Harley," Pocotaligo's Beretta, Pocotaligo's Pony, UH HR CH Pocotaligo's Bailey, and HR CH MHR Pocotaligo's Coffee—all raised and trained by Kim Parkman of Pocotaligo Kennels in Sumter, South Carolina. In 2000 this photograph by veteran wildlife photographer Phillip Jones was reproduced on a popular poster. By permission of *South Carolina Wildlife*

A Boykin pup scratching, one of two identical bronze miniatures cast in 1995 by Mariah Kirby-Smith. By permission of Mariah Kirby-Smith, Camden, South Carolina

Brambles and Rascal, Boykin spaniels in the family of Edward and Alice Eatmon, as painted in 1988 by Dr. Don Stauffer, then of Ephrata, Pennsylvania. By permission of Edward Eatmon, Kingstree, South Carolina

Be Still, by Robert Hickman, a limited-edition print released in 2005, depicting three state symbols: state dog, state bird (Carolina wren), and state flower (Carolina jessamine). By permission of Robert W. Hickman, Lexington, South Carolina

Pocotaligo's Coffee, owned by Kim and Jule Parkman, an outstanding and legendary performer in the early days of Boykin spaniel national field trials, winner of national champion titles in 1988, 1989, 1990, and 1992 as well as many field titles. Photograph courtesy of Kim Parkman, Sumter, South Carolina

Owing to his small size, Lucky is always the "meat" for a couple of nasty golden retrievers. So Lucky is crossed with an Airedale, and one of those pups is then crossed with a South Georgia animal that is half pit bull and half alligator. In this delightful whopper, the offspring from that cross—Lucky's "grand-doggator"—proceeds to take care of the offending golden retrievers while grandsire Lucky gloats from the back of his owner's pickup truck.

That Charleston Belle

In February 1997 Ben McCutcheon Moïse, a retired natural-resources officer from Charleston, wrote a memoir of his favorite Boykin spaniel for Mike Creel:

Southern Belle, her official name, was number 164 foundation stock on the Boykin registry. I, of course, think she was the prettiest Boykin dog ever born, and she was my ever present companion on land and water, in all weather, in all seasons, day and night for thirteen years. Most people recognized her before they recognized me.

Her photograph was published in many newspapers and magazines, including one portrait with me in the Junior League cookbook *Charleston Receipts Repeats*. One of her pups, Sarge, was the subject of a well-known painting by wildlife artist Burton E. Moore Jr. And her portrait appeared as a remarque on print editions. She lies now on Moïse Island by the campfire she loved so much, marked by a granite stone inscribed: "Belle, Old Girl."

She loved to perch right up on the bow of my boat, snout to the wind, ears blown back like the hood emblem on Jaguar automobiles. She persisted in doing this even though she was launched several times when I ran aground in the myriad shelltops and mud flats hidden just beneath the high tide. Usually when she saw a wave or a wake coming she would turn and dash to the rear. She had good sea legs.

She became a good law enforcement dog and helped to find many contraband ducks and doves hidden by errant hunters. She was trained to respond to my "suggestion" "Find the Bird!" When she heard that, she immediately went into search mode, and if there were any birds around, buried or stashed, she found 'em. One time I pulled alongside a crabber I knew, and while we chatted Belle, up front, began acting antsy. I could swear she was almost on point. She suddenly jumped into the crabber's boat, went under the bow and pulled out a freshly killed out-of-season coon.

Ben Moïse with his legendary Southern Belle. Photograph courtesy of Ben Moïse

Belle was an excellent swimmer. She could even figure out the direction to swim to hit a certain point going tangent to the tide. One night I was in Ashley River opposite Charleston City Marina waiting for a boat suspected of night trawling for shrimp in the river. Belle snorted against my leg (indicating her need for a pit stop). Not wanting to move the boat, I ignored her several times until she gave two snorts, her "can't wait" signal. I cranked up, and when my boat reached shore, she disappeared in the darkness shortly before I saw against the marina lights a dark running boat come from behind the seawall and proceed up river.

I called for Belle a few times, and when she didn't come, I left without her. I followed the reed line along the west side of the river all the way up to the power plant and located the suspects' boat. With spotlight and throttle in one hand and steering wheel in the other, I showered down on the gas and in seconds was on the boat. They were in full tow. I wrote citations and told them to follow me to the marina, where I was going to seize their boat, motor, trailer, net, and catch. I was concerned about Belle but had to finish my work before I picked her up.

As I approached the floating dock by the ramp inside the marina, an old man I was familiar with was there throwing a cast net for shrimp. He told me that about forty-five minutes earlier a dog swam in, walked up the ramp, shook itself off, and disappeared into the dark parking lot. I walked to my truck, and she was underneath. She was glad to see me and stuck her nose between my knees for a pat. She had crossed the Ashley River against the tide, swum around the breakwater and through the marina up to the boat ramp.

One day I had taken a visiting dignitary over to Caper's Island. We docked on the back side and walked across to the scenic tree-strewn "Boneyard" beach. As we neared the Caper's Inlet side of the beach, the visitor commented on what a well-behaved dog Belle was. Things escalated to full bragging mode, and I told him Belle would do anything I "suggested" to her even, for instance, if I told her to go back to the boat, some two miles away.

"Oh, bull," he said. Matching wagers came out of our pockets, and it was time to prove it or shut up. I pointed my finger at her and said, "Go get in the boat, Belle." She looked at me with an air of disbelief. I repeated, "Go hop in the boat," whereupon she started slowly retracing our path to the dock but kept looking back over her shoulder. With a few more commands to "hop in the boat" for encouragement, she finally faded from our sight. About an hour and a half later we took the woods road back, and there was Belle sitting up on the bow of the whaler and glad to see us. It was the sweetest twenty dollars I ever got.

She was a good hunting dog too, although her abilities were largely wasted on me since I seldom had time to go hunting, and consequently my aim left much room for improvement. Some friends and I—Belle included—had been drawn for a hunt on Samworth Waterfowl area near Georgetown, S.C. As we were taken by boat that morning to the lower Middleton ricefields, we were cautioned that wild pigs roamed the dike and to keep our dog away from them. We split up into two blinds, set out our decoys, and patiently waited.

Just before legal shooting hours a flight of mallards swooped into the decoys. Old Belle was ready to go then! We waited six or seven minutes more and each dropped a nice greenhead, all dutifully retrieved by Belle, who was very pleased with herself and the recipient of generous pats and praise.

Those were the last ducks we saw that morning, and thinking the hunt was over we picked up the decoys. I was going to ride around with a biologist who said he would check each embarkation point at nine, ten, and eleven o'clock. My friend went to sit in the blind with the other two hunters, and Belle and I began walking to the dock to await the biologist.

Belle had run a little distance ahead, knowing the hunt was over and her duty done. As I walked down the dike with the decoy bag and shotgun, I remembered the caution about the pigs and shouted for Belle. At that moment a large flock of wood ducks arose from the canal to my right. I dropped the decoy bag, shouldered the double barrel and shot the closest duck to my left. The flock disappeared through the cypress trees, and I walked to an opening near the canal. Belle was already in the water to fetch the downed duck but heading in the wrong direction.

I called her back and "suggested" that she find the bird, but again she went in the wrong direction. I called her, pointed out the duck and sent her a third time. Once again she went in the other direction. I let her go, figuring I could throw a stick near the duck to attract her attention. When, lo and behold, here she comes with another woody in her mouth—fresh killed—one that I had not seen ahead of the one I had dropped. She brought it to my feet, put it down, re-entered the canal, swam straight to the other, and brought it to me with a look of smugness.

Ben Moïse's Southern Belle with Rosebud the raccoon.
Photograph courtesy of Ben Moïse

To me Belle exemplified everything I ever expected in a dog. She was good looking and nice acting. She picked up, in class acts, everything I ever shot (ducks, marsh hens, and doves), slept in the bed with my wife and me, helped raise and protect my two girls, listened to all my griping and carrying on without complaining, and could sense when I needed a lift or needed to be left alone. I, in turn, understood her wave lengths. Most of the time we did for each other without having to say it. How I miss her.

By 2008 Moïse had a new Southern Belle, age eleven, but he could never forget the original. As the photograph of the original Belle and her pet baby raccoon Rosebud shows, she was truly a special dog.

A Guide Dog for a Dog

Banker Neil Raiford and his wife, Karen, a medical student, from Greenville, North Carolina, acquired their Boykin, Maggie, in January 1996 to be a guide and companion for their ten-year old deaf Cavalier King Charles spaniel, Nickey. The average life span for Cavaliers is only nine. "These dogs are our children, and Maggie is a pet. Both are inside dogs," said Karen Raiford in a 1997 interview. "They play, live, and sleep together. Before Maggie came into our lives, Nickey seemed depressed and lonely. He's gotten a lot more lively, and she's really intuitive. Maggie always looks for Nickey and lets him know when we come in. He feeds off her reaction, her vitality, and follows her lead. They are inseparable."

Boykin Turtle Hunters

John Rucker—a former English teacher in Greensboro, North Carolina, who by 2008 was residing in Bluff City, Tennessee—has several Boykin spaniel turtle hunters. During a nature hike in the late 1990s, Rucker's Boykin spaniel Buster Brown was retrieving just about anything his master told him to get. Rucker pointed out a box turtle munching mushrooms. "Buster, what's that?" he asked. Buster sniffed, and the walk continued. Not a hundred yards down the trail, Buster appeared with a different box turtle in his mouth. Trained to be soft mouthed, Buster dropped the turtle into Rucker's open hands, and "a new sport was born." A second Boykin named Sparky and then two others—Jake and Greta—joined the family, and each in turn learned the sport of turtle hunting from Buster.

The new sport of doggy turtle hunting is even helping to advance science. A turtle-hunting dog can cover a larger area in less time and more effectively than human searchers. Rucker's dogs have been invited to hunt box turtles for scientific studies and educational projects in Massachusetts, Maryland, Tennessee, the Virginias, and the Carolinas. If no funding is available, Rucker and his dogs work for free. Sometimes pay is "just a tank of gas," he says. Since 2006 Rucker's "turtle dogs" have helped annually to train high-school students in biological fieldwork for the Clinch River Environmental Studies Organization, which is conducting a study of the box-turtle population in a thirty-acre clear-cut at the University of Tennessee Arboretum's research facility near Oak Ridge.

Box turtles are in danger throughout their range because of the loss and fragmentation of their habitat, highway-traffic and land-clearing mortalities, and their removal from the wild for use as temporary pets or for sale in the pet trade and on the black market to Asia. Rucker emphasizes that dogs trained to be turtle hunters should have their skills employed solely to benefit the continuation of the species. Rucker's dogs have assisted the North Carolina Zoo herpetologist John Groves with a continuing box-turtle study on the zoo's site. The dogs have also been used in a study conducted near Efland, North Carolina, in which high-school herpetology students from all over the state participate in a summer camp on reptiles and amphibians. The dogs found a large population of reproducing box turtles on the campgrounds.

By August 2008 Rucker and his current Boykin spaniels had made their third trip to the Washington, D.C., area for what he called a "big

John Rucker with his Boykin spaniel "turtle dog" Buster holding a box turtle in its mouth. Photograph by Steve O'Neil, Earthshine Mountain Lodge

turtle job" for the Maryland State Highway Administration, to inventory and radio-tag box turtles living in the planned eighteen-mile corridor for the intercounty connector from Laurel, Maryland, to the United States capital. The tagged turtles were relocated behind a turtle-excluder fence along the highway.

The dogs also participated in a September 2007 eastern box turtle study at Earthshine Mountain Lodge in Lake Toxaway, North Carolina, and were featured in *Wildlife Adventures with Steve: John Rucker's Turtle Dogs*, a video produced by naturalist Steve O'Neil. Internet searches will find the latest You-Tube videos and news about these dogs. The dogs' turtle abilities have been covered in newspapers too, including the *Washington Post* and the *Knoxville News Sentinel*.

The Parr Family's Boykin Traditions

Like his father, David B. Parr Sr., David B. "D.B." Parr Jr., a native of Newberry, South Carolina, has served two terms on the Boykin Spaniel Society board of directors. At eleven he got his first Boykin after his father convinced his mother that she really did not want a cocker spaniel. The Boykin, out of Nat Gist's Sumter kennel, was named Cheney, D.B.'s maternal grandmother's middle name. When he was fifteen, D.B. and his family moved from Newberry to a farm in Jalapa, where Cheney loved the outdoors as much as D.B. did. After school D.B. had to corral and feed his father's black Angus cattle. "After doing this several times with me, Cheney figured it out, started racing to the creek ahead of me and would herd the cows by herself," said D.B., adding with a smile: "We stopped doing this after Cheney got a little too excited one day and herded the cows through the fence." At the farm, D.B.'s father began to raise Boykins. His kennel earned a high reputation for producing dogs such as Scarlet and Lady.

After he completed college, D.B. had two more Boykins that he hunted with. In 2008 Parr and his wife, Nancy Blair, both Clemson-educated engineers, were living in the Columbia area raising two active young sons. "At the time we got married, I didn't have a dog and Nancy Blair wanted a cocker spaniel (sound familiar?)," D.B. said. They ended up, however, with a Boykin, Ida II, who became both an in-house pet and a wonderful

Sarah Creel sledding South Carolina–style on a cafeteria tray with Boykin spaniel Governor Riley during a rare snowy Christmas at her family's home in Red Bank, South Carolina. Photograph by Mike Creel

hunter. "Ida loved to hunt," said D.B., and was even included in an article in the July 1999 issue of the *American Hunter* magazine. After Ida died at age thirteen, Reesie Peacey came into the Parr household, principally as a pet for the boys. With the exception of Reesie Peacey and a male Boykin named Jefferson Davis, D.B.'s Boykins had all been named after his mother's sisters: Penn, Agnes, and Ida. "In my family to have a dog named after you is a compliment," he says.

It takes a Boykin to get things done in D.C.

As governor of South Carolina, Richard W. "Dick" Riley proclaimed September 1, 1984, as Boykin Spaniel Day and the following year signed the act making the Boykin spaniel the official state dog—a story told in detail in the next chapter. When he signed the Boykin Spaniel Day proclamation, Governor Riley was presented with *South Carolina's Own*, a print by Burton E. Moore Jr., which Riley took with him to Washington, D.C., after he was appointed U.S. Secretary of Education in 1992.

For one of his key initiatives—Goals 2000: Educate America Act, a reform bill establishing improved national standards for public education nationwide—Secretary Riley needed the support of Representative Bill Ford of Michigan, then chair of the House Education and Labor Committee. During a tense period in the formation of the bill, Ford, a devoted Boykin spaniel owner, saw Riley's print of *South Carolina's Own*. Riley promised that, if Ford's stewardship of Goals 2000 got the bill through committee and to a vote, Riley would consider giving the print to Ford. Goals 2000 was signed into law on March 31, 1994, and Riley presented the print to Chairman Ford. Prior to the publication of this book, Riley has never publicly shared this story of how a mutual appreciation for Boykin spaniels was instrumental in the passage this major piece of legislation.

The stories in this chapter are representative of many that over the years have become part of Boykin lore. With such a rich heritage of stories and testimonials to document this short-tailed dog's value, Boykin owners have understandably been boosters for their breed. Since 1977 Boykin spaniels and their masters have been unified under a national organization; word has been spread across the nation of this multitalented, home-loving retriever; breed standards have been set; the national field trial has become an institutionalized annual event; and sound genetic practices have become the bedrock of Boykin breeders' principles. Given the distinguished career achievements of this little retriever, it seems perhaps only natural that it would enter the political arena as a candidate to become the official state dog of South Carolina.

6

Steps to State Doghood

If you pick up a starving dog and make him prosperous,
he will not bite you. That is the principal difference
between a dog and a man.

Mark Twain, *Pudd'nhead Wilson's Calendar for 1894*

From the time of Alec White's first encounter with Dumpy outside the church in Spartanburg, Boykin spaniels have been demonstrating their power over human affairs. The rise of the Boykin spaniel from obscurity to South Carolina's official state dog is a story of the breed's development and exercise of power among humans. It is a good story, packed with humor, some serious political fighting, and even a wisp of intrigue.

In electoral politics the politically ambitious, serious candidates emerge only when they are considered (at least by their admirers) to have strong interpersonal qualities that draw affection and attention to themselves, almost like a magnetic force. They do not start life as candidates but rather come to see themselves and be seen by others as having the ability to endure hard campaigns, show their mettle, ingratiate themselves with the crowds, and demonstrate grace under pressure. So it was with the emerging candidate status of the Boykin spaniel.

Important as the qualities of good looks, charm, and beguiling grace might be, they are nevertheless insufficient by themselves for modern successful campaigns. Another essential ingredient for assuring electoral success is instant recognition by a wide-ranging audience who can never hope to know the candidate personally but must feel that they "identify with each other."

All in the Family

In the South Carolina political arena, the Boykin spaniel had the advantage of a large, well-organized "family" to promote the eventual candidacy of their "favorite son." Descendants of Lemuel Whitaker "Whit" Boykin and related families were instrumental in the founding of the Boykin Spaniel

Society. While it might be argued that the Boykin family could benefit by having their namesake canine become state dog, the record demonstrates that sincere devotion to the animal was and continues to be their incentive.

The elements necessary for the Boykin's political success came to a head in late 1975 with the publication of Mike Creel's lengthy cover story on the breed in the September–October 1975 issue of *South Carolina Wildlife*, a state magazine with a national readership and a national reputation for excellence. Creel's article had the dual effect of placing the Boykin spaniel in the limelight and heightening interest in the dog's preservation and standardization. The article and the issue's cover, which features a photograph by Art Carter showing a "Boykin spaniel at work" with a waiting hunter in the background, made a powerful statement. The article's success in raising public awareness was reinforced when it was followed so quickly by the formation of the Boykin Spaniel Society. These events promoted the animal's image while also providing a solid base for getting the

Cover for the issue of *South Carolina Wildlife* that sparked a revival of interest in the Boykin spaniel. Photograph courtesy of *South Carolina Wildlife*

breed on a sound genetic track that would protect its superb looks and its superior record of achievement as a working dog.

Why a State Dog?

At this time in the breed's history, at least some people had already begun thinking about the prospect of official status for the Boykin. The record is not clear about who came up with the idea to push for making the Boykin spaniel the state dog. The Boykin Spaniel Society's minutes show that in early 1978 some discussion took place about the possibility, but no action was taken.

The idea of memorializing animals through official legislative acts is anything but foreign to the Palmetto State. There is plenty of evidence to show South Carolinians' fondness for honoring even living humans. In every direction one looks in the state, there are buildings, streets, stretches of highway, bridges, and highway interchanges named for currently serving state and federal legislators, college presidents, and other notables. Many of the state's residents consider that the laws naming these entities were passed for reasons much less compelling than the one that honored their favorite dog.

Boykin spaniel devotees researched previously named official animals of the Palmetto State and also looked at other states that had named official canines. By the late 1970s, five other states had passed legislation to create state dogs: the Chesapeake Bay retriever in Maryland (1964), the Great Dane in Pennsylvania (1965), the American foxhound in Virginia (1966), the Boston terrier in Massachusetts (1979), and the Catahoula leopard dog in Louisiana (1979). By the time the Boykin spaniel became state dog in 1985, South Carolina already had five other official animals: the Carolina wren, voted state bird in 1948 (replacing the mockingbird, so named in 1939); the white-tailed deer, named state game animal in 1972; the striped bass, which became state fish in 1972; the wild turkey, approved as state game bird in 1976; and the lettered olive, recognized as state seashell in1984. Since the passage of the Boykin spaniel legislation in 1985, there have been still more official state animals added: the loggerhead turtle (state reptile, 1988), the Carolina mantid (state insect, 1988), the eastern tiger swallowtail (state butterfly, 1994), the spotted salamander (state amphibian, 1999), the wolf spider (state arachnid, 2000), and the northern right whale (state migratory marine mammal, 2009).

Seeing the array of impressive creatures that had already consumed many hours of the General Assembly's valuable time by the late 1970s, a few Boykin spaniel proponents became gradually emboldened to mount an initial campaign to make their beloved liver-brown ball of energy the state dog.

First Try for State Dog

The first legislative effort to give the Boykin spaniel official status was made in the General Assembly's 1978 session, when Charleston-area state senator Arnold Goodstein, introduced a bill to make the Boykin spaniel the official state dog, giving the Senate its first opportunity to debate the issue. Because of the breed's origins in Camden area, some 120 miles from Charleston, the idea of a Charlestonian introducing such legislation may seem surprising. Goodstein, however, was well aware of the breed's endearing attributes, and he had ties to the Boykin's home region. "My mother was a native of Camden," he says, "and she introduced me to Boykin spaniels in my early childhood. I grew up with this breed and love them to this day."

Since the late 1940s, Boykin spaniels had worked their way into the hearts of Charleston society, where they rank right up there with magnolias, moon mist, and the houses on Rainbow Row. Weekend bird-hunting expeditions with Boykins to local marshes, fields, and the coastal rivers had become a revered tradition for the families of Frank Ford, Bob Russell, Jack Mitchell, Sherrill Poulnot, and others. So the idea that a Charleston legislator might introduce a bill to make the Boykin spaniel the state dog was not a far stretch after all. Besides the senator's wife was a veterinarian and had considerable interest in Boykins as well.

"Senator Goodstein was also well known to Alex Sanders," said one insider. Later president of the College of Charleston, Sanders was a Richland County state senator when the first Boykin spaniel bill was introduced "and a good hunting buddy" of people connected with the Boykins. Sanders's mother, Henrietta Thomas Sanders of Columbia, and her family were from the Camden area, so he was well acquainted with Boykin spaniels.

Goodstein remembered introducing the bill after a conversation with state Representative Archie Hardy, a brother of Boykin spaniel supporter "Beaver" Hardy and great-grandson of Whit Boykin Sr.'s brother Allen Jones Boykin. The 1978 bill was not, however, part of an organized push from the Boykin Spaniel Society. "We followed the news of this bill's introduction with some interest, naturally," said one society founder. "But, we didn't know a thing about it before it happened." While the society's main focus then was on assuring the breed's genetic future, records show that at least some society members were happy to keep interested people current on the bill's progress.

Goodstein's bill encountered significant problems in the Senate when Senator Rembert Dennis, the most powerful state senator at that time, declared his opposition to naming any domestic animal to an official state position. The April 5, 1978, issue of the *State* newspaper included an article titled "Dennis Wants No More Animals in Menagerie: Boykin Spaniel as State Dog Debated." Senator Dennis's position still sounds humorous today: "I ask you whether we should get in the field of including domestic animals. If we do, what kind of state cat are we going to have, and what kind of state chicken? Where are we going to stop?" Dennis and Goodstein had "an exchange" over the merits of the bill, which was the closest thing to a debate in that day's session.

By early May, however, Senator Dennis had not only removed his objection but also recanted publicly, stating that he had not known how few dog breeds originated in the United States and how important this made the Boykin spaniel. A June 2, 1978, memorandum in the Boykin Spaniel Society archives shows that at least some of the society's leadership actively supported the measure as individuals. With Senator Dennis's objections removed, the Goodstein bill sailed through the Senate in mid-May and then went before the House of Representatives.

Once it entered the lower house, the bill became bottled up in the House Agriculture and Natural Resources Committee and died at the session's end. There are some people who say that the Boykin Spaniel Society's lack of organization caused the demise of the bill, but others point to the deep-seated objections of a few powerful legislative figures. A principal opponent was Representative John Wood from Greenville. To Wood, a former high-school principal, it was outrageous that the General Assembly should waste its time on trivial pursuits such as a debate on a state dog when serious issues confronting the state were being ignored daily. "The first thing you know, we'll have a state everything—a state criminal. . . . We'll have state cows and hogs and everything else," he fumed in the press. (In 2008 the General Assembly passed—and the governor signed—a bill to make indigo the state's official color. The state previously had designated an official waltz, an official dance, and other such non-animal symbols.)

When the legislative session ended, Representative Wood had prevailed for the time being. The Goodstein bill had failed, and there were some feelings of deep disappointment among Boykin spaniel devotees. Several years passed before the introduction of another bill proposing the naming of the breed as official dog. In the meantime the Boykin Spaniel Society was organizing with increased effectiveness.

The Second Attempt

The dedicated efforts of Kitty Beard and others to create a strong Boykin Spaniel Society were beginning to pay off by the early 1980s. The mailing lists and the membership list were growing. In late 1978 a committee on breed standards had produced a report that gave an official definition of the dog's appearance for the first time ever.

By 1978 the society already had more than three hundred members. A few years later it could boast more than one thousand dues-paying members. In South Carolina or elsewhere, any local political leader would be envious of a candidate with a thousand supporters who were willing to make an annual contribution simply to receive four newsletters and learn about events where their "star" might next perform.

Much work went into planning the state-dog campaign before the 1984 session of the South Carolina General Assembly. When the South Carolina Wildlife and Marine Resources Commission met on April 20, 1984, Dr. James A. Timmerman Jr., executive director of the South Carolina Department of Wildlife and Marine Resources (later Department of Natural Resources) stated that private citizens and the Harry Hampton Memorial Wildlife Fund had asked the commission to endorse the Boykin spaniel as the state dog. Commissioner James P. "Preacher" Harrelson of Walterboro made the motion, and Commissioner Charles L. "Chuck" Compton of Laurens seconded it. The Wildlife Commission then adopted the motion unanimously with a recommendation that the commission staff pursue the effort in the coming legislative year. News of the commission's action went out immediately to the press. Groundwork to counter potential legislative indifference or opposition had been well laid because Wildlife Commission support carried substantial weight in matters of South Carolina's time-honored outdoor heritage.

State dog campaigner and Boykin Society founder Beaver Hardy recalled later that the thrust of the legislative campaign was directed toward making the Boykin spaniel stand out in the legislators' minds. "Most members of the General Assembly were basically benign or wholly inattentive toward this idea," Hardy said. "It was really what some might call frill legislation, so unless a legislator owned a Boykin spaniel and cared deeply about the dogs, he wouldn't know much about them. It was our job to let them know about these South Carolina dogs and to tell them they had constituents who cared."

By the time of the 1984 legislative session, Kitty Beard was serving as president of the Boykin Spaniel Society. "Beaver" Hardy, who had served

Larry Cartee, executive director of the Harry Hampton Memorial Wildlife Fund, presenting Governor Dick Riley *South Carolina's Own,* a limited-edition print by Burton E. Moore Jr., on the occasion of the governor's signing a proclamation making September 1, 1984, Boykin Spaniel Day. Also present are Sarge Pendarvis, the Boykin spaniel depicted in the print; Laurens attorney Charles L. "Chuck" Compton, chairman of Hampton Fund and S.C. Wildlife commissioner; Greenville businessman David Cline, a member of the Hampton Fund board; and Dr. James A. Timmerman Jr., executive director of the South Carolina Wildlife and Marine Resources Department. SCWMRD photograph by Mike Creel

as president in 1980–81, was heading the committee responsible for promoting the Boykin for designation as state dog. He was determined that the work would be successful. The society has records of contacts made in communities throughout the state, where residents were asked to write to or call their state legislators. Each member of the society's board had been given a number of influential Senate and House members to contact.

As interested as the society was in having the legislation introduced in 1984, they decided to ask the committee not to send it forth. More organizational work was needed because it was clear that legislative hurdles—including specific objections of important legislators—still existed. No one in the society cared to see a repeat performance of the fate that the 1978 bill had suffered.

Boykin Spaniel Day, 1984

Meanwhile the Boykin Spaniel Society's quiet, effective campaign was gaining an endorsement from Governor Richard Riley, who signed a proclamation making September 1, 1984, Boykin Spaniel Day. This celebration coincided with opening day of South Carolina's dove-hunting season. Because the General Assembly was not in session, the slow-news environment gave Boykin supporters a splendid opportunity to present the public once again with the Boykin spaniel as the logical candidate for state dog.

At the Boykin Spaniel Day proclamation signing in the governor's office on August 17, 1984, a Boykin spaniel named Sarge (owned by Judy and Butch Pendarvis of Edgefield, South Carolina) sat on the governor's desk, delighting the press corps and the governor. Governor Riley and Sarge were photographed amid members of the executive committee of the Boykin Spaniel Society, State Wildlife commissioners, and staff. In the background of one of these photographs is *South Carolina's Own*, a swamp-scene print featuring Sarge by Burton E. Moore Jr. of Charleston. This limited-edition print was a fund-raising project for the Harry Hampton Memorial Wildlife Fund.

Although Governor Riley was from Greenville, his popular wife, Ann Yarborough "Tunky" Riley, had grown up in the Pee Dee region east of Camden, and she is rumored to have been most influential in securing the governor's support for making the Boykin spaniel the state dog. During the ceremonies Governor Riley suggested that Sarge be invited to sit in governor's chair, and Sarge promptly did. From the photograph that was published throughout the state, there could be no doubt that the state's top elected official had just thrown his considerable influence behind the Boykin spaniel's candidacy. The day ended with Boykin advocates wreathed in smiles over their progress in getting official recognition for the Boykin spaniel.

The Second Boykin Bill

House of Representatives Bill 2403 was introduced by Representative Robert J. Sheheen of Camden, with a total of fifty-four cosponsors, on February 13, 1985. It was immediately referred to the Agriculture and Natural Resources Committee, which was chaired by Representative John. J. "Bubber" Snow of Williamsburg County, another supporter of the bill. The large number of cosponsors included politically influential legislators.

"Lots of us signed on for the passage of that bill, but Bob Sheheen was the one who made it work," remembered Justice Jean Toal, who was then a representative from Richland County. (Later she became the first woman on the Supreme Court of South Carolina and then its first female chief justice.) "He was the legislator-kingpin without whose leadership the bill was not going anywhere."

Even in 1985 Sheheen, who later became speaker of the House of Representatives for several terms, was—as chairman of the powerful House Judiciary Committee—a legislator to be reckoned with and a man actively involved in constituent service. In the late 1990s Sheheen said he really did not remember much about the effort to get the bill passed. A 1985 newspaper article quoted him as saying that the House of Representatives sometimes took itself a little too seriously and needed to lighten up and see the value of designating the Boykin spaniel as the state dog.

Boykin Democrat or Republican?

Although the introduction of the bill was never meant to be a partisan issue, Republicans and Democrats alike good-naturedly joke that the Boykin spaniel is a card-carrying member of one or the other party. Some Democrats have claimed that the dog's common, working-class origins and its inclusive ancestry suggest that the Boykin spaniel is a real Democrat. According to one Democrat, "Some of my Republican friends try to claim this dog as theirs, because in the summer the fur on a Boykin's ears bleaches out to a Tang-color, which proves the Boykin spaniel admires Strom Thurmond [legendary for having dyed red hair into his nineties]. But, I'm telling you Strom only started getting this color of hair when he found out that Boykin spaniels were his constituents, and he wanted to do what appeared to be the popular thing among those with lots of energy and vitality."

Republicans have counterclaimed the dog as their own. "The facts are impressive that the dog has to be member of the GOP," says one partisan. "From the day that dog was discovered, he has been a self-made, entrepreneurial kind of guy who thrives in an unregulated environment. All he has ever asked government for has been fair recognition of his contributions, never for a hand-out." Humor aside, the Boykin Spaniel Society had no interest in how the Boykin spaniel might vote. By early 1985 all concern among Boykin fans for the dog's political life was riveted on how to get legislators to elect the Boykin spaniel as the official state dog. Of course neither the society nor General Assembly had any interest in making the state-dog issue into a partisan cause. The notion of elevating the Boykin spaniel to official status was representative of South Carolina's unity, not partisan gain or divisiveness.

Even with the bipartisan unity that the Boykin Spaniel Society and its legislative supporters had demonstrated, there were still political disappointments in 1985. "Despite all our preparatory work in the 1984 session the bill was apparently going nowhere again, just like when Senator Goodstein introduced it," recalls Hardy. The society's board and others were aware of a "dark horse" candidate that had its own legislative supporter. The Walker foxhound was being promoted by Representative Larry Koon, a Republican from Lexington County who was a great devotee of that breed. While he had not introduced legislation to nominate the Walker foxhound as the state's official dog, his service on the Agriculture and Natural Resources Committee guaranteed that, if the Boykin bill came to a vote in that committee, it had no chance of passing legislatively unless Koon either supported the bill or remained neutral. Thus the chairman, Representative Snow, chose to withhold a vote and hope for a better day.

Koon felt strongly that the Walker foxhound should be the official South Carolina dog. He was a member of the state fox hunters' association and had a kennel full of foxhounds. Furthermore he could argue with some historical accuracy that the foxhound had been a resident breed in South Carolina much longer than the Boykin spaniel. Koon was not alone in his opposition. The influence of John Wood's views remained in the minds of legislators even after Wood was out of the legislature. But under the sharp eyes of Hardy and Representative Sheheen promotional efforts directed toward securing the crown for the Boykin spaniel continued.

Under Hardy's leadership, the Boykin Spaniel Society had organized a Boykin spaniel "walk-in" before the State Wildlife Commission in 1984. With the legislation before the House Agriculture and Natural Resources Committee, a repeat performance was orchestrated. Owners Nat Gist of Sumter, John Chappell of Batesburg-Leesville, and Ned and Meta Beard of Camden appeared on February 27, 1985, walking their dogs in front of the committee in the hearing room. While some stuffier individuals sniffed as if they smelled something bad, others (Boykin spaniel devotees included) feared what they might sniff. The Boykin spaniels, however, were so well behaved in the legislative chambers that some pundits began to compare them favorably both in manners and intelligence to the legislators themselves.

Opposition Removed

On February 27, 1985, the same day as the "walk-in," Representative Koon suddenly and inexplicably removed his opposition to the bill. Supporters of the bill opined that Koon had pretty much decided that continued resistance in the face of growing support for the Boykin spaniel was not helping him gain any recognition for his foxhound. The Boykin bill was quickly acted upon and reported favorably to the floor of the House, where it had a successful second reading on February 28 and passed after third reading on March 1. Representative Snow and others shared great joy in having the bill finally pass the committee.

Robert Ariail's March 6, 1985, editorial cartoon for the *State* newspaper depicting a self-confident Boykin spaniel ("state dog"), eyeing the State House dome (labeled "state fire hydrant"). By permission of Robert Ariail

When the bill went next into the Senate, it had smooth sailing. No effective opposition remained. The bill was introduced in the Senate on March 5. By Tuesday, March 12, 1985, it had had its third reading and was ordered enrolled. Ratified on March 20 by the General Assembly, the bill was sent to Governor Riley for his signature.

Senator Don Holland of Camden was the floor leader to shepherd the bill through the Senate. Holland was a veteran of earlier symbolic legislation as a chief supporter of the successful bill that made the praying mantis (Carolina mantid) the state insect. In a 1996 interview, Senator Holland (now deceased) was quick to give credit for passage of the Boykin spaniel bill to Representative Sheheen. "After Senator Rembert Dennis had joined the Boykin spaniel forces in 1978, no senator had really opposed the idea. But Bob Sheheen really had to work in the House to get this bill passed," said Senator Holland. Then he added, "I guess there's no state in the Union that has more of a record than South Carolina of making it official when we want to tell the world about something we really like and want to claim as special for our own."

Governor Riley Makes It Official

Governor Riley wasted no time in promulgating the Boykin spaniel bill once it had been passed by both houses of the General Assembly. With a stroke of Governor Riley's pen on March 26, 1985, Act 31 of the 1985 Session of the General Assembly became law, raising the status of the little brown canine to that of official state dog of South Carolina. In approximately eighty years the Boykin spaniel had emerged from total obscurity as a foundling on the steps of a church in Spartanburg, to become the Beau Brummel of Camden society, and finally to be proclaimed through the legislative process as the official dog for all South Carolinians.

Since its rise to official status in 1985, the Boykin spaniel has received vastly increased attention—in part from its becoming state dog but also from its remarkable lines, physical agility, and noble character. Some of the nation's finest wildlife artists have painted the Boykin spaniel in hunting and playful domestic settings. These good-looking little reddish-brown dogs are now also found in calendars, editorial cartoons, sculpture, videos, novels and all over the Internet. As the next chapter shows, visual artists and Boykin spaniels have found each other more with each passing decade.

7

Boykin Images

From Fine Art to Fiction

Dogs are not our whole life, but they make our lives whole.

Roger Caras

Images of South Carolina's state dog, the Boykin spaniel, are no longer in short supply. They seem to surface everywhere and in every form. By the 1990s hardware stores in places such as Lexington, South Carolina, were proudly displaying gray sweatshirts bearing the image of the first South Carolina Migratory Waterfowl Stamp featuring the Boykin spaniel. Scores of professional artists have immortalized the dog in their works since 1978. Photographs of this little retriever are appearing in national magazines, photography contests, calendars, and most abundantly in the Boykin's home-state periodical *South Carolina Wildlife*. On the Internet several Web sites are devoted to Boykin spaniels, and a topic search will locate other images and items. South Carolina Educational Television has produced a video on the Boykin community with a short segment devoted to the breed and its origins.

As the Boykin spaniel became a fixture of households and hunting lodges in South Carolina and beyond, the search for images by which to remember these animals became a driving a force for owners and admirers of the breed. Photographs, framed art prints, shirts, caps, and coffee mugs became personal mementos that kept the little brown dogs in the minds of their masters, signaled human enthusiasm for the Boykin, and served as magnets to bring people with common interests together.

The First Boykin Paintings

The earliest images of Boykins are photographs taken during the 1920s. Several decades passed before the emergence of any appreciable number of other kinds of artwork depicting the Boykin spaniel. Inevitably they began to appear because there was a market among owners and admirers for lifelike images of this dog. The best pieces of art capture the Boykin in familiar settings, such as waiting by a dove-hunter's stool or perched attentively in a duck boat. The dog's master is usually out of the scene, which makes it possible for each viewer to mentally step into the empty space next to the Boykin.

Formation of the Boykin Spaniel Society became a major impetus for the production of Boykin artworks. By giving lovers of the breed a center of interest, the society has proved a magnet for Boykiniana of all sorts. Society minutes from early 1978 show it considered endorsing a head portrait of a Boykin by Prescott S. "Sonny" Baines, a Lexington, South Carolina, wildlife artist, as a first official portrait. The proposal did not gain approval, probably because of its timing. The Boykin Spaniel Society had not yet established a breed standard, and a visual depiction endorsed by the society might have been construed as the standard itself.

This minor setback did not quell Baines's enthusiasm to capture the Boykin on canvas. He produced three paintings in late 1977 and early 1978. The head portrait, which became the basis for a limited edition print released in 1981, became the property of McKee Boykin Jr. and Margaret "Susie" Boykin of St. Matthews, South Carolina, each of whom has been an avid collector of Boykin spaniel art. Susie Boykin said in 1997 that the painting by Baines was an authentic representation of the dog "because of the sensitivity in the eyes, the rendering of the fur, and the general coloration. . . . it is a very fine example of what a good Boykin spaniel should look like." This portrait (reproduced as the frontispiece for this book) was based on several dogs, including those of Baynard Boykin and Mike Creel's first dog, Booger.

McKee Boykin's brother, Hamilton Boykin, owns another of Baines's Boykin spaniel trilogy, *The Cornfields of Boykin*. This painting shows a Boykin spaniel in a cornfield near the hamlet of Boykin with doves flying above in an azure sky. The third Baines painting belongs to Baynard and Matilda Boykin and depicts their own dog sitting amid shotgun shells with several bagged mourning doves close by.

Other early examples of high-quality Boykin portraiture include works by Randy McGovern, Matilda "Tillie" Boykin, and Jim Killen. Collectors such as McKee Boykin have found numbered prints of Boykins marketed in shops and art fairs as far away as New Orleans. With the growth of the Internet, it is difficult to say where Boykin items are most marketed today although South Carolina sites are still prominent.

McKee Boykin stated that "paintings of these little guys add a wonderful regional twist to life in South Carolina," adding that, "Of course, it is especially meaningful if you carry the name Boykin in your own family . . . you kind of transfer all those wonderful feelings you have for your animal onto the painting itself."

Boykin Notecards

In early 1978 Kitty Beard, then executive secretary of the Boykin Spaniel Society, tracked down an illustration of a Boykin spaniel that she and other executive committee members admired. Vim, a little dog owned by Mrs. Carl J. Gilbert of Dover, Massachusetts, had been painted by Evelyn S. Cunningham of Needham, Massachusetts. The society requested permission to use this image on its postcards "to help the Boykin spaniel become nationally recognized." Ms. Cunningham agreed for a nominal fee of $275. Since then Vim's likeness has appeared countless times on society postcards.

Jim Killen's Boykin Images

The most prolific and dedicated of Boykin spaniel artists is Jim Killen. A Minnesota native, Killen, has been associated with the South Carolina wildlife art community since February 1987, when his painting *School Daze* was featured on the poster for the Southeast Wildlife Exposition in Charleston. Depicting a variety of retriever puppies waiting for instruction, *School Daze* was an instant success. The *School Daze* original sold for $10,000, and poster sales were brisk. Unfortunately the Boykin spaniel puppy was not included in the class, but public disappointment with the Boykin pup's absence persuaded Killen to paint *Late for School,* of just a Boykin spaniel puppy. The painting features Robert Russell's puppy Pooshee's Box of Chocolates, nicknamed "Boxer," staring forlornly at a little blue ball and a leash. This little Boykin has apparently missed the bell, and the other pups in his class have been taken afield for an education without him.

Killen endeared himself further to the Boykin-adoring public when his painting of a Boykin spaniel (based on his friend Bob Russell's Pooshee's Buckshot) won the 1988–89 South Carolina Migratory Waterfowl Stamp competition. The South Carolina state duck stamp for 1988–89 season was the first to feature an animal other than a duck or goose. The design shows the head of a Boykin spaniel holding a well secured widgeon, proud trophy of the hunt. This stamp remains South Carolina's best-selling duck-stamp design. The 1988 Governor's Edition print and stamp matted and framed with a metallic seal, which sold originally for $350, has been known to fetch $1,500 in the resale market.

Minnesota wildlife artist Jim Killen holding his winning entry in the 1988–89 South Carolina Migratory Waterfowl Stamp competition

Interest in Killen's art is often ascribed to his consistent attention to detail. This quality is particularly evident in the Boykin design for the 1988–89 South Carolina Migratory Waterfowl Stamp, where he extends the same exactness to the dog and to the widgeon the dog holds. Owners of Boykin spaniels agree that this Minnesota artist captures the breed's enthusiasm for retrieving. As one Boykin devotee put it, "Killen only depicts the head and neck of the dog in his duck stamp, but he does it with such intensity you can almost see the dog's docked tail wagging when you look at the painting."

In the early 1990s Killen followed his Boykin duck stamp with a Carolina Heritage series of paintings, commissioned by the South Carolina Waterfowl Association. The association's 1993–94 duck-stamp print from the series features an adult Boykin spaniel in the field with a pair of wood ducks flying overhead and a Mason wood duck decoy on the ground. His representation of the good life of gentlemanly hunting in South Carolina's coastal marshes evokes powerful emotions in the state's devotees of the sport. Boykin sweatshirts, T-shirts, and a variety of other products bearing Killen's designs are still marketed.

In 1996 Killen returned to the Southeastern Wildlife Exposition in Charleston with another Boykin painting, *Pride and Joy.* This time the dog is a puppy seated in an open field and gazing to the foreground at a Carolina wren. In whatever scene he chooses to cast the Boykin spaniel, Killen has had the ability to please Boykin spaniel lovers by fusing native landscape scenes with realistic portrayals of South Carolina's dog.

By the late 1990s, Killen had assured himself a place in the wildlife art market in South Carolina. His wife, Karen, stated at that time that Killen had been commissioned to paint at least one Boykin spaniel per year for each of the past ten years. His Web site displays various recent Boykin paintings. Many but not all of the patrons for these works came from South Carolina. At the same time, Killen contributed a design to the Franklin Mint for a decorative plate featuring a variety of retrievers, including a Boykin spaniel, ensuring a place for the little brown dog from South Carolina on fine porcelain as well as canvas. Most recently Killen painted a Boykin in the ACE Basin marshland with two wood ducks flying above. This image will appear on the thirtieth annual South Carolina Migratory Waterfowl Commemorative stamp (2010–11 hunting season). The stamp and a poster are scheduled for release in July 2010.

Boykin Swamp Scene

One of the earliest paintings of the Boykin spaniel, still a favorite among Boykin lovers, is *South Carolina's Own, the Boykin Spaniel,* created in 1984 by Burton E. Moore Jr. to benefit the Harry Hampton Memorial Wildlife Fund and the South Carolina chapters of Ducks Unlimited. According to Moore, who lives in Mount Pleasant, South Carolina, the painting was the first one endorsed by the Boykin Spaniel Society as an accurate representation of the breed. The work features Sarge, the same dog who sat in Governor Riley's chair during the August 1984 proclamation of Boykin Spaniel Day.

Sarge was not only a great model for a painting, but also a son of Ben Moïse's Southern Belle. In Moore's painting light filters through cypress boughs in a southern swamp to reveal a Boykin spaniel in a weathered wooden boat beside four bagged wood ducks, the apparent result of the dog's work. The original painting was sold at auction for $10,000. Nine-hundred and fifty signed and numbered limited edition prints were originally sold for $125 each and now command much higher prices. Moore donated the money from Boykin print sales to Ducks Unlimited and the Harry Hampton Memorial Wildlife Fund and feels some pride that his art benefited the early conservation of the Congaree Swamp, now South Carolina's only National Park.

Other South Carolina Boykin Artists

Charleston artist John Carroll Doyle has specialized in marine fish life, character studies of people such as musicians and fishermen, and local scenes, but in 1981 his painting *Boykin Spaniel*, he "went to the dogs" in the best sense of the word when he depicted two bright-eyed Boykin spaniels in a fall coastal scene of golden oaks, sand, and marsh. Artist Barbara Shipman of Beaufort, South Carolina, found inspiration for her 1989 Boykin spaniel painting *Boykin Playpen* in an experience at the Southeastern Wildlife Exposition, where she watched a "full of himself" Boykin pup named Cody making several forays into the crowd and even grabbing the tail of a man in an alligator costume and refusing to let go. Published by Tidwell Galleries in Charleston as a signed and numbered series of 1,450 prints, *Boykin Playpen* shows a playful Boykin pup in command of his surroundings, peering over the side of a boat with a background of crab pots and a blue sky with billowy white clouds.

An Ohio native, Robert Hickman of Lexington, South Carolina, has lived in South Carolina since 1977 and became a full-time artist in 1996. In 1998 he began focusing on wildlife and sporting dogs, but did not "discover" Boykin spaniels until 2002. "I knew they were our state dog, but really did not know much about them. . . . After getting to know several owners and trainers of Boykins and being educated by them about the breed, I knew that I had to add this breed to my portfolio." Hickman developed a series of seven limited-edition Boykin art prints. Among them is *Be Still*, which shows a Boykin puppy watching a Carolina wren perched in yellow jessamine—three popular state symbols in one work. Hickman's *Boykin Spaniel Portrait*, a head and neck view of a Boykin with a background of winter cattails, is being used by the Boykin Spaniel Society as

When I Grow Up, by Robert Hickman, a limited edition print
released in 2003. By permission of Robert HIckman

Image 18 X 24 $75.00 S/N

The Boykin Spaniel: South Carolina's Native Son, by Julia Horner,
a limited-edition print released in 1997. By permission of Julia Horner

its logo. *Faithful* is another head and neck portrait of a Boykin, this time holding a mourning dove in its mouth. *Boykin Graphite—Double Image* is a head and neck view of a male and a female Boykin, which can be framed together or separately.

Hickman's *When I Grow Up* (2003) is the first in his series of sporting-dog prints that depicts an adult dog and an admiring pup. In this work, an adult Boykin spaniel is shown with a retrieved dove while the pup at his side carries a small dove feather in the corner of his mouth. "I have come to know many [Boykin] owners and have found them to be very passionate about their little brown dogs," Hickman says; "I have really enjoyed painting Boykins and am glad to play a small part in introducing people around the country to this very special bred through my artwork."

A Boykin Art Link to President Carter

Julia Horner, a journalist and freelance writer who has spent much of her career in North Carolina and Virginia, developed an appreciation for things from South Carolina through her parents, an alumna of Converse College and a graduate of the Citadel. "I gave my heart to Boykin spaniels in the early 1980s," Ms. Horner has said. In 1997, while "working as a Boykin Spaniel Rescue recruit for local dog transport," she began to take an interest in Boykin art. Because she "wanted to provide Boykin lovers with a representation that was not the same hunting motif, she created a print called *The Boykin Spaniel: South Carolina's Native Son.*

Ms. Horner's great-great-grandfather and President Jimmy Carter's great-great-grandmother were brother and sister, so when she took her mother to a family reunion in 1980s, Ms. Horner had the privilege of presenting one of the prints to President Jimmy Carter. She refers to her Boykin spaniels as "my boys" and has featured them in interpretive New

Julia Horner presenting her portrait of a Boykin spaniel to her cousin President Jimmy Carter. Photograph courtesy of Julia Horner

Year's cards. She has also illustrated Bill Crites's *Piper Anne Crabby Pants's First Big Adventure*, a children's story about Boykin spaniel manners, which should be available for purchase in late 2009.

An Amateur Effort

The popularity of Boykin spaniels and the affection they engender have led to an increasing number of amateur efforts to reflect the feelings of owners for their own dogs and for the breed as a whole. One such painting is *Lord Berkeley, the Boykin*, which Lynn Kelley originally created for the amusement of his family and friends. In 2001, Kelley remembered, "Our family decided to have a big party for Lord Berkeley (AKA 'Berke') to celebrate his tenth whelping day. We were surprised and delighted when twenty-nine people and five dogs from four states accepted the invitation to the party." Because he was named after one of the Carolina Colony's Lords Proprietor, Berke is depicted wearing an eighteenth-century British military officer's dress uniform and a medallion for the "Order of the Top Dog" hanging from a sash. Friends began suggesting humorously that Kelley should enter the painting in the 2002 State Fair art contest. "It's hard to tell who was more surprised when it was juried for inclusion in the 'amateur' class—my friends or me," said Kelley, "but I like to think that Berke enjoyed that painting. After all, he lived until he was fifteen

Lord Berkeley, the Boykin, by Lynn Kelley, a juried selection for the 2002 State Fair amateur division. Courtesy of Lynn Kelley

plus, so he sure heard a lot about it for the next five years." Lord Berkeley's successor, Mary Boykin Chesnut "Mugsy" has already developed an artistic trail of her own while still a puppy. At less than one year in age, she has been the subject of scores of photographs.

The tradition of painting the Boykin spaniel is not a long one. Nevertheless, as the pieces of art described here indicate, the acceptance of the breed by a large and growing public has been accompanied by a growing demand for both humorous and aesthetically rich images that capture the aristocracy of form, the exquisite coloration, and endearing emotional qualities of the compact retriever from Camden. Without any fear of false prophecy, one can say that the heyday of Boykin art had only begun by the late 1980s and early 1990s and that the classics of the 1970s and 1980s will become increasingly sought after even as new images of Boykins proliferate and become readily available for sale on the Internet.

A Pennsylvania Boykin Artist

There is something about the bold and noble face and lines of a Boykin spaniel that attracts artists. Jocelyn Beattie, a wildlife artist who lives in the small town of West Middlesex in northwestern Pennsylvania, met a Boykin spaniel from Randy Good's Nickelson Run Kennel in Kittaning, Pennsylvania, shortly after her good friend Thomas G. Hunt had purchased it. She immediately fell in love with "Roadie" (Trumpeter's Roadie Oh), and waited for ten months for the pup to mature before beginning a painting of the dog's head. The painting was completed in time for Ms. Beattie to display it at the prestigious Chestertown Wildlife Art Show on Maryland's Eastern Shore. The painting sold very quickly and now has a new home in Maryland. A limited edition of two hundred numbered prints of Roadie is also selling well.

Boykin Spaniel Sculpture

At least four original sculpted pieces of Boykin spaniels stand out amid a variety of mass-produced items. One of these, which was sold in a limited edition in 1991, is a stoneware miniature cast from an original clay model sculpted by Mary Deas Boykin (Mrs. Tom) Worley of Middleton, Ohio, daughter of the late L. W. "Whit" Boykin II of Camden and great-granddaughter of breed founder Whit Boykin. She patterned her sculpture after her father's favorite dog, Bucky.

Mariah J. Kirby-Smith, a professional sculptor whose business is Certified Palmetto Bug Castings in Camden, has been commissioned to create three different Boykin sculptures. Her first is a half life-size bronze of Sam Boykin's beloved Boykin spaniel Murdock with empty shotgun shells at

Bucky (*left*), a stoneware miniature sculpted before 1991 by Mary Deas Boykin Wortley. Photograph reprinted from the *Boykin Spaniel Society Newsletter,* by permission of the Boykin Spaniel Society

Murdock (*below*), sculpted in 1989 by Mariah Kirby-Smith. Image courtesy of Mariah Kirby-Smith

Boykin Girl, Mariah Kirby-Smith's bronze of a girl and her Boykin spaniel, located at the Kershaw County Public Library in Camden, South Carolina. Photograph by Mike Creel, courtesy of Mariah Kirby-Smith

his feet, which was commissioned as a birthday gift for Sam in 1989 by Sam's wife, Nancy, of Sewanee, Tennessee. This sculpture is now owned by Boykin master and avid hunter Howard Nichol of San Antonio, Texas. One additional casting is in Kirby-Smith's personal collection.

In 1995 Kirby-Smith did a sculpture of a Boykin puppy scratching itself, which is displayed with a Missouri mule and other images on the interior of the World of Unity Globe, commissioned by the Unity School of Christianity in Lee's Summit, Missouri. Kirby-Smith's most recent Boykin spaniel work was commissioned in 2004 by the Friends of Kershaw Library for Kershaw County Library. Placed in the main library at 1304 Broad Street in Camden, the life-size bronze sculpture depicts a young girl reading a book about dogs and petting her Boykin spaniel. Unveiled in late June 2006, the 380-pound sculpture was placed atop a solid mahogany base. Kathy Hill, president of the Friends of the Kershaw Library, told the *Camden Chronicle* at the unveiling that three young Camden ladies modeled for Ms. Kirby-Smith: Virginia and Margaret Lackey and Sophie Sweet.

Photography

Photography of the Boykin spaniel has evolved from an age of snapshots into an art form of its own. While all Boykin spaniel owners probably photograph their dogs, some are producing near-professional shots of their favorite canines in posed and candid scenes. The Boykin's dark hair and unquenchable vitality pose a challenge for high-definition photography. Even when they manage to get a Boykin to hold still for as little as a split second, professionals as well as amateurs regularly fail to capture the complex, nuanced textures and coloration of the dog's coat, since the lighting and camera angle must be perfect to meet the challenge. As the photographs in this book show, however, when these challenges have been met, the results are frequently amazing. Fostering the quest for better and better photographs are publications such as *South Carolina Wildlife*, which probably has the record for publishing excellent Boykin images and holds an annual photography contest that draws in good, new Boykin photographs. A number of other state and national magazines, as well as South Carolina newspapers, have also featured good Boykin spaniel photographs.

In the 1997 *South Carolina Wildlife* photography competition, held at the Palmetto Sportsmen's Classic in Columbia, two quality Boykin works by amateur photographers were displayed. One was a photograph of Lizzie, a smooth Boykin, shown in the split second of her leap into the water. Now deceased, Lizzie was owned by Ernestine Player of Columbia and photographed by her nephew, William Aston of Latta, South Carolina. Aston's photograph captures the dog's enthusiasm, and the viewer can almost hear the splash of the water.

In the same contest David P. Smith of Blythewood, South Carolina, exhibited two photographs of a Boykin puppy investigating two mounted wood ducks, thus displaying the budding of its primal instincts toward his future quarry of the hunt. The puppy's sleekness is played off against the flamboyant colors of South Carolina's most abundant summer duck.

While amateur photographers continue to produce impressive images of Boykin spaniels, professional photographers have set the highest standards. Since the mid-1970s *South Carolina Wildlife* has led the field by providing Boykin spaniel fans with increasing numbers of photographs. They include Ted Borg's shot of Kim Parkman's Pocotaligo's Coffee in front of a haystack near Sumter, published with Rick Leonardi's story "Gun Pups" in the September–October 1993 issue. Equally impressive are shots of various Boykins by Robert Clark and Michael Foster with Gigi Huckabee's article "Owner's Choice" in the November–December 1986 issue.

Cover Dogs and Calendar Dogs

Boykin spaniels have made it onto *South Carolina Wildlife*'s cover on at least two occasions. The first was the September–October 1975 issue, for which Art Carter snapped an action shot of a Boykin charging through corn stubble straight at the camera. The September–October 1983 issue had Boykins on both front and back covers: Phillip Jones's photographs of Coach Campbell's Cocoa and Flea Baggins retrieving dummies in Dillon, South Carolina, to support Pat Robertson's article "First in the Field" about field-trial champions.

Boykins have made it three times into the *Sportsman's Calendar* published by *South Carolina Wildlife*. Phillip Jones's photograph of George Brown Campbell's Cocoa splashing into the water was the November choice in the 1984–85 calendar. Mike Creel's photograph of young Ryan Jordan of Florence and his puppy, Swamp Fox, were on the February page of the 1986–87 calendar. Another Phillip Jones photograph, this time of Kim Parkman's Pocotaligo's Colt under a Christmas tree like a present was on the December page in the 1996–97 calendar.

South Carolina Poster Art

Well worth mentioning is the educational poster printed by the Harry Hampton Memorial Wildlife Fund to promote the March 18–20, 1988, Palmetto Sportsmen's Classic outdoor show in Columbia. The poster features the Boykin spaniel and other South Carolina official symbols, including the whitetail deer, the wild turkey, the Carolina wren, the striped bass, and yellow jessamine with a fact-filled narrative on the reverse side. Since this poster is now a collector's item, it would be well worth reprinting.

Phillip Jones, who is on the staff of the South Carolina Department of Natural Resources, took the photograph *Generations*, which was used on a poster printed in 2000. The fifteen hundred copies sold out in a matter of months. The photograph features five generations of Boykin spaniel bitches: the grande dame Pocotaligo's Coffee, Harlequin of Pocotaligo, Pocotaligo's Beretta, Pocotaligo's Pony, and Pocotaligo's Bailey. The Boykins are sitting on the back of a lemon-yellow pickup truck in a South Carolina field with a bright blue autumn sky behind them. The breeder of these dogs, Kim Parkman of Pocotaligo Kennels in Sumter, remembers that Jones thought of photographing the dogs on the truck for a very practical reason—the difficulty of getting five generations of spirited Boykins to sit still for a long photo shoot.

The Most Familiar Image?

Until 2008 probably the mostly widely circulated photograph of a Boykin ever taken was of Chris Bishop's dog Clark, which was featured on the dust jacket of the first edition of this book in 1997. Clark's image also appeared on the cover of the free 1996–97 hunting and fishing rules and regulations published by the South Carolina Department of Natural Resources. Some four hundred fifty thousand copies of this booklet were printed and distributed to hunters and fishermen across the Palmetto State and along its borders.

The South Carolina regulations booklet featuring Chris Bishop's Boykin spaniel Clark on its cover. Photograph of booklet by Mike Creel

A Boykin as a Commercial Model

An "all-points bulletin" went out among a few Boykin groups in June 2008 when a twelve-page advertising supplement for Home Depot appeared in the *State* newspaper in Columbia. (The following month it appeared in the North Carolina *Raleigh News and Observer.*) The excitement came from the fact that the cover of this supplement featured a golden-eyed Boykin spaniel wearing a red bandanna and lounging amid patio furniture. The same dog reappeared in a center spread, this time wearing a blue bandanna and lounging on a lawn with a display of lawn furniture and a gas grill.

Boykin enthusiasts sought information about the dog and its owners, but the company was careful to protect their privacy. Eventually a former

A Boykin spaniel as a commercial model for Home Depot,
June 2008. Courtesy of Home Depot

newspaper reporter in North Carolina was able to find out that the newspaper insert had been distributed nationwide and that the dog's name is Sally. Sally is probably from Atlanta, but her masters are not identifying themselves, just as many parents of child models choose to maintain distance from media probes. The Home Depot circular represents a debut for Boykin spaniels in commercial advertising, but undoubtedly this will not be the last time that a Boykin is featured in commercial photography. Boykins are probably easier to work with as models than many other breeds—or human children.

Boykins as Subjects of Cartoons

It might be considered flattery enough to be painted, photographed, and selected as state dog, but in South Carolina the Boykin spaniel also has been appropriated into editorial cartoons by one of the South's premier award-winning editorial cartoonists, Robert Ariail, whose work appeared from the 1980s through 2009 in the *State,* one of South Carolina's oldest newspapers and its largest-circulating one.

In 1985, twenty days before Governor Riley signed the bill and just after Representative Koon lifted his objection to making the Boykin spaniel the state dog, Ariail's first Boykin spaniel cartoon appeared on the editorial page of the *State.* The cartoon shows a Boykin spaniel sauntering with more than casual interest by the dome of the State House, drawn to the size of a fireplug. An arrow points to the "state dog," which is looking toward the dome, leaving readers to imagine what the dog is thinking. The message seems to be that the little brown dog, after an embarrassing defeat the year before, has finally mastered his political adversaries in the State House. Ariail sent a signed copy of the cartoon to Robert Sheheen, author of the successful act to make the Boykin spaniel state dog. Sheheen had the cartoon framed and placed it on the wall of his Camden law office.

The second Ariail Boykin cartoon, which appeared on the editorial page of the July 9, 1996, issue of the *State,* stemmed from a political dispute between Governor David Beasley and Boykin Rose, whom the governor had appointed as state director of public safety (also the great-grandson of breed founder Whit Boykin and son of a leading member of the Boykin Spaniel Society). The cartoon shows the governor all ready for a day of hunting but hampered by a dog leash wrapped around his legs. A smug Boykin spaniel with the name "Rose" on its collar is attached to the business end of the leash. Both critics of the governor and lovers of the breed appreciated the humor in this cartoon, which found a place on refrigerators and bulletin boards across South Carolina.

Robert Ariail's July 9, 1996, editorial cartoon using the state dog to illustrate a political dispute between Governor David Beasley and Director of Public Safety Boykin Rose. By permission of Robert Ariail

Boykins on Television

Although the Boykin spaniel has not yet appeared in Hollywood movies, it has broken into South Carolina television. Joanna Angle, host producer of the *Palmetto Places* series on the South Carolina Educational Television network taped a program on the Boykin community in fall 1995. The twenty-seven-minute program, which first aired on September 14, 1996, features several minutes on Boykin spaniels with the breed founder's grandson, Baynard Boykin, telling the story of the breed's origins and letting a Boykin spaniel do his stuff. The segment has been rebroadcast several times.

Boykins in Fiction

Though Beaver Hardy described the Camden party where he brought his pups to sell in the 1950s as a scene out of *The Great Gatsby* (1925), no Boykin spaniel appeared in works by F. Scott Fitzgerald or any other fiction writer until the very end of the twentieth century, when the Boykin wriggled itself into American letters as stealthily as a Boykin puppy works its way across a room, first in John Culler's short story "The Retriever from

Hell" (1995). A decade later, in 2005, Anne Rivers Siddons became the first nationally recognized author to give a starring role to a Boykin spaniel in fiction. The Boykin, named Elvis, is a critically important character in her acclaimed novel, *Sweetwater Creek*, which is set along the lowcountry coast of South Carolina. Ms. Siddons is a friend of Pat Conroy, another lowcountry author and aficionado of the Boykin spaniel.

In 2004, just before Ms. Siddons's novel was released, a children's book was published on Boykin spaniels. Written by Lynn Kelley and illustrated in color by Lisa Gardiner, *The First Boykin Spaniels: The Story of Dumpy and Singo* tells the story of the breed from the time of Dumpy's appearance in Spartanburg and his mating with Singo to the proclamation of the Boykin spaniel as the official state dog of South Carolina. The story in the book is narrated by a Boykin spaniel named Sweet Carolina Hershey because Liz Spragens—then a young girl and one of Hershey's owners—convinced Kelley that children would find the book more interesting and credible if the story were told by a Boykin family member showing readers an old family album.

Imagery in photography, painting, sculpture, film, and commercial advertising affects us through what we see. Literature allows us to "see" landscapes and creatures—dogs included—in our heads. There is another, much more primitive, art—one created even by little children to help them make sense of their emerging world. This art is called "naming," and, as we shall see in the next chapter, Boykin spaniel owners have long been experts at it.

8

The Art of Naming Boykin Spaniels

Boykin spaniel names such as "Brown Sugar," "Sweet Carolina Hershey," and "Russell Stover" tantalizingly mix confection with affection.

Lynn Kelley

If naming something is an art form in its own right, the oldest Boykin art form continues to flourish with no shortage evident in the creativity used to illustrate the special personalities so evident in this breed. If you asked the time-worn question "would a rose by another name smell so sweet?" in regard to the developing tradition of naming Boykin spaniels, the answer would probably be "No!" As stories in this book demonstrate, most names for Boykins seem so suited to that dog's personality, appearance, or heritage that any other name would have been inadequate by comparison. Could a dog called Booger, for example, get any more rascally in his antics? Certainly not. The naming of these vivacious spaniels has become an art in itself and should be celebrated.

Named For A Friend

One long-standing, but unwritten, tradition is that a Boykin spaniel should be given a name that befits its place of origin, its forbears both canine and human, its appearance, or some aspect of its special personality. Naming of Boykin spaniels falls into a number of categories. First are dogs named for a close friend or family member, such as Sam, Lizzie, Lucy, Molly Brown, and Bessie. A good example is the time Kitty and Henry Beard named a beautiful female Boykin spaniel puppy "Deasie" (pronounced "Daisy") in honor of Deas Boykin, Henry Beard's great-uncle who had given Kitty's family their first Boykin spaniel, Patty, when Kitty was a child.

Local Flavor in Names

The geography and traditions of South Carolina and the southern region in general account for Boykin names with local and historic flavor, including Black River Buster, Pee Dee, Belle Island Beau, Rice Field, and Marshland. Champion dogs such as Bubba Pope's Dixie Blair in Columbia and Richard Coe's Hubba Bubba in Summerville fit right in with southern traditions. State legislator Bill Cork's Boykin Geechee, was named for the patois spoken on South Carolina's barrier islands and coastal towns such as Beaufort.

The story of Catherine Ceips's naming of her Boykins illustrates the power of Palmetto State geography in naming Boykin spaniels. A South Carolina state representative (2003–7) and later state senator (2007–8) from Beaufort, Ms. Ceips has also had two very important Boykin spaniels in her life: Cooper and Bay. In 1988 while living in North Carolina, she got Cooper, whom she named after the Cooper River in South Carolina. Later, after moving to Beaufort, South Carolina, she got Bay, a female who was named for Beaufort Bay. "Cooper and Bay were great buddies," Ms. Ceips said in 2008. "Cooper passed away at the age of fifteen. Bay had always been with Cooper or someone, never alone." This was of concern to Ms. Ceips, who had been elected to the South Carolina House of Representatives and was spending three days a week in Columbia. She decided to bring Bay to Columbia. To make sure Bay had a good home life, she changed her Columbia residence from one of the hotels to the historic Chesnut Cottage on Hampton Street, which had been the Columbia town home of well-known Civil War diarist Mary Boykin Chesnut, a native of Camden. Bay only was at Chesnut Cottage during the evenings. During the day she went—as might well have been expected of the official state dog—with Representative Ceips to the Blatt Building, where the state representatives have their offices. "People loved her. She even had her own fan club. I would be in a committee meeting or in the State House and return to my office and find her 'in a meeting with many guests,'" Ceips said.

Ceips's favorite story about Bay proves why her name fits her so well as a working dog who loves the waters of South Carolina and their bountiful bird populations. "Bay walked down the hall one day to another Representative's office and located the trophy ducks on his wall. She sat and stared at the ducks for what seemed like forever, then calmly left and returned to my office."

When Representative Ceips was elected to the State Senate, she moved her office to the Gressette Building, where the well-known and well-named

Bay continued to make new friends with her daily briefings and politicking by roaming the halls of her new building. Senator Ceips mused, "You know, they say in politics, 'if you want a friend, get a dog.'" As the senator discovered, it also helps to bestow on such a good friend an appropriate name, rooted in the geography of the state that cared enough about the Boykin spaniel to make it official.

Kennel Bloodlines

Kennel names pinpoint a dog's origin to Boykin spaniel breeders and their bloodlines. Dogs such as Edisto Luke were probably whelped at John Chappell's kennel in Leesville, South Carolina. Pocotaligo's Coffee hearkens from the Sumter kennel of Kim Parkman. Goose Pond Malcolm is immediately linked to the Gresham, South Carolina, kennel of Chris Bishop and his wife, Joni. Pooshee's Bigfoot is linked both to Robert Russell's home at Bonneau on Lake Marion, once part of the old Pooshee plantation, and to the Pooshee line of Boykin spaniels that was begun by Russell and continued by his daughter, Nancy Updegrave of Awendaw, South Carolina. (Pooshee is a Native American name of undetermined origin.)

Brown Sugar And Other Sweets

The Boykin's liver-brown coat probably accounts for more names than any other naming scheme. The Boykin Spaniel Society's foundation stock list includes many dogs named Cocoa. The list is also strongly flavored with Ginger, Brandy, Brownie, and Brown Sugar. Other names—such as Sweet Carolina Hershey, Fudge Royal, Chocolate, Nestle, Reesie Peacey, and Russell Stover—add to the Boykin "sampler" for a dog that is brown and sweet. (For many years Russell Stover candies were manufactured in Marion, South Carolina, a small town east of Florence.)

Personality Kids Match Their Names

Some Boykin spaniel names speak directly to the dog's personality. Kirby Tupper's Balls of Fire possessed uncontainable energy, which is well documented by the tales told about the animal. Personality is also reflected in names such as Rascal, Mischief, Trouble, Happy, Pert, Murphy's Law, Dandy, Boomer, Bandit, Bad Billy, and Floozy. People who knew these dogs often attest to the good fit between the dogs' names and their personalities.

The names of the thousands of Boykin spaniels on record with the Boykin Spaniel Society encompass every naming scheme we have discussed and probably others. Given the creativity of the human mind, the southern influence, and the breed's affect on people, this naming tradition has a future without bounds. It has given to South Carolinians and others a sense of pride, a dose of humor, and tremendous jolts of joy just to hear calls such as "Go fetch, Cocoa, Brownie, Balls, Rascal, and Clark!"

Conclusion

On April 18, 1997, the day before the annual Boykin Spaniel Society's national hunt test, the first page of the "Celebrations" section of the *State* newspaper in Columbia featured a story on Boykin spaniels by Pat Berman with old photographs of Whit Boykin and A. L. White and color photographs by Eric Seals of champion Boykins from the Pocotaligo line. Berman recounted the breed's history and quizzed Boykin owners about experiences with their dogs. Marking the twentieth anniversary of the Boykin Spaniel Society's formation, the *State* celebrated the breed with this credible and entertaining tribute, which is still worth reading in the newspaper's electronic archives.

In the present a significant number of events have been centered on the Boykin spaniel as a breed. The care that has been showered on this dog through the efforts of the Boykin Spaniel Society, as well as many considerate owners and breeders, has demonstrated that a very good breed can become better with each passing generation through careful selection. The breed's continued success in the marketplace of potential buyers is in large measure owed to those ethical Boykin breeders who have shown themselves consistently willing to place long-term improvement of the breed ahead of the short-term profit motive. Owners of Boykins have carried out their own special mandate to provide their canine charges proper care and training, making sure that new generations of Boykin spaniels will be raised in good environments and will receive the nurturing to which any good dog is entitled.

Over the past century many different kinds of people have fallen under the spell of Boykin spaniels. One person hunts. Another paints. One creates postcards. Another tosses frisbees. One lets his little canine buddy ride shotgun in his truck. Another teaches tricks. The little wonder dogs take it all in stride bringing their special style to every new challenge. Whatever the basis of their enthrallment with the Boykin spaniel, virtually all people who come in contact with the breed accept the fact that the breed's special character is a result of its selection for the outdoors and rural settings. The continuing challenge in the future will be to assure a consistent bettering of the Boykin spaniel's genetic strengths, so that it will remain a great working dog and a family favorite.

Just as each generation of Boykin spaniels has changed since Dumpy and Singo produced the first litter in the early 1900s, so has the state of South Carolina changed dramatically in the past one hundred years. The one-industry textile town of Spartanburg has become a thriving twenty-first century metropolis, a part of what is called "Greenville-Spartanburg" with a diversified economic base, including a world-class automobile manufacturing facility. Camden with its easy-going, bucolic lifestyle is being drawn closer into the fabric of the city of Columbia, thirty-five miles away, as each new housing development emerges in Richland and Kershaw counties. With continuing "development" and the disappearance of what developers sometimes call "vacant land" comes not only the loss of rural vistas but also the fouling of the water supply, the pollution of the air, and the irreversible loss of native wildlife habitat. It is ironic that creating economic diversity often means the lessening of ecological diversity.

More than thirty years ago the founders of the Boykin Spaniel Society were inspired to act to save the breed by careful stewardship. Today the kind of joint action that those visionary individuals took upon themselves is required for saving what remains of the rural environment and the habitat in which the Boykin spaniel has developed and thrived. Statewide initiatives through legislation to establish rural-use zones of cropping, recreation, and hunting are only one possible means for addressing the need to maintain large tracts of unspoiled rural environments. Not to face the issue will inevitably lead more and more to a patchwork quilt of slivers of rural land where it is less and less possible to sustain hunting and other rural recreation. When the landscape becomes so cut up that it is no longer desirable for hunting, the reason for breeding the Boykin spaniel as a "hunting dog first" will disappear. How we deal with preserving the rural landscape will have a significant impact on the breed and its owners.

The Boykin Spaniel Society Breed Standard

General Description. The Boykin spaniel is medium in size, sturdy, and typically spaniel. He is first and foremost a hunting dog with proven retrieving flushing abilities characterized by boundless enthusiasm and endurance, moderate speed and agility. Being intelligent and possessing a great desire to please make the Boykin easy to train. He is a strong swimmer, taking to water easily, and is valuable for water retrieving as well as field retrieving. **Temperament.** The typical Boykin is friendly and eager to please. As a pet and companion, he is exceptional with an amicable disposition. Faults: Hostility towards other dogs or people in normal situations or excessive timidity or hyperactivity is not in keeping with the Boykin's character. **Size and Proportion.** The Boykin is built to cover rough ground and swim in all conditions with agility and reasonable speed. His appearance should be a sturdy dog with good but not too heavy bone. He should be kept to medium size—neither too small nor too large and heavy to do the work for which he is intended.

Dog: Height—15 ½" to 18" Weight—30 to 40 lbs.
Bitch: Height—14" to 16 ½" Weight—25 to 35 lbs.

The height at the shoulders should approximately equal the length of the body from the top of the shoulders to the base of the tail. Faults: Over-heavy, large-boned specimens. Leggy individuals, too tall for their length and substance. Oversize or undersize specimens (more than 1" over or under the breed ideal). **Head.** The head, comprising the muzzle and skull, is impressive without being heavy or snipey and is proportionally in balance with the rest of the dog's body. The skull to be of medium length, fairly broad, flat on top, slightly rounded at the sides and back. The muzzle to be approximately the same length as the skull. Viewed from the top, the width of the muzzle is approximately one half the width of the skull. Viewed in profile, the nasal bone is straight with a moderate stop and subtle rise at the junction of the muzzle and skull forming two parallel planes between the top lines of the skull and muzzle. The distance from the tip of the nose to the base of the skull is about the same length as the neck. The forehead is covered with smooth, short hair. The jaws are sufficient length to allow the dog to easily carry game. The nose to be dark liver in color with nostrils well-opened and broad for good scenting power. Faults: Pointed or heavy skull, over-heavy muzzle, muzzle too short or narrow.

Teeth. Teeth should be straight and meet in a close scissors bite (the lower teeth touching behind the upper incisors). An even bite (incisors meet each other edge to edge) is acceptable but not preferred. Faults: Over- or undershot jaws.

Eyes. The eyes are yellow to brown to harmonize with the coat, set well apart, expression alert, intelligent and trusting. Darker shades of yellow preferred over lighter shades. Faults: A prominent or pop eye.

Ears. The ears are set slightly above the level of the eyeline and reach the tip of the nose when pulled forward. They lie flat and close to the head.

Neck. The neck is moderately long, muscular, slightly arched at the crest and gradually blends into sloping shoulders without being abruptly angled or excessively throaty.

Body Structure. The body is sturdily constructed but not too compact. Sloping shoulders, chest well developed but not barrel, the back is strong, straight and level except for a slight arch in the loin area. Faults: High hindquarters reach back (too much arch over the loin extending forward into the middle section), sway back (dip in back).

Legs and Feet. The legs are strong, of medium length and well boned, but too short as to handicap for field work. Legs should be straight when viewed from the front or rear. The feet are round to slightly oval, firm, and well-padded, turning neither in nor out. Faults: Fiddle front (front legs out at elbow, pasterns close, and feet turned out). Cowhocks (hocks on rear legs turning towards each other).

Tail. The tail should be docked so that at maturity it is $2\frac{1}{2}$ to 3 inches long. (Leave $\frac{1}{3}$ of the tail plus $\frac{1}{4}$" when pup is 3–5 days old.)

Coat. The coat is flat to moderately curly with medium length, fine hair with light feathering acceptable on the legs, feet, ears, chest, and belly. A short straight coat without feathering is acceptable.

Color. The color is a solid, rich liver (reddish brown) or dark chocolate allowing for a small, white spot on the chest. No other white markings are allowed.

Gait. The Boykin spaniel moves freely with good reach in front and strong drive from the rear with no tendency for the feet to cross over or interfere with each other. Viewed from the rear, the hocks should follow on a line with the forelegs, neither too widely nor too closely spaced. As speed increases, the feet converge towards a center line. Because the Boykin spaniel has been bred primarily for hunting and retrieving, it is essential that there be proper balance between the front and rear assemblies for endurance and efficient use of energy in the field.

The Boykin Spaniel Society Code of Ethics

The Boykin Spaniel Society endorses the following code of ethics for its members. It is the purpose of the BSS to encourage its members to perfect through selection, breeding, and training the type of dog most suitable in all respects for work as a companionable gun dog and to do all in its powers to protect and advance the interests of Boykin spaniels in every endeavor.

Responsibilities as a Member of the Boykin Spaniel Society

Members' responsibilities include educating the public about the breed, keeping in mind that they and their dogs represent the breed, the BSS, and the sport of purebred dogs in general. Members are urged to accept the written breed standard as approved by the Boykin Spaniel Society as the standard description of physical and temperamental qualities by which the Boykin spaniel is to be judged. Members are required to maintain good sportsmanship at all events and competitions, abiding by the applicable rules and regulations set forth by the governing bodies for such events and competitions. Members' conduct should always be in accord with the purposes and intent of the BSS constitution and bylaws.

Responsibilities as a Breeder

BSS members who breed Boykin spaniels are encouraged to maintain the purpose of the breed. Owners of breeding animals shall provide appropriate documentation to all concerned regarding the health of dogs involved in a breeding or sale, including reports of examinations such as those applying to hips, eyes, and heart. If any such examinations have not been performed on a dog, this should be stated.

Breeders should understand and acknowledge that they may need to take back, or assist in finding a new home for, any dog they produce at any time in its life, if requested to do so.

Members who breed should sell puppies, permit stud service, and/or lease any stud dogs or brood bitches only to individuals who give satisfactory evidence that they will give proper care and attention to the animals concerned and who may be expected generally to act within the intent of the statements of this code of ethics. Members are encouraged to use clear, concise written contracts to document the sale of animals, use of stud dogs, and lease arrangements, including the use, when appropriate, of nonbreeding agreements. Members of the Boykin Spaniel Society should not sell dogs/puppies at auction or sell or donate dogs/puppies that will be awarded in raffles. The Boykin Spaniel Society considers auctions and raffles not to be reasonable and appropriate methods to obtain or transfer dogs. Additionally members of the Boykin Spaniel Society should not sell, barter, or transfer dogs/puppies to brokers, commercial dealers, retail pet stores, or retail distribution outlets.

The Boykin Spaniel Society, as of May 25, 2006, will no longer register dogs to multiple owners. The ONLY type of ownership recognized going forward will be single ownership. This change in registration procedure is a direct result of continuing problems associated with multiple owners that have entered into co-ownership arrangements. Dogs that are currently registered with multiple or co-owners will not be affected by this change. BSS registration application forms and certificates of registration will be modified to reflect the recommended changes. Policies with respect to the registration and transfer of dogs may be adopted from time to time by the BSS board of directors or an appropriate committee thereof, which policies should take into account the interests of the BSS, its members, and the Boykin spaniel.

For the reasons described above, purchasing a dog outright from a breeder or an individual that endorses and adheres to the responsibilities and guidelines as described and defined in this code of ethics of the Boykin Spaniel Society is the recommendation from the Boykin Spaniel Society.

Advisory Guidelines

Breeding stock should be selected with the following objectives in mind:

Recognizing that the Boykin spaniel breed was developed as a useful gun dog, to encourage the perfection by careful and selective breeding of Boykin spaniels that possess the appearance, structure, soundness, temperament, natural ability and personality that are characterized in the standard of the breed, and to do all possible to advance and promote the perfection of these qualities.

BSS members are expected to follow BSS requirements for record keeping, identification of animals, and registration procedures.

Animals selected for breeding should:
1. Be of temperament typical of the Boykin spaniel breed; stable, friendly, trainable, and willing to work. Temperament is of utmost importance to the breed and must never be neglected;
2. Be in good health, including freedom from communicable disease;
3. Possess the following examination reports in order to verify status concerning possible hip dysplasia or hereditary eye disease:

   Hips: appropriate report from Orthopedic Foundation for Animals; PennHip; or at least a written report from a board-certified veterinary radiologist (Diplomate of the American College of Veterinary Radiologists).
   Eyes: appropriate report from a Diplomate of the American College of Veterinary Ophthalmology (ACVO).
   Hearts: appropriate certificate from OFA.

Consideration should be given also to other disorders that may have a genetic component, including, but not limited to, epilepsy, hypothyroidism, skin disorders (allergies), and orthopedic disorders such as elbow dysplasia and patellar luxation.

APPENDIX 3

Grooming Your Boykin Spaniel:
Boykin Spaniel Society Guidelines

Boykin owners often ask how to clip or groom their dogs. There is no one set way as it comes down to personal preference. Some owners like to clip their dogs all the way down, all over, so that the dog looks smooth coated. Others prefer to leave the feathers on the legs, ears, and belly. Still others just like to brush the coats and leave them natural.

If you clip your Boykin short all over, use a #7 blade and only run the blade with the grain of the hair, not against it. That way you get a nice even clip without any choppy areas. The top of the head and the feet can be trimmed with a #10 blade to get a cleaner look. Carefully trim around the ears with scissors. Put your fingers between the scissors and the ear leather to prevent accidents.

If you are going to work your Boykin in dove fields or on upland game then a clip is recommended to keep the briar damage to a minimum. The soft coat of the Boykin acts like Velcro to cockleburs, foxtails, and sand-spurs as well as blackberry brambles that wreak havoc on your Boykin's coat as well as your fingers when you tried to pry them loose. A coating of cooking spray, like PAM, sprayed before you go into the field will help ease the combing out if you leave the coat intact.

If you decide to clip your Boykin but want to keep some of the feathers then most clip them like a springer spaniel. The top of the head, the sides and down the back of the neck, down the back and the sides, the fronts of the legs, and the top of the tail are clipped using a #7 or #10 blade. The underside and the base of the ears are clipped to reduce matting. The armpits and inside flanks are clipped as well. The feet and between the toes are clipped using a #10 blade. Male dogs often need to have the hair trimmed around their testicles to reduce matting. What is left is the feathers on the ears, the backs of the legs, the chest, and the belly. If your Boykin has a short tail then clip it all over. If your pup has a longer tail then you can leave the feathers on the underside of the tail.

The main advantage to clipping your Boykin at least once a year is that you can see any blemishes on the skin, possibly dry, flaky conditions, and correct any problems with fleas and ticks that could be hidden in a heavy coat. If you find your dog has dry, flaky skin consider changing his diet and/or adding a teaspoon of vegetable oil to his food each day.

Of course the best time to clip your Boykin is in the late spring or early summer. Don't clip your pups' entire coat off late in the fall if he is going to spend the winter outside.

Whether you clip or don't clip, brush your Boykin's coat once a week to keep the shedding down to a minimum. It's recommended not to bathe your dog more often than once a month and then to only use pet shampoos. Never use dishwashing detergent as it will dry out your dog's skin.

Keep your Boykin's nails trimmed as well. A battery operated Dremel-type tool with a sanding bit works wonders to grind down the sharp edges and keep the nails short without cutting to the quick. If you trim your pups' nails with toenail clippers, make sure you have some Quik-Stop handy in case you cut too short.

While you are grooming, check the inside of your pups' ears. Some spaniels have chronic ear problems and a once weekly application of a veterinary-recommended ear solution will help keep the ears dry and clean.

Whether you clip or don't clip, start grooming habits with a puppy—messing with his feet, making him sit or stand still—and your pup will look forward to being groomed (making your job not only easier, but enjoyable for both of you). Happy grooming.

Choosing a Breeder:
Boykin Spaniel Society Guidelines

Before you fall in love with the first adorable Boykin puppy you see, take the time in an initial phone call to ask the questions listed below. You may not find a breeder who fits 100 percent of these criteria, but if you receive more than two negative responses, consider another breeder. At the end of the list you will find questions to ask yourself. You should be able to answer all of them affirmatively before you begin your search.

Remember: You are adding a new member to your family for the next 10–15 years. NOW IS NOT THE TIME TO BARGAIN HUNT!

Prepare to spend five hundred dollars and up or more for a well-bred puppy. You may have known someone who has (or you may yourself have purchased) a "backyard" bred dog, a pet-store or puppy-mill dog and had great success. However, the incidence of problems in the breed makes it prudent to be on guard. Among the undesirable traits are temperament problems including aggression, shyness, or hyperactivity, hip dysplasia, and eye problems causing early blindness. Responsible breeders do all they can to avoid these problems by researching pedigrees and screening parents for certain inherited problems before breeding.

Breeders are expected to produce Boykins to high standards. They are entitled to respect and courtesy from the people they are trying to please, so always be on time for any appointments and be honest in explaining your lifestyle, family activity level, experience with dogs, and knowledge of Boykin spaniels. Keep this checklist by the phone when you make your calls. Good luck with your search for a quality puppy!

1. Where did you find out about this breeder? Responsible breeders usually have a waiting list of puppy buyers. They rarely find it necessary to advertise in newspapers or with a sign out in the front yard.

2. Do both parents (the sire and dam) have hip clearances from the OFA (Orthopedic Foundation for Animals) or PennHip? Ask to see the certificates. "My vet okayed the X-ray" is not a valid clearance.
3. Do both parents have current eye clearances? This must be performed every year. Ask to see the certificates.
4. Are both parents at least two years old? OFA hip clearances cannot be obtained before that age. PennHip determines hip conditions at an earlier age.
5. How often is the dam bred? Breeding every heat cycle IS TOO OFTEN and may indicate that profit is the primary motive for the breeding.
6. Do all four grandparents, siblings of the parents, and any other puppies that they may have produced have these clearances? A responsible breeder will keep track of these statistics and honestly discuss any problems that have occurred in the lines and what has been done to prevent them from recurring.
7. Are both parents free of allergies or epilepsy?
8. On what basis was the sire chosen? If the answer is "because he lives right down the street" or "because he is really sweet," it may be that sufficient thought was not put into the breeding.
9. Is the breeder knowledgeable about the breed? Is he or she involved in competition or hunting with their dogs?
10. Are the puppy's sire and dam available for you to meet? If the sire is unavailable can you call his owners or people who have his puppies to ask about temperament or health problems? You may also be provided with pictures or videos.
11. Have the puppies been raised in a clean environment?
12. Is the breeder knowledgeable about raising puppies, critical neonatal periods, and proper socialization techniques? Puppies that are raised without high exposure to gentle handling, human contact, and a wide variety of noises and experiences, or are removed from their dam or litter mates before at least seven weeks may exhibit a wide variety of behavioral problems! Temperament, a genetic trait carried over from the parents, still needs development from the early beginnings of a puppy's life. The breeder should provide extensive socialization and human interaction to the puppies in the litter.
13. Does the breeder provide a three-to-five generation pedigree, copies of all clearances, the guarantee, and health records?
14. Have the puppies' temperaments been evaluated, and can the breeder guide you to the puppy that will best suit your lifestyle? A very shy puppy will not do well in a noisy household with small children,

just as a very dominant puppy won't flourish in a sedate, senior-citizen household.

15. Do the puppies seem healthy, with no discharge from eyes or nose, no loose stools, no foul-smelling ears? Are their coats soft, full, and clean? Do they have plenty of energy when awake yet calm down easily when gently stroked?
16. Do the puppies have their first shots, and have they been wormed?
17. Does the breeder have only one or at most two breeds of dogs and only one litter at a time? If there are several breeds of dogs, chances are the breeder cannot devote the time it takes to become really knowledgeable about the breed. If there is more than one litter at a time, it is very difficult to give the puppies the attention they need and may indicate that the primary purpose for breeding is profit, rather than a sincere desire to sustain and improve the breed.
18. Does the breeder belong to the Boykin Spaniel Society?
19. Do you feel comfortable with this person? If you feel intimidated or pressured, keep looking! It's worth the effort.

Before becoming a new dog owner there are several questions you need to ask yourself. Are you prepared to do the following?

1. Take full responsibility for this dog and all its needs for the next ten to fifteen years? This is NOT a task that can be left to children!
2. Invest the considerable time, money, and patience it takes to train the dog to be a good companion? This does not happen by itself!
3. Always keep the dog safe; no running loose, riding in the back of an open pickup truck, or being chained outside?
4. Make sure the dog gets enough attention and exercise? (Boykin puppies need several hours of both, every day!)
5. Live with shedding, retrieving, drooling, and high activity for the next ten to fifteen years?
6. Spend the money it takes to provide proper veterinary care, including but certainly not limited to vaccines, heartworm testing and preventative, spaying or neutering, and annual check ups?
7. Keep the breeder informed and up to date on the dog's accomplishments and any problems that may arise? Take your questions to the breeder or other appropriate professional before they become problems that are out of hand?
8. Have the patience to accept and enjoy the trials of Boykin puppyhood, which can last for three or more years, and each stage afterward? Continue to accept responsibility for the dog despite

inevitable life changes such as new babies, kids going off to school, moving, or returning to work?

9. Resist impulse buying and instead have the patience to make a responsible choice?

If you answered yes to ALL of the above, you are ready to start contacting breeders. Start early because most responsible breeders have a waiting list ranging from a few months to several years. Remember, the right puppy or adult dog IS worth waiting for!

A word about rescue dogs—rescue dogs may or may not have been responsibly bred. However, since they are adults, we are able to evaluate them for any signs of a problem before you fall in love, something that can't be done with a puppy. We consider this only one of the many advantages to adopting an older dog! If you think a puppy may not be right for you and would like to be considered for an adult dog, contact the Boykin Spaniel Rescue for information.

State Dog Act

Act 31, 1985
South Carolina General Assembly
106th Session
Bill 2403
(A31, R50, H2403)
An Act to Provide That the Boykin Spaniel Is the Official Dog
of the State.

Whereas, the Boykin Spaniel is the only dog which was originally bred for South Carolina hunters by South Carolinians; and

Whereas, the Boykin Spaniel has developed into a breed of superb hunting instincts and mild temperament; and

Whereas, the Boykin Spaniels in existence today are the descendants of an original dog bred by Mr. L. Whitaker Boykin of Kershaw County, South Carolina; and

Whereas, the Boykin Spaniels can now be found throughout the United States and are highly regarded as pets and hunting dogs; and

Whereas, the Boykin Spaniel registry is now headquartered in Kershaw County, South Carolina, and has published guidelines for the registry of Spaniels; and

Whereas, the South Carolina Wildlife and Marine Resources Commission endorsed the Boykin Spaniel as South Carolina's State Dog on April 20, 1984; and

Whereas, Richard W. Riley, Governor of the State, proclaimed September 1, 1984, as Boykin Spaniel Day. Now, therefore,

Be it enacted by the General Assembly of the State of South Carolina:

Official State Dog

Section 1. The Boykin Spaniel is the official dog of the State.

Time effective

Section 2. This act shall take effect upon approval by the Governor.

Organizations of Interest to
Boykin Spaniel Owners and Admirers

The Boykin Spaniel Society (BSS)

Founded in 1977 with its headquarters office in Camden, South Carolina, the BSS is the original and oldest organization promoting the breed. The BSS has grown to more than 2,700 members from all fifty states in the United States and from Canada. The BSS maintains registries for litters and individual dogs. These registries contain more than 22,800 individual Boykin spaniels and 7,055 litters, including 667 foundation stock dogs.

The BSS annually hosts two major field events: the BSS National Field Trial in March or April and the BSS National Upland Field Trial in January. Annual membership dues are $35; sponsor membership is $75 (includes a silver pin with a Boykin spaniel head); and life membership is $750 (includes an antique-silver pin with a gold Boykin spaniel head). Tax-deductible donations to help with Boykin spaniel health issues may be made to the Boykin Spaniel Foundation, which has the same executive committee as BSS.

BSS headquarters are located in the Village at Dusty Bend on North Broad Street (Highway 521) in Camden, South Carolina. The office may be reached by telephone at 803-425-1032 or fax at 803-425-5458 from 8 A.M. to 12 P.M. and 1 P.M. to 4 P.M., Monday through Friday. The mailing address is The Boykin Spaniel Society, P.O. Box 2047, Camden, S.C. 29020. The e-mail address is boykinss@boykinspaniels.org. The society's Web site is www.boykinspaniels.org (accessed March 26, 2009).

Boykin Spaniel Rescue, Inc. (BSR)

Boykin Spaniel Rescue, Inc., is a nonprofit 501(c) 3 organization that was chartered for the sole purpose of rescuing purebred Boykin spaniels from shelters or owners who can no longer care for them and saving Boykins that are abandoned or roaming free without identification. Learn more about the BSR by visiting their Web site: www.boykinrescue.org (accessed March 26, 2009). Their toll-free telephone number is 877-LBD-DOGS (877-523-3647), and their e-mail address is bsr@boykinrescue.org.

The adoption fee in 2008 was $250 per dog. This fee helps to cover BSR costs for veterinary care, microchipping, and incidentals for the dog. Donations to BSR are appreciated. Checks may be made payable to "Boykin Spaniel Rescue, Inc." and sent to: Boykin Spaniel Rescue, Inc. c/o Katherine Garstang, 1624 Yorktown Drive, Charlottesville, Va. 22901.

Carolina Boykin Spaniel Retriever Club (CBRSC)

The CBRSC welcomes all Boykin owners and Boykin spaniel clubs. The CBRSC was formed to promote the breeding of purebred Boykin spaniels with the goal of bringing out their natural qualities, to encourage hunting with trained Boykin spaniels while hunting with the aim of preserving game, and to advance the interest of the Boykin spaniel breed by encouraging sportsmanlike competition at hunting tests. The CBRSC holds field trials six times a year; the rules for these trials are similar to those of the BSS National Field trial. The club also holds UKC/HRC-sanctioned hunt tests, which are not affiliated with the BSS. The club's Web site is www.boykinspaniel.net (accessed March 26, 2009).

Midsouth Boykin Spaniel Retriever Club (MSBSRC)

The MSBSRC is made up of Boykin owners from Alabama, Louisiana, Georgia, Florida, Mississippi, and Tennessee. The club hosts a variety of events for the benefit of the membership, including training seminars for hunt tests, general hunting, and obedience; a social gathering with fun activities for the dogs; a dove shoot; and a mock hunt test to prepare for the Boykin Spaniel Society's National Field Trial. Learn more about the club by visiting their Web site: www.midsouthboykinspaniel.net (accessed March 26, 2009).

Dang Yankee Boykin Spaniel Club

A group of Boykin spaniel enthusiasts in the northeast are setting up their own Boykin club to organize training, competition, and social events in their area. Learn more about the club by visiting their Web site: www

.yankeeboykinspaniel.net (accessed March 26, 2009). For general information e-mail them at info@yankeeboykinspaniel.net. The group also provides e-mail addresses for regional contacts: ksass@yankeeboykinspaniel.net (New York, Connecticut, Massachusetts, New Jersey, Delaware, and Maryland); and klk@yankeeboykinspaniel.net (Indiana, Ohio, Pennsylvania, and West Virginia).

Boykin Spaniel Club and Breeders Association of America (BSCBAA)

The BSCBAA is a nonprofit group "dedicated to all the things you do with your Boykin spaniel." Incorporated in South Carolina in 1997, the organization states it is dedicated to preserving and improving the hunting and working instincts of the Boykin spaniel through education of owners in the areas of training, health, events, and breeding.

The BSCBAA is currently the official American Kennel Club (AKC) national parent club for the Boykin spaniel. Annual membership levels and dues for the BSCBA are breeder member $75; member (voting) $35; and member at large (nonvoting) $25. The mailing address is: BSCBAA, P.O. Box 107, Sargent, Ga. 30275. Their e-mail address is INFO@Boykin SpanielClub.org. Learn more about the organization by visiting its Web site: www.boykinspanielclub.org (accessed March 26, 2009).

Hunting Retriever Club, Inc. (HRC)

Affiliated with the United Kennel Club (UKC), the HRC puts on hunt tests open to all gun-dog breeds. (See appendix 9 for more information.) The HRC's address is P.O. Box 3179, Big Spring, Tex. 79721. Its Web site is http://www.huntingretrieverclub.org (accessed April 2, 2009).

American Wild Turkey Hunting Dog Association (AWTHDA)

This group is a voluntary association for people interested in preserving the legality and the tradition of wild-turkey hunting using dogs. On its Web site (www.turkeydog.org) the "Tales" page features many Boykin spaniel stories.

Dog/Kennel Registry

The South Carolina Department of Natural Resources issues tattoo-registration numbers for a modest fee for individual dogs and for kennels. Application forms may be obtained by writing to Dog/Kennel Registry, SCDNR, P.O. Box 11710, Columbia, S.C. 29211. The registry office is on the first floor of the Rembert Dennis State Office Building at 1000 Assembly Street in Columbia. The telephone number is 803-734-3833.

American Kennel Club Companion Animal Recovery (AKC CAR)

AKC CAR registers all brands of microchips. It has a one-time registration fee per owner per pet, but it does charge a small transfer fee when the ownership changes. The link to the registration site is http//www.akccar .org (accessed March 18, 2009). stories about Boykins: www.turkeydog .org (accessed March 19, 2009).

Orthopedic Foundation for Animals (OFA)

A private, nonprofit foundation established in 1966, OFA continues its original focus on canine hip dysplasia, but it has expanded its focus to other inherited diseases and to other companion animals, such as cats. Its mission is "to improve the health and well-being of companion animals through a reduction in the incidence of genetic disease."

All breeders should accept the responsibility of breeding healthy puppies. The OFA databases provide breeders a research tool for implementing better breeding practices. OFA maintains databases on hip dysplasia, elbow dysplasia, patellar luxation, autoimmune thyroiditis, congenital heart disease, leg-calve-perthes disease, sebaceous adenitis, congenital deafness, and shoulder OCD—as well as DNA-based databases on Von Willebrand's disease and progressive retinal atrophy.

The OFA Web site is www.offa.org (accessed March 26, 2009).

Canine Eye Registration Foundation (CERF)

CERF was founded by purebred-dog owners and breeders who were concerned about the effect of hereditary eye disease on the quality of their dogs' lives. Established in conjunction with cooperating board-certified, veterinary ophthalmologists, CERF has as its goal the elimination of hereditary eye disease.

In its national registry CERF includes all dogs that have been certified as free of hereditary eye disease by members of the American College of Veterinary Ophthalmologists (ACVO). It also maintains a database on all dogs examined by ACVO diplomates. This database many be used for researching trends in eye disease and breed susceptibility. This data valuable not only to clinicians and students of ophthalmology but also to interested breed clubs and individual breeders and owners of specific breeds. Learn more about CERF by visiting their Web site: www.vmdb .org (accessed March 26, 2009).

Purina Club Partnership Program (PCPP)

Eradicating diseases that afflict dogs so that they can live longer and healthier lives is a key priority of Purina. The Boykin Spaniel Society participates in the Purina Parent Club Partnership (PPCP) Program, which works through Purina's loyalty program, Pro Club. Pro Club members who are also members of the Boykin Spaniel Society or an affiliate club, earn dollars that the club may use for health studies, rescue, and/or educational efforts. To enroll in Purina Pro Club, call their toll-free number: 877-PRO-CLUB (877-776-2582) between 7 A.M. to 5 P.M. central time, Monday through Friday. When calling, let the representative know that you want to join Pro Club as part of the PPCP Program. You can also enroll through the Web site: www.purinaproclub.com (accessed March 26, 2009).

Boykin Spaniel Society
National Field Trial Records, 1980–2009

1980

1st Field Trial, 3rd Annual Meeting
May 24
Hardy's Rice Pond, Elgin, S.C.

Open Dove
1st: Rusty Triever—Allan Fallaw,
Batesburg, S.C.
2nd: Cricket—Nat Gist, Sumter, S.C.
3rd: Barney—William Tetterton,
Camden, S.C.
4th: Smokey—David Parker,
Hemingway, S.C.

JAM (Judges' Award of Merit)
Cheney Parr—D. B. Parr Jr.,
Newberry, S.C.
Candy—W. B. Boykin, Camden, S.C.
Turk—Hugh G. Baiden, Columbia, S.C.
Cocoa—George Campbell, Dillon, S.C.
Pooshee's Big Foots—R. B. Russell,
Charleston, S.C.
Alexander Hamilton Boykin—Dr. Cantey
Haile, Columbia, S.C.
Elmore—F. Simons Hane,
Columbia, S.C.
Charlie Brown—Nat Gist, Sumter, S.C.
Dixie—Nat Gist, Sumter, S.C.
Cocoa—Manly Hutchinson,
Columbia, S.C.
Tosh-A-Lov—Earl Watts, Camden, S.C.

Open Dove-Duck
1st: Cricket—Nat Gist, Sumter, S.C.
2nd: Elmore—F. Simons Hane,
Columbia, S.C.
3rd: Pooshee's Bigfoot—R. B. Russell,
Charleston, S.C.
4th: Cocoa—George Campbell,
Dillon, S.C.

JAM (Judges' Award of Merit)
Barney—William Tetterton,
Camden, S.C.
Dixie—Nat Gist, Sumter, S.C.
Cocoa—Manly Hutchinson,
Columbia, S.C.

Puppy Dove-Duck
1st: Bo—Alton Yeargin,
Simpsonville, S.C.
2nd: Pooshee's Eggs Benedict—
Michele Fisser, Charleston, S.C.
3rd: Susie—Marion Simmons,
Walterboro, S.C.

JAM (Judges' Award of Merit)
Brandi—Taylor Clarkson,
Summerville, S.C.

Puppy Dove
1st: Bo—Alton Yeargin,
Simpsonville, S.C.
2nd: Travis—Sharon Parker, Murrells
Inlet, S.C.

3rd: Pooshee's Eggs Benedict—
Michele Fisser, Charleston, S.C.

JAM (Judges' Award of Merit)
Poppy—Tom Lord, Columbia, S.C.
Susie—Marion Simmons,
Walterboro, S.C.
Dan Dee—William Tetterton,
Camden, S.C.

1981

**2nd Annual Boykin Spaniel Society
Retriever Trial
May 9
Mill Creek Park, Pinewood, S.C.**

Open Champion
Elmore—Dr. Simons Hane,
Columbia, S.C.

Open Dove
1st: Al's Beau—Alton Yeargin,
Simpsonville, S.C.
2nd: Wendy—Beaver Hardy,
Columbia, S.C.
3rd: Elmore—Dr. Simons Hane,
Columbia S.C.
4th: Banjo—E. B. Beard, Camden, S.C.

Open Duck
1st: Lucky—John Culler, Camden, S.C.
2nd: Elmore—Simons Hane,
Columbia, S.C.
3rd: Banjo—E. B. Beard, Camden, S.C.
4th: Princess Widgeon—Tom Pate,
Burlington, N.C.

Puppy Champion
Coach Campbell's Trouble—
George Campbell, Dillon, S.C.

Puppy Duck
1st: Coach Campbell's Trouble—
George Campbell, Dillon, S.C.
2nd: Bubba—J. Stevens Dukes,
Johnsonville, S.C.
3rd: Dynamite—Nat Gist, Sumter, S.C.
4th: Pappy—William Tetterton,
Camden, S.C.

Puppy Dove
1st: Grizzly—Jon Christopher Bishop,
Florence, S.C.
2nd: Buckshot—Eugene Griffith,
Newberry, S.C.
3rd: Chief—Harold A. Loyacano Jr.,
Pearl River, La.
4th: Riverdale's Beau—Buddy Rivers,
Oswego, S.C.

1982

**3rd Annual Boykin Spaniel Society
National Retriever Trial
May 8
Mill Creek Park, Pinewood, S.C.**

Open Champion
Bull Island Beau—Mark R. Shields,
Mount Pleasant, S.C.

Open Land
1st: Bull Island Beau—Mark R. Shields,
Mount Pleasant, S.C.
2nd: Banjo—Ned Beard, Camden, S.C.
3rd: Snuffy Smith—Carl Cheely,
Milledgeville, S.C.
4th: Kate—Joni C. Bishop, Florence, S.C.

Open Water
1st: Bull Island Beau—Mark R. Shields,
Mount Pleasant, S.C.
2nd: George Dog—Rusty Harley,
Charleston, S.C.
3rd: Chloe—Dick Bishop, Gresham, S.C.
4th: Dixie Two—Nat Gist, Sumter, S.C.

Puppy Champion
Dixie Two—Nat Gist, Sumter, S.C.

Puppy Land
1st: Rebel—Nat Gist, Sumter, S.C.
2nd: Fox's Princess Margaret—
Russell Fox, Batesburg, S.C.
3rd: Dixie Two—Nat Gist, Sumter, S.C.
4th: Brown Sugar—Van K. Richardson,
Heath Springs, S.C.

Puppy Water
1st: Joshua—Steven C. Moore,
Darlington, S.C.
2nd: Dixie Two—Nat Gist, Sumter, S.C.

3rd: JC's Elizabeth—Mr. and Mrs. Robert Caulder, Camden, S.C.
4th: JC's Meggie—Mr. and Mrs. Robert Caulder, Camden, S.C.

1983
4th Annual Boykin Spaniel Society National Retriever Trial
May 21
Mill Creek Park, Pinewood, S.C.

Open Champion
Grey Wood's Woody—Tom Lord, Columbia, S.C.

Open Land
1st: Buck—Clay Hasty, Camden, S.C.
2nd: Rhastus Beene—Bill Johnson, Corpus Christi, Tex.
3rd: Snuffy Smith—Carl Cheely, Milledgeville, Ga.
4th: Woody—Tom Lord, Columbia, S.C.

Open Water
1st: Widgeon—Elizabeth Riley, Elgin, S.C.
2nd: Coach Campbell's Cocoa—George Campbell, Dillon, S.C.
3rd: Woody—Tom Lord, Columbia, S.C.
4th: George Dog—Rusty Harley, Charleston, S.C.

Puppy Champion
Coach Campbell's Flea Baggins— George Campbell, Dillon, S.C.

Puppy Land
1st: Flea Baggins—George Campbell, Dillon, S.C.
2nd: Buddy—Keith Hendrickson, Greensboro, N.C.
3rd: JC's Dee Dee II—Janice Caulder, Camden, S.C.
4th: Edisto Nicholas—James Baxley Jr., Columbia, S.C.

Puppy Water
1st: JC's Miss Tillie—Janice Caulder, Camden, S.C.
2nd: Flea Baggins—George Campbell, Dillon, S.C.
3rd: JC's Dee Dee II—Janice Caulder, Camden, S.C.

4th: Addie—Wallace Scarborough, Charleston, S.C.

1984
5th Annual Boykin Spaniel Society National Retriever Trial
May 12
Mill Creek Park, Pinewood, S.C.

Open Champion
Rebel—Nat Gist, Sumter, S.C.

Open Land
1st: Rebel—Nat Gist, Sumter, S.C.
2nd: Widgeon—Elizabeth Riley, Elgin, S.C.
3rd: Indian Chad Hale—Ray Styles, Wichita Falls, Tex.
4th: Goldrush Digger—Don Odom, Sumter, S.C.

Open Water
1st: Dixie Two—Nat Gist, Sumter, S.C.
2nd: Boykin's Thunder—Cue D. Boykin, Austin, Tex.
3rd: Rebel—Nat Gist—Sumter, S.C.
4th: Edisto Nicholas—J. Ed Baxley Jr., Royston, Ga.

Puppy Champion
Pooshee's Wade Hampton—H. Grady Phillips III, White Oak, S.C.

Puppy Land
1st: Pooshee's Wade Hampton— H. Grady Phillips III, White Oak, S.C.
2nd: Gibson's Peach Brandy— Walter Gibson, Denmark, S.C.
3rd: Cojo Chappell—Jack Farrer, Tavares, Fla.
4th: Edwin McGee's Fudge— Edwin McGee, Florence, S.C.

Puppy Water
1st: Pooshee's Wade Hampton— H. Grady Phillips III, White Oak, S.C.
2nd: Cojo Chappell—Jack Farrer, Tavares, Fla.
3rd: Greywood's Paddle Oar— Thomas A. Lord, Columbia, S.C.
4th: Gibson's Peach Brandy— Walter Gibson, Denmark, S.C.

1985

6th Annual Boykin Spaniel Society
National Retriever Trial
May 11
Mill Creek Park, Pinewood, S.C.

Open Overall Champion
Boykin's Thunder—Cue D. Boykin,
Austin, Tex.
Open Class Runner-Up: Goldrush
Digger—Millie Odom, Sumter, S.C.

Open Land
1st: Mason Dixon—Jerry Butler,
Quinby, S.C.
2nd: Goliath—Tom Evans, Sumter, S.C.
3rd: Molly—Carl Lathrop,
Douglasville, Ga.
4th: Buck—Clay Hasty, Camden, S.C.

Open Water
1st: Savannah Trapper—William E.
Poteat, McCormick, S.C.
2nd: Cooper Kelly—Richard and
Ann Christie, Moncks Corner, S.C.
3rd: Goldrush Digger—Millie Odom,
Sumter, S.C.
4th: Calhoun's Best Buddy—Keith
Hendrickson, Greensboro, N.C.

Overall Derby Champion
Randy Weston—H. Victor Weston,
Springfield, Ga.

Derby Land
1st: Crane Creek Jabo—Don Odom,
Sumter, S.C.
2nd: White Oak's Nick—Galen Grider,
Fernandina Beach, Fla.
3rd: Jake—Mark Duffee, Florence, S.C.
4th: Randy Weston—H. Victor Weston,
Springfield, Ga.

Derby Water
1st: Gibson's Peach Brandy—
Walter E. Gibson, Denmark, S.C.
2nd: Randy Weston—H. Victor Weston,
Springfield, Ga.
3rd: Jake—Mark Duffee, Florence, S.C.
4th: Buster—John Trenary, Moncks
Corner, S.C.

Overall Puppy Champion
Little Charlie Brown—Richard F. Coe,
Summerville, S.C.

Puppy Land
1st: Little Charlie Brown—
Richard F. Coe, Summerville, S.C.
2nd: Amos—Amelia Skipper, Pine
Mountain, Ga.
3rd: Ruark's Reminiscence—
Tom Harrison, Plymouth, N.C.
4th: Duchess—David Carmichael,
Darlington, S.C.

Puppy Water
1st: Pocotaligo's Coffee—Kim Spigner,
Sumter, S.C.
2nd: Little Charlie Brown—Richard F.
Coe, Summerville, S.C.
3rd: Buster—Jimmy Lowery, Sumter, S.C.
4th: Pooshee's Secret Weapon—Michele
Russell, Charleston, S.C.

1986

7th Annual Boykin Spaniel Society
National Retriever Trial
May 3, 1986
Swift Creek Kennels, Camden, S.C.

Open Overall Champion
Pooshee's Wade Hampton—H. Grady
Phillips III, White Oak, S.C.

Open Land
1st: Pooshee's Wade Hampton—
H. Grady Phillips III, White Oak, S.C.
2nd: Pocotaligo's Coffee—Kim Parkman,
Sumter, S.C.
3rd: Banjo—Ned Beard, Camden, S.C.
4th: Mason Dixon—Jerry Bennett,
Quinby, S.C.

Open Water
1st: Buster—John S. Trenary, Moncks
Corner, S.C.
2nd: B.J.—Frank T. West Jr., Marion,
S.C.
3rd: Little Charlie Brown—Richard F.
Coe, Summerville, S.C.
4th: Pooshee's Wade Hampton—
J. Grady Phillips III, White Oak, S.C.

Novice Overall Champion
Pooshee's Bo Derek—Lewis Smoak, Florence, S.C.

Novice Land
1st: Pooshee's Bo Derek—Lewis Smoak, Florence, S.C.
2nd: John C. Calhoun—David B. Parr Sr., Newberry, S.C.
3rd: Brambles—Edward F. Eatmon, Kingstree, S.C.
4th: Kirby's Wildwood Walker—Kirby Jordan Jr., Florence, S.C.

Novice Water
1st: Brambles—Edward F. Eatmon, Kingstree, S.C.
2nd: Curly Bill—Mark L. Chapman Jr., Taylors, S.C.
3rd: Pooshee's Bo Derek—Lewis S. Smoak, Yonges Island, N.C.
4th: John C. Calhoun—David B. Parr Sr., Newberry, S.C.

Puppy Overall Champion
Firestone—Charles Jurney, Mooresville, N.C.

Puppy Land
1st: Firestone—Charles Jurney, Mooresville, N.C.
2nd: Sammy—Monica and Annie Oakley, Clinton, S.C.
3rd: Rapp—Robert G. Boyle, Columbia, S.C.
4th: Buckshot Doc—Trip Chavis, Chapin, S.C.

Puppy Water
1st: Sam—Robert Clark, Birmingham, Ala.
2nd: Firestone—Charles Jurney, Mooresville, N.C.
3rd: Mace's No Show Jones—Lewis S. Smoak, Florence, S.C.
4th: Southern Comforts Super Smoker—Joe and Sheila Migliore, Boaz, Ala.

1987

8th Annual Boykin Spaniel Society National Retriever Trial
May 9
Raley's Mill Pond, Camden, S.C.

Overall Open Champion
Pooshee's Wade Hampton—H. Grady Phillips III (handler and owner), White Oak, S.C.

Open Land
1st: Firestone—Charles Jurney (handler and owner), Mooresville, N.C.
2nd: Pooshee's Wade Hampton—H. Grady Phillips III (handler and owner), White Oak, S.C.
3rd: B.J.—Jerry Bennett (handler), Ty West (owner), Marion, S.C.
4th: Kirby's Wildwood Walker—Kirby Jordan Jr. (handler and owner), Florence, S.C.

Open Water
1st: Pocotaligo's Coffee—Kim S. Parkman (handler), Kim and Jule Parkman (owners), Sumter, S.C.
2nd: Banjo—Ned Beard (handler and owner), Camden, S.C.
3rd: Clark's Sam—Joe Migliore (handler), Robert Clark (owner), Birmingham, Ala.
4th: Pooshee's Wade Hampton—H. Grady Phillips III (handler and owner), White Oak, S.C.

Novice Overall Champion
JC's Meggie—Robert Caulder (handler and owner), Camden, S.C.

Novice Land
1st: Fellow's Little Dog—Kirby Jordan Sr. (handler and owner), Florence, S.C.
2nd: Lady—Sheila Migliore (handler), Bruce Payton (owner), Birmington, Ala.
3rd: JC's Meggie—Robert Caulder (handler and owner), Camden, S.C.
4th: Buster—Robert Lowery (handler), James Lowery (owner), Sumter, S.C.

Novice Water
1st: Firestone—Charles Jurney (handler and owner), Mooresville, N.C.
2nd: JC's Meggie—Robert Caulder (handler and owner), Camden, S.C.
3rd: Strider—Bruce Payton (handler and owner), Birmington, Ala.
4th: Willie—Kelly Mahone (handler), Kathy and Kelly Mahone (owners), Hot Springs, Ark.

Puppy Overall Champion
Pocotaligo's Juice—Jule Parkman (handler), Jule and Kim Parkman (owners), Sumter, S.C.

Puppy Land
1st: Pocotaligo's Juice—Jule Parkman (handler), Jule and Kim Parkman (owners), Sumter, S.C.
2nd: Virginia's Molly—Jule Parkman (handler), Cliff Goodson (owner), Thomson, Ga.
3rd: Bramblewood Rascal—Jim Avent (handler), Edward F. Eatmon (owner), Kingstree, S.C.
4th: Second Mill Pleiku—Millie Odom (handler), Don and Millie Odom (owners), Sumter, S.C.

Puppy Water
1st: Second Mill 3-Toes Bear—Millie Odom (handler), Don and Millie Odom (owners), Sumter, S.C.
2nd: Bramblewood Rascal—Jim Avent (handler), Edward F. Eatmon (owner), Kingstree, S.C.
3rd: Socks—Marvin Blount Jr. (handler and owner), Greenville, N.C.
4th: Second Mill Pleiku—Millie Odom (handler), Don and Millie Odom (owners), Sumter, S.C.

1988

9th Annual Boykin Spaniel Society National Retriever Trial
May 14
South Ranch Winns, Winnsboro, S.C.

Open Overall Champion
Pocotaligo's Coffee—Kim S. Parkman (handler), Kim and Jule Parkman (owners), Sumter, S.C.

Open Land
1st: Pocotaligo's Coffee—Kim S. Parkman (handler), Kim and Jule Parkman (owners), Sumter, S.C.
2nd: Buster—Jimmy Lowery (handler), Robert Lowery (owner), Sumter, S.C.
3rd: Buster—John Trenary (handler and owner), Moncks Corner, S.C.
4th: Drum—Ned Beard (handler and owner), Camden, S.C.

Open Water
1st: B.J.—Chris Bishop (handler), Ty West (owner), Marion, S.C.
2nd: Buster—John Trenary (handler and owner), Moncks Corner, S.C.
3rd: Pocotaligo's Coffee—Kim S. Parkman (handler), Kim and Jule Parkman (owners), Sumter, S.C.
4th: Bramblewood Belle—Edward Eatmon (handler and owner), Kingstree, S.C.

Novice Overall Champion
Millie's Hunting Boots—Millie Odom (handler and owner), Sumter, S.C.

Novice Land
1st: Barney Boy—Jody Branham (handler and owner), Matthews, N.C.
2nd: Second Mill Pleiku—Don Odom (handler), Don and Millie Odom (owners), Sumter, S.C.
3rd: Pooshee's Secret Weapon—Michele F. Russell (handler and owner), Charleston, S.C.
4th: Millie's Hunting Boots—Millie Odom (handler and owner), Sumter, S.C.

Novice Water
1st: Pocotaligo's Cruise Control—John Iler (handler), Jule and Kim Parkman (owners), Sumter, S.C.
2nd: Joe's Alabama Bear—Joe Cox (handler and owner), Livingston, Ala.
3rd: Millie's Hunting Boots—Millie Odom (handler and owner), Sumter, S.C.
4th: Socks—Marvin Blount Jr. (handler and owner), Greenville, N.C.

Puppy Overall Champion
Little Cricket—Nat Gist (handler and owner), Sumter, S.C.

Puppy Land
1st: Smoaks Incredible Rusty—Jack Sims (handler and owner), Charleston, S.C.
2nd: McInnis B-Boy—John D. McInnis (handler and owner), Dillon, S.C.
3rd: The Incredible Hamp—Bill Cochran (handler), Lewis S. Smoak (owner), Yonges Island, S.C.
4th: Little Cricket—Millie Odom (handler), Nat Gist (owner), Sumter, S.C.

Puppy Water
1st: Socks Casey—Marvin Blount Jr. (handler and owner), Greenville, N.C.
2nd: Little Cricket—Millie Odom (handler), Nat Gist (owner), Sumter, S.C.
3rd: Jake—Samuel J. Deery IV (handler and owner), Greenville, N.C.
4th: Black Creek Woody—Greg Askins (handler), Ronna Askins (owner), Darlington, S.C.

1989

10th Annual Boykin Spaniel Society National Hunting Test
May 13
Webb Creek, Santee, S.C.

Overall Open
1st: Pocotaligo's Coffee—Kim S. Parkman (handler), Kim and Jule Parkman (owners), Sumter, S.C.
2nd: HR Clark's Sam—Joe Migliore (handler), Robert J. B. Clark (owner), Birmingham, Ala.

3rd: Bramblewood Belle—Edward Eatmon (handler and owner), Kingstree, S.C.
4th: Firestone—Charles Jurney (handler and owner), Mooresville, S.C.

Open Land
1st: Black River Buster—Bobby Lowery (handler), Jimmy Lowery (owner), Sumter, S.C.
2nd: Bramblewood Belle—Edward Eatmon (handler and owner), Kingstree, S.C.
3rd: HR Clark's Sam—Joe Migliore (handler), Robert J. B. Clark (owner), Birmingham, Ala.
4th: Pocotaligo's Coffee—Kim S. Parkman (handler), Kim and Jule Parkman (owners), Sumter, S.C.

Open Water
1st: Pocotaligo's Coffee—Kim S. Parkman (handler), Kim and Jule Parkman (owners), Sumter, S.C.
2nd: Pooshee's Wade Hampton—Grady Phillips (handler and owner), Winnsboro, S.C.
3rd: Chattahoochee Chaser—Jim Biggs (handler and owner), Marietta, Ga.
4th: HR Clark's Sam—Joe Migliore (handler), Robert J. B. Clark (owner), Birmingham, Ala.

Overall Intermediate
1st: Socks—Marvin Blount Jr. (handler and owner), Greenville, N.C.
2nd: Bramblewood Rascal—Edward Eatmon (handler and owner), Kingstree, S.C.
3rd: Fiddle—Ned Beard (handler), Meta Beard (owner), Camden, S.C.
4th: Chattahoochee Chaser—Jim Biggs (handler and owner), Marietta, Ga.

Intermediate Land
1st: Bramblewood Rascal—Edward Eatmon (handler and owner), Kingstree, S.C.
2nd: Socks—Marvin Blount Jr. (handler and owner), Greenville, N.C.
3rd: Dolly—Donald Smith (handler and owner), Winnsboro, S.C.

4th: Fiddle—Ned Beard (handler), Meta
Beard (owner), Camden, S.C.

Intermediate Water
1st: Socks—Marvin Blount Jr. (handler
and owner), Greenville, N.C.
2nd: Pocotaligo's Bailey—John Iler
(handler), Jule and Kim Parkman
(owners), Sumter, S.C.
3rd: Willie—Kelly Mahone (handler),
Kathryn Mahone (owner), Hot
Springs, Ark.
4th: Crane Creek Jabo—Don Odom
(handler and owner), Sumter, S.C.

Overall Novice
1st: Wade's Monticello Bud—Keith Cain
(handler and owner), Jenkinsville, S.C.
2nd: B.J.—Chuck Granner (handler),
C. J. Mahaffey (owner), Paducah, Ky.
3rd: Sally—David Johnson (handler),
Mert Johnson (owner), Florence, S.C.
4th: Harpeth's Dauntless Duke—
W. Pat Williams (handler and owner),
Franklin, Tenn.

Novice Land
1st: B.J.—Chuck Granner (handler),
C. J. Mahaffey (owner), Paducah, Ky.
2nd: Wade's Monticello Bud—
Keith Cain (handler and owner),
Jenkinsville, S.C.
3rd: Pooshee's Mr. Jack—Robert Mielke
(handler and owner), Lancaster, S.C.
4th: Sally—David Johnson (handler),
Mert Johnson (owner), Florence, S.C.

Novice Water
1st: Wade's Monticello Bud—Keith Cain
(handler and owner), Jenkinsville, S.C.
2nd: Walt's Little Buddy—Walter Johnson
(handler and owner), Florence, S.C.
3rd: B-Boy—Jack McInnis (handler),
John D. McInnis (owner), Dillon, S.C.
4th: Smoaks Incredible Rusty—Jack Sims
(handler and owner), Charleston, S.C.

Overall Puppy
1st: Casey Jones—Olin Lee (handler and
owner), Cheraw, S.C.
2nd: E.'s Baby Brewster—Elizabeth Cox
(handler and owner), Livingston, Ala.
3rd: Bear Eli Parnell—William Lynch
(handler), Eli and Eleanor Parnell
(owners), Sumter, S.C.
4th: Punkie—Betsy Harrington (handler
and owner), Hartsville, S.C.

Puppy Land
1st: Casey Jones—Olin Lee (handler
and owner), Cheraw, S.C.
2nd: Kiss Me Kate—Bob King (handler
and owner), Charleston, S.C.
3rd: Punkie—Olin Lee (handler), Betsy
Harrington (owner), Hartsville, S.C.
4th: Triever B Bosco—Edith Baker
(handler and owner), Kingstree, S.C.

Puppy Water
1st: E's Baby Brewster—Elizabeth Cox
(handler and owner), Livingston, Ala.
2nd: Big Mikee Duzz—Sandy King
(handler and owner), St. Augustine, Fla.
3rd: Casey Jones—Olin Lee (handler
and owner), Cheraw, S.C.
4th: Bear Eli Parnell—William Lynch
(handler), Eli and Eleanor Parnell
(owners), Sumter, S.C.

1990

**11th Annual Boykin Spaniel Society
National Retriever Trial
May 19
Wateree Correctional Institution,
Camden, S.C.**

Overall Open
1st: Pocotaligo's Coffee—Kim S. Parkman (handler), Kim and Jule Parkman
(owners), Sumter, S.C.
2nd: Bert—Olin Lee (handler and
owner), Cheraw, S.C.
3rd: Black River Buster—Robert Lowery
(handler and owner), Sumter, S.C.
4th: Bramblewood Belle—Edward
Eatmon (handler and owner),
Kingstree, S.C.

Open Land
1st: Pocotaligo's Coffee—Kim S. Parkman (handler), Kim and Jule Parkman (owners), Sumter, S.C.
2nd: Bramblewood Belle—Edward Eatmon (handler and owner), Kingstree, S.C.
3rd: The Incredible Bear— Lewis Smoak (handler and owner), Yonges Island, S.C.
4th: Bert—Olin Lee (handler and owner), Cheraw, S.C.

Open Water
1st: Bert—Olin Lee (handler and owner), Cheraw, S.C.
2nd: Pocotaligo's Coffee—Kim S. Parkman (handler), Kim and Jule Parkman (owners), Sumter, S.C.
3rd: Buster—John Trenary (handler and owner), Moncks Corner, S.C.
4th: Black River Buster—Robert Lowery (handler and owner), Sumter, S.C.

Intermediate Overall
1st: Dixie Blair—Bubba Pope (handler and owner), Columbia, S.C.
2nd: Beau Jiminy—Chuck Granner (handler and owner), Paducah, Ky.
3rd: Goose Pond Jessie—Chris Bishop (handler), Joni Bishop (owner), Gresham, S.C.
4th: The Incredible Bear— Lewis Smoak (handler and owner), Yonges Island, S.C.

Intermediate Land
1st: Goose Pond Jessie—Chris Bishop (handler), Joni Bishop (owner), Gresham, S.C.
2nd: Dixie Blair—Bubba Pope (handler and owner), Columbia, S.C.
3rd: Beau Jiminy—Chuck Granner (handler and owner), Paducah, Ky.
4th: The Incredible Bear—Lewis Smoak (handler and owner), Yonges Island, S.C.

Intermediate Water
1st (tie): Dixie Blair—Bubba Pope (handler and owner), Columbia, S.C.
1st (tie): Bert—Olin Lee (handler and owner), Cheraw, S.C.
2nd: McInnis B-Boy—Jack McInnis (handler and owner), Dillon, S.C.
3rd: Beau Jiminy—Chuck Granner (handler and owner), Paducah, Ky.
4th: Southern Comfort's Chantilly— Joe Migliore (handler), Joe and Sheila Migliore (owners), Boaz, Ala.

Novice Overall
1st: Casey Jones—Olin Lee (handler and owner), Cheraw, S.C.
2nd: Pooshee's Brandywine— Bob King (handler), Eric King (owner), Charleston, S.C.
3rd: Dixie Blair—Bubba Pope (handler and owner), Columbia, S.C.
4th: Bear Creek Dusty—Jim West (handler and owner), Little Mountain, S.C.

Novice Land
1st: Honey Hill's Hannah—Nancy Updegrave (handler), Doug and Nancy Updegrave (owners), Awendaw, S.C.
2nd: Casey Jones—Olin Lee (handler and owner), Cheraw, S.C.
3rd: Benchmark—Edward C. Moore (handler and owner), Roanoke Rapids, N.C.
4th: Pooshee's Brandywine—Bob King (handler), Eric King (owner), Charleston, S.C.

Novice Water
1st: Casey Jones—Olin Lee (handler and owner), Cheraw, S.C.
2nd: Dixie Blair—Bubba Pope (handler and owner), Columbia, S.C.
3rd: A.J.—Armond Groves (handler and owner), Seneca, S.C.
4th: Pooshee's Brandywine—Bob King (handler), Eric King (handler and owner), Charleston, S.C.

Overall Puppy

1st: Lynch's Comin' To Daddy—William Lynch (handler and owner), Moncks Corner, S.C.

2nd: Tai O'Conner—Nancy Updegrave (handler), J. Fitzgerald O'Conner Jr. (owner), Columbia, S.C.

3rd: Peppermint Patty—Stancil Gaither (handler and owner), Scottsboro, Ala.

4th: Socks Amos—Marvin Blount Jr. (handler and owner), Greenville, S.C.

Puppy Land

1st: Lynch's Comin' To Daddy—William Lynch (handler and owner), Moncks Corner, S.C.

2nd: Tai O'Conner—Nancy Updegrave (handler), J. Fitzgerald O'Conner Jr. (owner), Columbia, S.C.

3rd: Howell's Hope—Madison P. Howell III (handler and owner), Ruffin, S.C.

4th: Peppermint Patty—Stancil Gaither (handler and owner), Scottsboro, Ala.

Puppy Water

1st: Lynch's Comin' To Daddy—William Lynch (handler and owner), Moncks Corner, S.C.

2nd: Tai O'Conner—Nancy Updegrave (handler), J. Fitzgerald O'Conner Jr. (owner), Columbia, S.C.

3rd: Deb's Brown Emma Girl—Craig Fulford (handler), Debbie Fulford (owner), Birmingham, Ala.

4th: Black River Bandit—Jimmy Lowery (handler), Robert Lowery (owner), Sumter, S.C.

1991

12th Annual Boykin Spaniel Society National Retriever Trial
May 18
Wateree Correctional Institution, Camden, S.C.

Open Overall

1st: Wade's Monticello Bud—Keith Cain (handler and owner), Jenkinsville, S.C.

2nd: WR Socks—Marvin Blount Jr. (handler and owner), Greenville, N.C.

3rd: MHR WR Pocotaligo's Coffee—Kim S. Parkman (handler), Kim and Jule Parkman (owners), Sumter, S.C.

4th: Beckoned By Cricket—Charles Granner (handler and owner), Paducah, Ky.

Open Land

1st: Wade's Monticello Bud—Keith Cain (handler and owner), Jenkinsville, S.C.

2nd: Beckoned By Cricket—Charles Granner (handler and owner), Paducah, Ky.

3rd: MHR WR Firestone—Charles Jurney (handler and owner), Mooresville, N.C.

4th: HR Beau Jiminy—Charles Granner (handler and owner), Paducah, Ky.

Open Water

1st: MHR WR Pocotaligo's Coffee—Kim S. Parkman (handler), Kim and Jule Parkman (owners), Sumter, S.C.

2nd: WR Socks—Marvin Blount Jr. (handler and owner), Greenville, N.C.

3rd: Wade's Monticello Bud—Keith Cain (handler and owner), Jenkinsville, S.C.

4th: Pocotaligo's Bailey—Kim S. Parkman (handler), Jule and Kim Parkman (owners), Sumter, S.C.

Intermediate Overall

1st: Wade's Monticello Bud—Keith Cain (handler and owner), Jenkinsville, S.C.

2nd: Incredible Rusty—Jack Sims (handler and owner), Charleston, S.C.

3rd: WR Nat's Reluck Butch—Larry Sterne (handler and owner), Tulsa, Okla.

4th: Socks Casey—Marvin Blount Jr. (handler and owner), Greenville, N.C.

Intermediate Land

1st: Incredible Rusty—Jack Sims (handler and owner), Charleston, S.C.

2nd: Wade's Monticello Bud—Keith Cain (handler and owner), Jenkinsville, S.C.

3rd: Socks Casey—Marvin Blount Jr. (handler and owner), Greenville, N.C.

4th: WR Nat's Reluck Butch—Larry Sterne (handler and owner), Tulsa, Okla.

Intermediate Water
1st: Wade's Monticello Bud—Keith Cain (handler and owner), Jenkinsville, S.C.
2nd: Beckoned By Cricket—Charles Granner (handler and owner), Paducah, Ky.
3rd: WR Nat's Reluck Butch—Larry Sterne (handler and owner), Tulsa, Okla.
4th: Benchmark—Edward C. Moore (handler and owner), Roanoke Rapids, N.C.

Novice Overall
1st: Socks Casey—Marvin Blount Jr. (handler and owner), Greenville, N.C.
2nd: B.J. (Buster Junior)—Rogers L. Moody Jr. (handler and owner), Columbia, S.C.
3rd: WR Nat's Reluck Butch—Larry Sterne (handler and owner), Tulsa, Okla.
4th: Doctor Fetchum—Robert H. Cox (handler and owner), Brandon, Fla.

Novice Land
1st: Lynch's Comin' To Daddy—William C. Lynch (handler and owner), Moncks Corner, S.C.
2nd: Pooshee's Superman—Bob King (handler), Nancy Updegrave (owner), Awendaw, S.C.
3rd: WR Nat's Reluck Butch—Larry Sterne (handler and owner), Tulsa, Okla.
4th: Black River Buckwheat—Robert L. Lowery (handler and owner), Sumter, S.C.

Novice Water
1st (tie): B.J. (Buster Junior)—Rogers L. Moody Jr. (handler and owner), Columbia, S.C.
1st (tie): Socks Casey—Marvin Blount Jr. (handler and owner), Greenville, N.C.
2nd: Gayle's Buddy Ray—Karl Buddenbaum (handler and owner), Harrisburg, N.C.

3rd: Doctor Fetchum—Robert H. Cox (handler and owner), Brandon, Fla.
4th: WR Nat's Reluck Butch—Larry Sterne (handler and owner), Tulsa, Okla.

Puppy Overall
1st: Jeb Stuart—Jack C. Evans (handler and owner), Charleston, S.C.
2nd: Dovewood's Woody—Roy Thompson (handler and owner), Summerville, S.C.
3rd: Lee's Decoy—Olin Lee (handler), Olin and Pat Lee (owners), Cheraw, S.C.
4th: Triever "B" Little Joe Cartwright—Edith A. Baker (handler and owner), Kingstree, S.C.

Puppy Land
1st: Jeb Stuart—Jack C. Evans (handler and owner), Charleston, S.C.
2nd: Dovewood's Woody—Roy Thompson (handler and owner), Summerville, S.C.
3rd: Lake Monticello Ripples—Keith Cain (handler and owner), Jenkinsville, S.C.
4th: Lee's Decoy—Olin Lee (handler), Olin and Pat Lee (owners), Cheraw, S.C.

Puppy Water
1st: Jeb Stuart—Jack C. Evans (handler and owner), Charleston, S.C.
2nd: Lee's Decoy—Olin Lee (handler), Olin and Pat Lee (owners), Cheraw, S.C.
3rd: Dovewood's Woody—Roy Thompson (handler and owner), Summerville, S.C.
4th: Triever "B" Little Joe Cartwright—Edith A. Baker (handler and owner), Kingstree, S.C.

1992

13th Annual Boykin Spaniel Society National Retriever Trial
May 16
Webb Creek, Santee, S.C.

Open Overall
1st: MHR WR Pocotaligo's Coffee—Kim S. Parkman (handler), Kim and Jule Parkman (owners), Sumter, S.C.

2nd: WR Socks—Marvin Blount Jr. (handler and owner), Greenville, S.C.
3rd: Wade's Monticello Bud—Keith Cain (handler and owner), Jenkinsville, S.C.
4th: Dixie Blair—William "Bubba" Pope (handler and owner), Columbia, S.C.

Open Land
1st: Bramblewood Rascal— Edward F. Eatmon (handler and owner), Kingstree, S.C.
2nd: WR Socks—Marvin Blount Jr. (handler and owner), Greenville, S.C.
3rd: Wade's Monticello Bud—Keith Cain (handler and owner), Jenkinsville, S.C.
4th: Dixie Blair—William "Bubba" Pope (handler and owner), Columbia, S.C.

Open Water
1st: MHR WR Pocotaligo's Coffee— Kim S. Parkman (handler), Kim and Jule Parkman (owners), Sumter, S.C.
2nd: Pocotaligo's Bailey—Kim S. Parkman (handler), Jule and Kim Parkman (owners), Sumter, S.C.
3rd: Beau Jiminy—Chuck Granner (handler and owner), Paducah, Ky.
4th: WR Socks—Marvin Blount Jr. (handler and owner), Greenville, S.C.

Intermediate Overall
1st: Pooshee's Superman—Nancy R. Updegrave (handler and owner), Awendaw, S.C.
2nd: Diamond Pete—Tim Blackwelder (handler and owner), Charleston, S.C.
3rd: Dovewood's Woody—Roy M. Thompson (handler and owner), Cross, S.C.
4th: Jalapa's Misty Morning Molly— W. Keith Midgette (handler and owner), Dahlgren, Va.

Intermediate Land
1st: Pooshee's Superman—Nancy R. Updegrave (handler and owner), Awendaw, S.C.
2nd: Diamond Pete—Tim Blackwelder (handler and owner), Charleston, S.C.

3rd: Jalapa's Misty Morning Molly— W. Keith Midgette (handler and owner), Dahlgren, Va.
4th: Dovewood's Woody—Roy M. Thompson (handler and owner), Cross, S.C.

Intermediate Water
1st: Dovewood's Woody—Roy M. Thompson (handler and owner), Cross, S.C.
2nd: Pooshee's Superman—Nancy R. Updegrave (handler and owner), Awendaw, S.C.
3rd: Buster Junior—Rogers L. Moody Jr. (handler and owner), Columbia, S.C.
4th: Diamond Pete—Tim Blackwelder (handler and owner), Charleston, S.C.

Novice Overall
1st: Bette's No Cotton—Ivey Sumrell (handler and owner), Weddington, N.C.
2nd: Diamond Pete—Tim Blackwelder (handler and owner), Charleston, S.C.
3rd: Lost Decoy's Cally Canvasback— Robert W. Norris (handler and owner), Charlotte, S.C.
4th: Sassie Sadie—Millie Odom (handler), Ella R. Calvert (owner), Lexington, S.C.

Chairman's Cup (for a young person with the highest scoring dog in a novice class): David Wright, handling Lady Ashley Kacey

Novice Land
1st: Bette's No Cotton—Ivey Sumrell (handler and owner), Weddington, N.C.
2nd: Diamond Pete—Tim Blackwelder (handler and owner), Charleston, S.C.
3rd: Big McEe Duzz—An McQuaig (handler and owner), St. Augustine, Fla.
4th: Holly—William D. Johnson (handler and owner), Lake View, S.C.

Novice Water

1st: Lost Decoy's Cally Canvasback—Robert W. Norris (handler and owner), Charlotte, S.C.

2nd (tie): Diamond Pete—Tim Blackwelder (handler and owner), Charleston, S.C.

2nd (tie): Dovewood's Woody—Roy M. Thompson (handler and owner), Cross, S.C.

4th: Bette's No Cotton—Ivey Sumrell (handler and owner), Weddington, N.C.

Puppy Overall

1st: Bette's No Cotton—Ivey Sumrell (handler and owner), Weddington, N.C.

2nd: Chocolate Chip—Clifford Taylor (handler and owner), Dalzell, S.C.

3rd: S-n-K's Burgandy Brandy—J. Steve Smith (handler and owner), Savannah, Ga.

4th: Sir Walter Raleigh—Tallulah McGee (handler), Robert C. Hagood (owner), Charleston, S.C.

Puppy Land

1st: Bette's No Cotton—Ivey Sumrell (handler and owner), Weddington, N.C.

2nd: Cody—David Carmichael (handler and owner), Florence, S.C.

3rd: Chocolate Chip—Clifford Taylor (handler and owner), Dalzell, S.C.

4th: S-n-K's Burgandy Brandy—J. Steve Smith (handler and owner), Savannah, Ga.

Puppy Water

1st: Bette's No Cotton—Ivey Sumrell (handler and owner), Weddington, N.C.

2nd: S-n-K's Burgandy Brandy—J. Steve Smith (handler and owner), Savannah, Ga.

3rd: Chocolate Chip—Clifford Taylor (handler and owner), Dalzell, S.C.

4th: Walker Creek's Jazzy—Patricia E. Labbe (handler), Marian G. Williams (owner), Columbia, S.C.

1993

14th Annual Boykin Spaniel Society National Hunting Test
April 24
Bennettsville, S.C.

Open

1st: Benchmark—Chris Bishop (handler), Edward C. Moore (owner), Roanoke Rapids, N.C.

2nd: Dixie Blair—William "Bubba" Pope (handler and owner), Columbia, S.C.

3rd: WR Socks—Marvin Blount Jr. (handler and owner), Greenville, N.C.

4th: MHR WR Pocotaligo's Coffee—Kim S. Parkman (handler), Kim and Jule Parkman (owners), Sumter, S.C.

Intermediate

1st: Hubba Bubba—Richard F. Coe (handler and owner), Summerville, S.C.

2nd: S-n-K's Burgandy Brandy—Steve Smith (handler and owner), Reidsville, Ga.

3rd: Chocolate Chip—Clifford Taylor (handler and owner), Dalzell, S.C.

Novice

1st: Sir Walter Raleigh—Robert C. Hagood (handler and owner), Charleston, S.C.

2nd: Hubba Bubba—Richard F. Coe (handler and owner), Summerville, S.C.

3rd: Lee's Decoy—Lee Smith (handler), Donnie Watts (owner), Lexington, S.C.

4th: Buster Brown—T. David Sligh (handler and owner), Martinez, Ga.

Puppy

1st: JR's Hunter Hershey—Jeff McCurry (handler), Jeff and Tracy McCurry (owner), Greenwood, S.C.

2nd: Mr. Mick—Curtis Hodge (handler and owner), Sumter, S.C.

3rd: Tripp—Robert A. Mielke (handler), Zane F. Rollings (owner), Lancaster, S.C.

4th: Monticello's White Oak "G'—Paul C. Holmes (handler and owner), Winnsboro, S.C.

1994

15th Annual National Hunt Test
April 16
Sandhills State Forest, Cheraw, S.C.

Open

1st: Dixie Blair—William "Bubba" Pope (handler and owner), Columbia, S.C.
2nd: Pocotaligo's Coffee—Kim S. Parkman (handler), Kim and Jule Parkman (owners), Sumter S.C.
3rd: Buster Junior (B.J.)—Kim S. Parkman (handler), Rogers L. Moody Jr. (owner), Fayetteville, N.C.
4th: Hubba Bubba—Richard Coe (handler and owner), Summerville, S.C.

Intermediate

1st: Alexander's Pride—Ackron Alexander (handler and owner), Summerville, S.C.
2nd: Bette's No-Cotton—Ivey Sumrell (handler and owner), Weddington, N.C.
3rd: Back Swamp Cody—David Carmichael (handler and owner), Florence, S.C.
4th: Palmetto—T. David Sligh (handler and owner), Martinez, Ga.

Novice

1st: Alexander's Pride—Ackron Alexander (handler and owner), Summerville, S.C.
2nd: Mr. Mick—Daulton C. Hodge (handler and owner), Sumter, S.C.
3rd: Florida's Fire Cracker—Becky Burney (handler and owner), St. Augustine, Fla.
4th: Erva's Sir Casey—Becky Burney (handler), Patricia and Erva Smith (owners), Leesville, S.C.

Puppy

1st: Lady Winchester—Ackron Alexander (handler and owner), Summerville, S.C.
2nd: Irene's Fancy Girl—Cliff Taylor (handler), Irene Sousa (owner), Columbia, S.C.

3rd: Riptide's Colonial Run— Michael O. Collins (handler and owner), Florence, S.C.
4th: Cricket-Three—Nat Gist (handler and owner), Sumter, S.C.

1995

16th Annual Boykin Spaniel Society National Hunting Test
April 22
Moree's Sportsman's Preserve, Society Hill, S.C.

Open

1st: Dixie Blair—Bubba Pope (handler and owner), Columbia, S.C.
2nd: Irene's Fancy Girl—Burke H. Dial (handler), Irene Sousa (owner), Columbia, S.C.
3rd: MHR WR HR Pocotaligo's Coffee—Kim S. Parkman (handler), Kim and Jule Parkman (owners), Sumter, S.C.
4th: Hubba Bubba—Richard Coe (handler and owner), Summerville, S.C.

Intermediate

1st: Unsinkable Molly Brown—Paul Sumner (handler), Marsha Sumner (owner), Chapin, S.C.
2nd: Freeman's Tom—Leonard Freeman (handler and owner), Ridgeville, S.C.
3rd: King's Curlee Gurlee—Kris Kadlec (handler), Pamela Kadlec (owner), Stark, Fla.
4th: Mr. Mick—Curtis Hodge (handler and owner), Sumter, S.C.

Novice

1st: Wyolina's Jacob's Ladder—Jeff Davis (handler), Jeff and Jennifer Davis (owners), Lewisville, N.C.
2nd: King's Curlee Gurlee—Kris Kadlec (handler), Pamela Kadlec (owner), Stark, Fla.
3rd: Haillie's Smokin Pooshee—Michael Langehans (handler), Sarah Langehans (owner), Florence, S.C.
4th: Freeman's Tom—Leonard Freeman (handler and owner), Ridgeville, S.C.

Puppy
1st (tie): Katy Sue Williams—Mary T. Dial (handler and owner), Columbia, S.C.
1st (tie): Sockson's Feather Finding Turk—Thomas H. Nickerson (handler and owner), Atlanta, Ga.
2nd: King's Curlee Gurlee—Kris Kadlec (handler), Pamela Kadlec (owner), Stark, Fla.
3rd: Pooshee's Big Gun—Michael D. Langehans (handler and owner), Florence, S.C.
4th: Pocotaligo's Sweet 16—Clifford Taylor (handler), Kim S. Parkman (owner), Sumter, S.C.

1996

17th Annual Boykin Spaniel Society National Retriever Trial
April 20
North Camden Plantation, Camden, S.C.

Open
1st: Hubba Bubba—Richard Coe (handler and owner), Summerville, S.C.
2nd: Dixie Blair—Rusty Pye (handler), Bubba Pope (owner), Columbia, S.C.
3rd: MHR WR HR Pocotaligo's Coffee—Kim S. Parkman (handler), Kim and Jule Parkman (owners), Sumter, S.C.
4th: Irene's Fancy Girl—Kim Parkman (handler), Irene Sousa (owner), Columbia, S.C.

Intermediate
1st: Wyolina's Jacobs Ladder—Jeff Davis (handler), Jeff and Jennifer Davis (owners), Lewisville, N.C.
2nd: Caymus Webber Hughes—Edwin Hughes (handler and owner), Charleston, S.C.
3rd: Buster Brown—T. David Sligh (handler and owner), Martinez, Ga.
4th: Ginger's Curly—Sam Mullican (handler and owner), Moncks Corner, S.C.

Novice
1st: Socks Jackson—Jan Blount (handler), Jan and Marvin Blount (owners), Greenville, N.C.
2nd: Maidstone's Kodiak—Paul Anderson (handler and owner), East Hampton, N.Y.
3rd: Caymus Webber Hughes—Edwin Hughes (handler and owner), Charleston, S.C.
4th: P.K. Maxwell Smart—Patricia Labbe (handler and owner), Batesburg, S.C.

Puppy
1st: Wednesday's Child of Ginger—Jay Anderson (handler), Gabe Anderson (owner), Sumter, S.C.
2nd: Rock'n Creek Watson—Jim Latimer (handler), Jim and Millie Latimer (owners), Leesville, S.C.
3rd: Consuela—William Reinecke (handler and owner), Charleston, S.C.
4th: Christie's Dixie Bell—David P. Smith (handler and owner), Blythewood, S.C.

1997

18th Annual Boykin Spaniel Society National Hunt Test
April 19
S.C. Waterfowl Association Wetlands Center, Rimini, S.C.

Open
1st: HR King's Curlee Gurlee—Pamela O. Kadlec (handler and owner), Stark, Fla.
2nd: Irene's Fancy Girl—Kim S. Parkman (handler), Irene Sousa (owner), Columbia, S.C.
3rd: Unsinkable Molly Brown—Paul A. Sumner Jr. (handler), Marsha L. Sumner (owner), Chapin, S.C.
4th: HR CH Pocotaligo's Bailey—Kim S. Parkman (handler), Jule and Kim Parkman (owners), Sumter, S.C.

JAM (Judges' Award of Merit)
Bramblewood Belle—Edward Eatmon (handler and owner), Kingstree, S.C.

Mr. Mick—Curtis Hodge (handler and owner), Sumter, S.C.
Bramblewood Rascal—Edward Eatmon (handler and owner), Kingstree, S.C.

Intermediate

1st: Sydney of Woodbine—Jake Rasor Jr. (handler and owner), Cross Hill, S.C.
2nd: Papa Joe's Joshua—James E. Watkins (handler and owner), Florence, S.C.
3rd: Riptide's Colonial Run— Michael O. Collins (handler and owner), Florence, S.C.
4th: Bird Dog Boone—Carl Howard (handler and owner), Charlotte, N.C.

JAM (Judges' Award of Merit)
Rountree's Sunflower Mocha Cola— Robert Rountree (handler and owner), Kansas City, Mo.

Novice

1st: Miggie McGirt—Charles M. Graham III (handler and owner), Mount Pleasant, S.C.
2nd: Dandy Firestone—Gene Putnam (handler and owner), Kings Mountain, S.C.
3rd: Rock'n Creek Bette—James Latimer (handler), James and Millie Latimer (owners), St. Matthews, S.C.
4th: Exeter Lord Dudley—Elizabeth Collins (handler and owner), Florence, S.C.

JAM (Judges' Award of Merit)
Pocotaligo's Wednesday—Lynn Wallace (handler), Kim S. Parkman (owner), Sumter, S.C.
Tanner Gaston Boyd—Chesley M. Hall (handler and owner), Charleston, S.C.
Sockson's Feather Findin' Turk—Thomas H. Nickerson (handler and owner), Atlanta, Ga.
Allyanna's Mighty Muddy—Jim Collins (handler and owner), Hinesville, Ga.

Puppy

1st: Pocotaligo's Camo—Bonnie Burney (handler and owner), St. Augustine, Fla.

2nd: Cricket—Patricia Grant (handler and owner), Camden, S.C.
3rd: Pocotaligo's Holland and Holland— Lynn Wallace (handler), Kim S. Parkman (owner), Sumter, S.C.
4th: Rock'n Creek Bird Boy—Millie Latimer (handler), James and Millie Latimer (owners), St. Matthews, S.C.

JAM (Judges' Award of Merit)
Hollow Creek's King Jake—Kenneth Faircloth (handler and owner), North Augusta, S.C.
Florida's Sugar Boogie—Pam Kadlec (handler), An E. McQuaig and Pam Kadlec (owners), Starke, Fla.
Pocotaligo's Southern Belle— Bill Biggerstaff (handler and owner), Clover, S.C.
Nassawango's Little Boy—John F. Wilkinson (handler and owner), Salisbury, Md.

1998

19th Annual National Boykin Spaniel Society Hunting Test
April 18
H. Cooper Black Jr. Memorial Field Trial and Recreation Area, Patrick, S.C.

Open (18 entries)

1st: Mr. Mick—Curtis Hodge (handler and owner), Sumter, S.C.
2nd: Goose Pond Malcolm—Chris Bishop (handler), Joni Bishop (owner), Gresham, S.C.
3rd: Unsinkable Molly Brown—Paul A. Sumner Jr. (handler), Marsha L. Sumner (owner), Chapin, S.C.
4th: HR CH King's Curlee Gurlee— Pamela Kadlec (handler and owner), Starke, Fla.

JAM (Judges' Award of Merit)
Bramblewood Rascal—Edward Eatmon (handler and owner), Kingstree, S.C.
HR Sydney of Woodbine—Kim S. Parkman (handler), Jake Rasor Jr. (owner), Cross Hill, S.C.

HR CH Pocotaligo's Bailey—Kim S. Parkman (handler and owner), Sumter, S.C.

Intermediate (16+ entries)
1st: Wateree Ralph—Curtis Hodge (handler and owner), Sumter, S.C.
2nd: HR Miggie McGirt—Charles M. Graham III (handler and owner). Mount Pleasant, S.C.
3rd: Pistol Pete Fetchum—Robert Cox (handler and owner), Brandon, Fla.
4th: Allyanna's Mighty Muddy— Jim Collins (handler and owner), Hinesville, Ga.

Novice (53 entries)
1st: Bette's Lulu—Carl Howard (handler), Ivey Sumrell (owner), Weddington, N.C.
2nd: Warren's 1st Scout—Billy Warren (handler and owner), Robersonville, N.C.
3rd: Just Ducky's Justasample—Pamela Kadlec (handler and owner), Starke, Fla.
4th: Monettes's Dutch Chocolate— Pamela Kadlec (handler and owner), Starke, Fla.

JAM (Judges' Award of Merit)
King's Tank Gunner Duzz—Roger Strickland (handler and owner), Gainesville, Fla.
Hollow Creek Gus—Patricia Smith (handler and owner), Leesville, S.C.
Pocotaligo's Camo—Bonnie Burney (handler and owner), St. Augustine, Fla.
Pocotaligo's Beretta—Welsey Rodgers (handler), Kim S. Parkman (owner), Sumter, S.C.

Puppy (20 entries)
1st: Just Ducky's Justasample—Pamela Kadlec (handler and owner), Starke, Fla.
2nd: Molly's Folly—Paul Sumner (handler and owner), Chapin, S.C.
3rd: Strick's Just Ducky Tao—Roger Strickland (handler and owner), Gainesville, Fla.
4th: Harlequin of Pocotaligo—Connie Wallace (handler), Connie and Lynn Wallace (owners), Sumter, S.C.

JAM (Judges' Award of Merit)
Just Caliente—Lynn Wallace (handler), Francis Hill (owner), Sumter, S.C.

1999
20th Annual National Boykin Spaniel Society Hunting Test
April 8–11
Boykin Mill Gun Club, Boykin, S.C.

Open (15 entries)
1st: HR CH King's Curlee Gurlee— Pamela O. Kadlec (handler and owner), Starke, Fla.
2nd: Goose Pond Malcolm—Chris Bishop (handler), Joni Bishop (owner), Gresham, S.C.
3rd: Caymus Webber Hughes— Eddie B. Hughes (handler and owner), Charleston S.C.
4th: HR Mr. Mick—Curtis Hodge (handler and owner), Sumter, S.C.

JAM (Judges' Award of Merit)
Bird Dog Boone—Charles Howard (handler), Charles and Melissa Howard (owners), Charlotte, N.C.
Wyolina's Jacob's Ladder—Jeff Davis (handler), Jeff and Jennifer Davis (owners), Lexington, S.C.
HR Sydney of Woodbine—Kim S. Parkman (handler), Jake Rasor Jr. (owner), Cross Hill, S.C.

Intermediate (17 entries)
1st: Pocotaligo's Wednesday—Kim S. Parkman (handler and owner), Sumter, S.C.
2nd: Rock'n Creek Bette—Millie Latimer (handler), James and Millie Latimer (owners), St. Matthews, S.C.
3rd: Zee—Harriett L. Clark (handler), Lee and Harriett Clark (owners), Wilson, N.C.

JAM (Judges' Award of Merit)
Dixie's Caper—Jim Harris (handler), Carrie and Jim Harris (owners), Deland, Fla.

HR Just Ducky's Justasample—Pamela O. Kadlec (handler and owner), St. Matthews, S.C.
Molly's Folly—Paul A. Sumner Jr. (handler and owner), Chapin, S.C.

Novice (43 entries)
1st: Shelby's Little Lulu—Lynn Wallace (handler), Julius D. Shivers (owner), Orange Beach, Ala.
2nd: Hannah Holt Schultz—Bradley D. Schultz (handler and owner), Clayton, N.C.
3rd: Pocotaligo's Philly—Lynn Wallace (handler), Lynn Wallace and Kim Parkman (owners), Sumter, S.C.
4th: Pocotaligo's Camo—Lynn Wallace (handler), Bonnie Burney (owner), St. Augustine, Fla.

JAM (Judges' Award of Merit)
P.K. Charlie Brown—Patty Labbe (handler), Karin Solis (owner), Batesburg, S.C.
Twisted Creek's Drake—Eddie Hughes (handler and owner), Charleston, S.C.
Mr. Mick's Flipside—Marie Hodge (handler), Curtis and Marie Hodge (owner), Sumter, S.C.
Widgeon of Pocotaligo—Lynn Wallace (handler and owner), Sumter, S.C.

Puppy (16 entries)
1st: Just Ducky's Sir Jaymes Mark— Millie Latimer (handler), Pamela O. Kadlec (owner), St. Matthews, S.C.
2nd: Rock'n Creek Just B.G.—James Latimer (handler), James and Millie Latimer (owners), St. Matthews, S.C.
3rd: Mossy Oak's Rhett—Richard F. Coe (handler and owner), Summerville, S.C.
4th: Hi-Brass Harley—Kevin K. Freeman (handler and owner), North Augusta, S.C.

JAM (Judges' Award of Merit)
Hollow Creek's Decoy II—Paul H. Pennell Jr. (handler and owner), Gastonia, N.C.

Chelsea's Woody Bear—John Inabinet (handler), John, Tessie, and Chelsea Inabinet (owners), Columbia, S.C.
Tom's Cee Gee—Millie Latimer (handler), Tommy Thompson and Pamela Kadlec (owners), Lexington, S.C., and St. Matthews, S.C.
Chewbaca—Walter L. Fink (handler and owner), Campobello, S.C.

2000

21st Annual Boykin Spaniel Society National Hunting Test
April 6–9
Moree's Sportsman's Preserve, Society Hill, S.C.

Open
1st: Bette's Lulu—Charles Jurney (handler), Ivey Sumrell (owner), Matthews, N.C.
2nd: Goose Pond Malcolm—Chris Bishop (handler), Joni Bishop (owner), Gresham, S.C.
3rd: HR Pocotaligo's Wednesday— Kim Parkman (handler and owner), Sumter, S.C.
4th: HR UH Sydney of Woodbine— Kim Parkman (handler), Jake Rasor Jr. (owner), Cross Hill, S.C.

JAM (Judges' Award of Merit)
Irene's Fancy Girl—Kim Parkman (handler), Burke H. Dial (owner), Columbia, S.C.

Intermediate
1st: Twisted Creek's Drake—Eddie Hughes (handler and owner), Wadmalaw Island, S.C.
2nd: HR Just Ducky's Justasample— Pamela O. Kadlec (handler and owner), Edgefield, S.C.
3rd: Dixie's Last Boy Scout—John Pollock (handler), John and Andrea Pollock (owners), Jacksonville, N.C.
4th: Cooper—A. Palmer Owings Jr. (handler and owner), Charleston, S.C.

JAM (Judges' Award of Merit)
Pocotaligo's Philly—Kim Parkman (handler), Lynn Wallace and Kim Parkman (owners), Sumter, S.C.

Novice
1st: Strick's JustDucky Tao—Roger Strickland (handler), Roger Strickland and Pamela Kadlec (owners), Gainesville, Fla., and Edgefield, S.C.
2nd (tie): Hi-Brass Harley—Kevin K. Freeman (handler and owner), North Augusta, S.C.
2nd (tie): Mossy Oak's Rhett—Richard F. Coe (handler and owner), Summerville, S.C.
3rd: Beal's Jig—Lynn Wallace (handler), Barry Beal (owner), Midland, Tex.
4th: Harlequin of Pocotaligo—Connie Wallace (handler), Connie and Lynn Wallace (owners), Sumter, S.C.

JAM (Judges' Award of Merit)
Twisted Creek's Drake—Edwin Hughes (handler and owner), Charleston, S.C.
Daisy—Harriett Clark (handler), Lee and Harriett Clark (owners), Wilson, N.C.
Chelsea's Mistletoe—Chelsea Inabinet (handler and owner), Columbia, S.C.
Hollow Creek's Rosey—Patricia L. Watts (handler and owner), Leesville, S.C.

Puppy
1st: Savannah Rose's Martha Duke—Gary Edmonds (handler), Gary and Rose Edmonds (owners), Columbia, S.C.
2nd: Fancy's Magnolia—Leslie Moats (handler and owner), Irmo, S.C.
3rd: Dawkins Pocotaligo Mojo—Lynn Wallace (handler), Ronald Dawkins (owner), Lexington, S.C.
4th: Pocotaligo's Cocomo Joe—Lynn Wallace (handler), Hector Snethen (owner), Sumter, S.C.

JAM (Judges' Award of Merit)
Heavy Duty's Brandy Jean—Connie Wallace (handler), Howard Harlan and Kim Parkman (owners), Nashville, Tenn., and Sumter, S.C.

Scape 'Ore Li'l Scarlett—Lori Melton (handler), S. F. Melton Jr. (owner), Timmonsville, S.C.
Pocotaligo's Carolina Wren—Lynn Wallace (handler), Eliza Weston and Kim Parkman (owners), Columbia, S.C., and Sumter, S.C.
Pocotaligo's Ruddy—Lynn Wallace (handler), Bruce Lanier and Kim Parkman (owners), West Point, Ga., and Sumter, S.C.

2001
22nd Annual Boykin Spaniel Society National Hunting Test
April 5–8
Tyger Ranch, near Buffalo, S.C.

Open (15 entries)
1st: HR CH Patton's Holy Moses—Joe Migliore (handler), Jowane Patton (owner), Birmingham, Ala.
2nd: HR Sydney of Woodbine, Kim S. Parkman (handler), Jake Rasor (owner), Cross Hill, S.C.
3rd: HR CH King's Curlee Gurlee—Pamela O. Kadlec (handler and owner), Edgefield, S.C.
4th: Goose Pond Malcolm—Chris Bishop (handler), Joni Bishop (owner), Gresham, S.C.

JAM (Judges' Award of Merit)
Pocotaligo's Philly—Kim S. Parkman (handler and owner), Sumter, S.C.

Intermediate
1st: Pocotaligo's Philly—Kim S. Parkman (handler and owner), Sumter, S.C.
2nd: HR Just Ducky's Tourbillion—Chris Meurett (handler and owner), Ocoee, Fla.
3rd: Fancy's Mighty Samson—Gene Putman (handler and owner), Kings Mountain, N.C.
4th: Mossy Oak's Rhett—Richard Coe (handler and owner), Summerville, S.C.

JAM (Judges' Award of Merit)
Daisy—Harriett Clark (handler), Lee and Harriett Clark (owner), Sutherlin, Va.

Novice (52 entries)
1st: Pocotaligo's Tasmanian Jake—Mack Smith (handler and owner), Galivants Ferry, S.C.
2nd: Alexander Beauregard—Alex Jim Pope (handler), Alex Pope (owner), Thomasville, N.C.
3rd: Hollow Creek's Mikie—Paul Pennell (handler), Patricia Watts and Paul Pennell (owners), Leesville, S.C.
4th: Craft's Shot of Jaegermeister—Chris Craft (handler and owner), Fayetteville, N.C.

JAM (Judges' Award of Merit)
Rock'n Creek Barney Google—Millie Latimer (handler), James and Millie Latimer (owners), St. Matthews, S.C.
Fancy's Mighty Samson—Gene Putnam (handler and owner), Kings Mountain, N.C.
Scape 'Ore Li'l Scarlett—S. F. Melton (handler), Frankie Melton (owner), Timmonsville, S.C.
Chelsea's Woody Bear—John Inabinet (handler and owner), Columbia, S.C.
Hollow Creek's Rosey O'Donnell—Patricia L. Watts (handler and owner), Leesville, S.C.
Chairman's Cup for highest scoring novice dog with a handler age sixteen or less: Alexander Beauregard with Alex Pope, Thomasville, N.C.

Puppy (21 entries)
1st: Chica—Ronnie Dawkins (handler), David Hull and Kim S. Parkman (owners), Houston, Tex., and Sumter, S.C.
2nd: Lori's Show-Me Trouble—Frankie Melton (handler), Lori Melton (owner), Timmonsville, S.C.
3rd: Amy's Pocotaligo Ellie—James Braswell (handler), Amy Braswell and Kim Parkman (owners), Pendleton, S.C., and Sumter, S.C.

4th: Dovewood's Major—Mike Branham (handler and owner), Elgin, S.C.

JAM (Judges' Award of Merit)
Pocotaligo's Firethorn Kate—Ronnie Dawkins (handler), Ancel Hamilton and Kim Parkman (owners), Blythewood, S.C., and Sumter, S.C.
Penny's Wooden Nickle—Randy McHugh (handler), Katie and Randy McHugh (owners), Evansville, Wis.
Just Ducky's CoCo Puff—Wayne Burnett (handler), Pamela O. Kadlec (owner), Edgefield, S.C.
Boulder Brook's Bandit—Bill Wright (handler), J. W. Wright (owner), Markham, Va.

Upland
HR Barthalamew—G. Vecchione, Blythewood, S.C.
Daisy—H. Clark, Southerlin, Va.
Kipper Ray—H. Clark, Sutherlin, Va.
Zee—H. Clark, Sutherlin, Va.
Penny's Wooden Nickle—R. McHugh, Evansville, Wis.
HR CH King's Curlee Gurlee—P. Kadlec, Edgefield, S.C.
Jack's Roux—J. Cafiero, Simpsonville, S.C.
Dannas's Darling Delight—E. Baker, Waco, Ga.
Walker Creek's Jazzy—P. Labbe, Batesburg, S.C.
P.K. Charlie Brown—K. Solis, Batesburg, S.C.
P.K. Maxwell Smart—P. Labbe, Batesburg, S.C.
Craft's Shot of Jaegermeister—C. Craft, Fayetteville, N.C.
Rock'n Creek Jaymes Mark—M. and J. Latimer, St. Matthews, S.C.
Mr. Mick—C. Hodge, Sumter, S.C.

Children's Handling Stake
Ben Makla and Show-Me Buster
Nathan Makla and Show-Me Buster
Whitney Berry and Walker Creek's Jazzy

2002

23rd Annual Boykin Spaniel Society
National Hunt Test
April 1–14
Tyger Ranch, near Buffalo, S.C.

Open
1st: HRCH King's Curlee Gurlee—
Pam O. Kadlec (handler and owner),
Edgefield, S.C.
2nd: Mr. Mick's Flipside—Curtis Hodge
(handler), Marie and Curtis Hodge
(owners), Sumter, S.C.
3rd: HR UH Fancy's Mighty Sampson—
Gene Putnam (handler and owner),
Kings Mountain, N.C.

Intermediate
1st: HR Hi-Brass Harley—Kevin Freeman (handler and owner), North
Augusta, S.C.
2nd: SHR Dawkins Pocotaligo Mojo—
Ronnie Dawkins (handler and owner),
Lexington, S.C.
3rd: Beal's Jig—Lynn Wallace (handler),
Barry Beal (owner), Midland, Tex.

Novice
1st: Pooshee's Summer Down—
Eddie Hughes (handler and owner),
Wadmalaw, S.C.
2nd: Cody—Jeff Spires (handler and
owner), Clearwater, S.C.
3rd: HR Hi-Brass Harley—Kevin
Freeman (handler and owner), North
Augusta, S.C.
4th: Beal's Jig—Lynn Wallace (handler),
Barry Beal (owner), Midland, Tex.

JAM (Judges' Award of Merit)
Just Ducky's Justmyluck—Gary Edmonds
(handler), Pam O. Kadlec (owner),
Edgefield, S.C.
Zena Warrior Princess—Marie Hodge
(handler and owner), Sumter, S.C.
Just Ducky's Law Partner—William C.
McMaster III (handler and owner),
Greenville, S.C.
Boulder Brook's Brille—Bill Wright
(handler and owner), Markham, Va.

Puppy
1st: Branson's Buddy Colonel—Jeff
Spires (handler), Stan Metz (owner),
Williamston, S.C.
2nd: Rock'n Creek Knocks—Millie
Latimer (handler), James and Millie
Latimer (owners), St. Matthews, S.C.
3rd: Rock'n Creek Miza Sue—Millie
Latimer (handler), James and Millie
Latimer (owners), St. Matthews, S.C.
4th: Marley—Ronnie Dawkins (handler),
Wade Collins (owner), Columbia, S.C.

JAM (Judges' Award of Merit)
Holland Ridge's Jeb Stuart—Mark Lee
(handler and owner), Seneca, S.C.
VSOP's de la Madgdelaine—Millie
Latimer (handler), John A. Wallace Jr.
(owner), Charleston, S.C.
Darby's Teal Boy—Chris E. Darby
(handler and owner), Goose Creek, S.C.

Roustabout (inaugural)
1st: Big Sky's Bessie Wayne—Phil
Hinchman (handler and owner),
Greenfield, Ind.
2nd: HRCH UH King's Curlee Gurlee—
Pam O. Kadlec (handler and owner),
Edgefield, S.C.
3rd: Addison's Big Riggs—Phil Hinchman
(handler and owner), Greenfield, Ind.
4th: Maggie's Lucky Penny—Larry
Hinchman (handler and owner),
Hammond, Wis.

Children's Handling Stake
Catelyn Anderson
Nathan Makla
Branson Metz

2003

Inaugural Boykin Spaniel Society
National Upland Field Trial
January 18–19
H. Cooper Black Jr. Memorial Field Trial
and Recreation Area, Patrick, S.C.

Open
1st: HRCH UH Fancy's Mighty
Sampson—Gene Putnam (handler
and owner)

2nd: HRCH UH King's Curlee Gurlee—Pam Kadlec (handler and owner)
3rd: HR UH Daisy—Harriett Clark (handler and owner)
4th: Warren's 1st Scout—Billy Warren (handler and owner)

Intermediate
lst: Beal's Jig—Kim Parkman (handler), Barry Beal (owner)
2nd: HR UH Pocotaligo's Philly—Kim Parkman (handler and owner)

Novice
1st: Rock'n Creek Webster—Millie Latimer (handler), James and Millie Latimer (owners)
2nd: Rock'n Creek Izabelle Many Feathers—Millie Latimer (handler), James and Millie Latimer (owners)
3rd: HR Pocotaligo's Wednesday—Kim Parkman (handler and owner)
4th: Just Ducky's Little Lass—Randy McHugh (handler), Katie and Randy McHugh (owners)

JAM (Judges' Award of Merit)
Pocotaligo's Taylor Made—Kim Parkman (handler and owner)

Completions
Rock'n Creek Jaymes Mark—Millie Latimer (handler), James and Millie Latimer (owners)
Penny's Wooden Nickle—Randy McHugh (handler), Katie and Randy McHugh (owners)
Hap Man Do—Dock Skipper (handler), Dock and Amelia Skipper (owners)

24th Annual Field Trial, Boykin Spaniel Society National Hunting Retriever Test April 10–13 Tyger Ranch, near Buffalo, S.C.

Open (10 entries)
1st: HR UH Daisy Ray—Harriett Clark (handler), Lee and Harriett Clark (owners)

2nd: HRCH Patton's Holy Moses—Kim Parkman (handler), Jowane Patton (owner)
3rd: HR UH Fancy's Mighty Sampson—Gene Putnam (handler and owner)
4th: HRCH Just Ducky's Justforkicks "Mule"—Chris Meurett (handler), Chris Meurett and Pam Kadlec (owners)

JAM (Judges' Award of Merit)
HRCH UH King's Curlee Gurlee—Pam Kadlec (handler and owner)

Intermediate (16 entries)
1st: Beal's Jig—Bill Crites (handler), Barry Beal (owner)
2nd: Just Ducky's Justforkicks—Chris Meurett (handler), Chris Meurett and Pam Kadlec (owners)
3rd: Just Ducky's Law Partner—William McMaster (handler and owner)
4th: UH HR Kipper Ray—Harriett Clark (handler), Harriett and Lee Clark (owner)

JAM (Judges' Award of Merit)
Savannah Rose's Martha Duke—Gary Edmonds (handler), Rose and Gary Edmonds (owners)
Dovewood's Major—Mike Branham (handler and owner)
Barthalamew—Gina Vecchione (handler and owner)

Novice (42 entries)
1st: Rock'n Creek Moye—Millie Latimer (handler), James and Millie Latimer (owners)
2nd: Boulder Brook's Brille—Bill Wright (handler and owner)
3rd: Chica—Bill Crites (handler), David Hull and Kim Parkman (owners)
4th: Pocotaligo's Finest Brandy—James Braswell (handler), Amy Braswell and Kim Parkman (owners)

JAM (Judges' Award of Merit)
SHR UH Darby's Teal Boy—Chris Darby (handler and owner)

Zena Warrior Princess—Marie Hodge (handler), Marie and Curtis Hodge (owners)

Craft's Shot of Jaegermeister—Chris Craft (handler and owner)

Rocky Ridge Bird Buster—Jamie Bedenbaugh (handler and owner)

Chairman's Cup for highest scoring novice dog with a handler age sixteen or less: Danny Bange of Ward, S.C. with Just Ducky's Just2cool4school "Fonzie"

Puppy (23 entries)
1st: Just Ducky's Just2cool4school "Fonzie"—Danny Bange (handler), Pam Kadlec (owner)
2nd: Rock'n Creek Howdy—Skip Nelson (handler and owner)
3rd: Drake—Sheila Johnson (handler), Sheila Johnson and Jaynie Redmond (owners)
4th: Boulder Brook's Indy—J. W. Wright (handler and owner)

JAM (Judges' Award of Merit)
Brownie Treat—Gene Meskan (handler), Gene and Chery Meskan (owners)
Jimmie Mac's Pocotaligo Itch—Mack Smith (handler), Mack and Jimmie Smith and Kim Parkman (owners)
Coltrane of Pocotaligo—Dawn Crites (handler), James Murray and Kim Parkman (owners)

Roustabout
1st: Penny's Wooden Nickle—Randy McHugh (handler), Kalie and Randy McHugh (owners)
2nd: UH SHR U-AG1 Pooshee's Dusa Lily Pad—Bill Crites (handler), Dawn and Bill Crites (owners)
3rd: Beal's Jig—Kim Parkman (handler), Barry Beal (owner)
4th: HR UH Fancy's Mighty Sampson—Gene Putnam (handler and owner)

Children's Handling Stake
Benjamin Duvall, 6, with Guinness
Catherine Duvall, 4, with Guinness
Marian Huggins, 9, with Drake

Rusty Scott, 9, with Cocoa
Elliott Lyles, 5, with Birdie

Natural Abilities (passing)
Susie Q—Al Bullington
Lady Bug—Al Bullington
Rock'n Creek Dixie Blaze—Mick Yannone
Unsinkable Molly Brown—Mary Ann Mathias
No Pink Promise—Dawn Crites
Just Ducky's Little Lass—Randy McHugh
Show-Me Baby Ruth—Bob Makla
Show-Me Big Mac—Bob Makla
Chessie—Bob Haux
P.K. Jazzy Jem—Patty Labbe
Tank—Gina Vecchione
Gunner—Christa Adamson
Drake—Marian Huggins
Maximus—Daniel Hoffman
Max—David Windell

2004

2nd Annual Boykin Spaniel Society National Upland Field Trial
January 17–18
H. Cooper Black Jr. Memorial Field Trial and Recreation Area, Patrick, S.C.

Open (7 entries)
1st: HR UH Daisy "Daisy"—Harriett Clark (handler and owner)
2nd: HRCH UH Fancy's Mighty Sampson "Sam"—Gene Putnam (handler and owner)
3rd: HRCH UH Curlee Gurlee "Gurlee"—Pam Kadlec (handler and owner)
4th: HR UH Kipper Ray "Kipper"—Harriett Clark (handler), Lee and Harriett Clark (owners)

Intermediate (9 entries)
1st: Just Ducky's Justmyluck "Lucky"—Pam Kadlec (handler and owner)
2nd: HR UH Kipper Ray "Kipper"—Harriett Clark (handler), Lee and Harriett Clark (owners)
3rd: Oyster Creek's Pistol Peat "Peat"—Scott Culbreth (handler and owner)

4th: HR UH Darby's Teal Boy—Chris Darby (handler), Chris and Susan Darby (owners)

Novice (22 entries)
1st: Pocotaligo's No Pink Promise "Promise"—Dawn Crites (handler), Dawn and Bill Crites (owners)
2nd: Hap Man Do "Hap"—Dock Skipper (handler), Dock and Amelia Skipper (owners)
3rd: Rock'n Creek Izabelle Many Feathers "Izzy"—handler Millie Latimer (handler), James and Millie Latimer (owners)
4th: Amy's Pocotaligo Ellie "Ellie"— James Braswell (handler), Amy Braswell and Kim Parkman (owners)

JAM (Judges' Award of Merit)
Just Ducky's Justmyluckybet "Wager"— Mark Lee (handler), Pam Kadlec (owner)
Holland Ridge's Jeb Stuart "Jeb"—Mark Lee (handler and owner)
Oyster Creek's Pistol Peat "Peat"—Scott Culbreth (handler and owner)
Pocotaligo's Tasmanian Jake "Jake"— Mack Smith (handler and owner)

25th Annual Field Trial, Boykin Spaniel Society National Hunting Retriever Test April 1–4
H. Cooper Black Jr. Memorial Field Trial and Recreation Area, Patrick, S.C.

Open (9 entries)
lst: HRCCH UH Fancy's Mighty Sampson—Gene Putnam (handler and owner)
2nd: HRCH UH Just Ducky's Justforkicks—Pam Kadlec (handler), Chris Meurett and Pam Kadlec (owners)
3rd: HR UH Pocotaligo's Philly—Kim Parkman (handler and owner)
4th: HR UH Daisy Ray—Harriett Clark (handler), Harriett and Lee Clark (owners)

JAM (Judges' Award of Merit)
HR Hi-Brass Harley—Kim Parkman (handler), Kevin Freeman (owner)
Warren's 1st Scout—Billy Warren (handler and owner)

Intermediate (11 entries)
1st: HR UH Darby's Teal Boy—Chris Darby (handler and owner)
2nd: Just Ducky's Law Partner—William McMaster III (handler and owner)
3rd: HR Pocotaligo's Tasmanian Jake— Mack Smith (handler and owner)

JAM (Judges' Award of Merit)
HR UH Kipper Ray—Harriett Clark (handler), Harriett and Lee Clark (owners)

Novice (31 entries)
1st: SHR Just Ducky's Ubetyourbippy "Bette"—Danny Bange (handler), Pam Kadlec (owner)
2nd: Oyster Creek's Pistol Peat "Peat"— Scott Culbreth (handler and owner)
3rd: Just Ducky's Guinness Stout— Patrick Duvall (handler and owner)
4th: SHR Just Ducky's Bookmark— Chris Meurett (handler and owner), Chris Meurett and Pam Kadlec (owners)

JAM (Judges' Award of Merit
Holland Ridge's Jeb Stuart—Mark Lee (handler and owner)
Lucky Bird Junior—Les Oliver (handler), Les and Page Oliver (owners)
SHR Gabriel Maxwell—Molly Moxley (handler), Rick Anderson (owner)
Caton's Rooty Toot Toot—Dan Caton (handler and owner)
Chairman's Cup for highest scoring novice dog with a handler age sixteen or less: Danny Bange with Just Ducky's Ubetyourbippy "Bette"

Puppy (27 entries)
1st: Just Ducky's Justaluckybet "Wager"—Chris Meurett (handler), Pam Kadlec (owner)

2nd: Just Ducky's Nike Air Jordan—Danny Bange (handler), Pam Kadlec (owner)
3rd: Lake Gaston's Buddy Bear—Mollie Moxley (handler), Fred Coates (owner)
4th: Justafloridacracker—Danny Bange (handler), Ed Gammons and Pam Kadlec (owners)

JAM (Judges' Award of Merit)
Just Ducky's Nike Air Vivacity—Danny Bange (handler), Pam Kadlec (owner)
Lady Lily Richey—Danny Bange (handler), Alan Richey (owner)

Roustabout Winner
Beal's Jig—Kim Parkman (handler), Barry Beal (owner)

Children's Handling Stake
Claire Brown, 6, with Mac
Mark Johnson, 6, with Molly
Chad Darby, 8, with Teal
Benjamin Duvall, 7, with Dutch
Kelsy Darby, 7, with Teal
Catherine Duvall, 5, with Dutch
Brantley Tart, 10, with Bette

Natural Abilities Test (passing)
Chessie—Bob Haux
Show-Me Sea Biscuits—Bob Makla
Show-Me Daisy—Bob Makla
Rudy—Ken Sass
Luke—Dave Abernathy
Lucky—Les Oliver
Drake—Marian Huggins
Gus—Richard Claybrooke
Thea—Joe Copeland
Isabelle—Chase Alderman
Burger—Chase Alderman
Molly's Girl—Marianne Wendl
Hershey's Kiss—Dave Wendl
Dixie—Robert Payne
Vader—Robert Payne
Cocoa—Welch Livingston
Jazzy—Cyndi Copeland
Sissy—Rich Mathias
Molly—MaryAnn Mathias

2005

3rd Annual Boykin Spaniel Society National Upland Field Trial
January 15–16
Carolina Star Gun and Hunt Club, Aiken State Park Natural Area, Windsor, S.C.

Open (9 entries)
1st: HRCH UH Fancy's Mighty Sampson "Sam"—Gene Putnam (handler and owner)
2nd: Caton's Rooty-Toot Toot "Toot"—Dan Caton (handler and owner)
3rd: Pocotaligo's Amazing Grace "Gracie"—Blake Waggoner (handler), Blake Waggoner and Kim Parkman (owners)
4th: HR UH Kipper Ray "Kipper"—Harriett Clark (handler), Lee and Harriett Clark (owners)

JAM (Judges' Award of Merit)
HR UH Daisy "Daisy"—Harriett Clark (handler), Lee and Harriett Clark (owners)

Intermediate (13 entries)
1st: HR UH Darby's Teal Boy "Teal"—Chris Darby (handler), Chris and Susan Darby (owners)
2nd: Pocotaligo's Amazing Grace "Gracie"—Blake Waggoner (handler), Blake Waggoner and Kim Parkman (owners)
3rd: Pocotaligo's No Pink Promise "Promise"—Dawn Crites (handler), Dawn and Bill Crites (owners)
4th: UR UH Pocotaligo's Philly—Kim Parkman (handler and owner)

JAM (Judges' Award of Merit)
Caton's Rooty-Toot Toot "Toot"—Dan Caton (handler and owner)
Woody's Cocoa GI "Cocoa"—Russell Scott (handler), Ann Scott (owner)
Boulder Brook's Brille "Brille"—Bill Wright (handler and owner)
Rock'n Creek Moye "Moye"—Millie Latimer (handler), James and Millie Latimer (owner)

Novice (21 entries)
1st: Brandywine's Amazing Grace—
Frank Semken (handler and owner)
2nd: Rock'n Creek Izabelle Many Feathers "Izzy"—Millie Latimer (handler),
James and Millie Latimer (owners)
3rd: H and P's Naughty Girl Belle
"Belle"—Robin Spriggs (handler and
owner)
4th: Show Me Big Mac "Mac"—
Bob Makla (handler and owner)

JAM (Judges' Award of Merit)
Hap Man Do "Hap"—Dock Skipper
(handler), Dock and Amelia Skipper
(owners)
Rock'n Creek Moye "Moye"—Millie
Latimer (handler), James and Millie
Latimer (owners)
Augustus Mars "Gus"—Richard
Claybrooke (handler and owner)
Just Ducky's First Edition "Edie"—
Anne Livingston (handler and owner)

*Gunners' Choice (the dog in each class
that the gunners would like to hunt
with)*
Novice: Brandywine's Amazing Grace—
Frank Semken (handler and owner)
Intermediate (tie): Woody's Cocoa GI—
Russell Scott (handler), Ann Scott
(owner); Moss Point's Elijah—Jack
Shannon (handler and owner)
Open: HRCH UH Fancy's Mighty
Sampson—Gene Putnam (handler and
owner)

**26th Annual Boykin Spaniel Society
National Hunting Retriever Test
April 1–3
South Carolina Wildlife Association
(SCWA) Camp Woodie, Rimini, S.C.**

Open (12 entries)
1st: HRCH UH Fancy's Mighty
Sampson—Gene Putnam (handler and
owner)
2nd: HR Pocotaligo's Amazing Grace—
Gene Putnam (handler), Blake Waggoner and Kim Parkman (owners)

3rd: HRCH UH Darby's Teal Boy—
Chris Darby (handler and owner)
4th: HR Hi-Brass Harley—Kim Parkman
(handler), Kevin Freeman and Kim
Parkman (owners)

JAM (Judges' Award of Merit)
HRCH Holland Ridge's Jeb Stuart—
Mark Lee (handler and owner)
HR Caton's Rooty Toot Toot—Gene
Putnam (handler), Dan Caton (owner)

Intermediate (23 entries)
1st: Pocotaligo's Finest Brandy—James
Braswell (handler), Jessica Braswell and
Kim Parkman (owner)
2nd: Oyster Creek's Pistol Peat "Peat"—
Scott Culbreth (handler and owner)
3rd: HR Caton's Rooty Toot Toot
"Toot"—Gene Putnam (handler and
owner), Dan Caton (owner)
4th: HR Pocotaligo's Amazing
Grace—Gene Putnam (handler), Blake
Waggoner and Kim Parkman (owners)

JAM (Judges' Award of Merit)
HR Salem Farm's Just Hot Ash—Robert
Wilhoit (handler and owner)
SHR Dawkins Pocotaligo Mojo—Kim
Parkman (handler), Ronnie Dawkins
(owner)
HR Pocotaligo's Tasmanian Jake—Kim
Parkman (handler), Malcolm Smith
(owner)
HRCH Holland Ridge's Jeb Stuart—
Mark Lee (handler and owner)

Novice
1st: SHR Fist Full of Dollars "Cash"—
Chad Funderburk (handler and owner)
2nd: SHR Just Ducky's Justagigalo
"Louie"—Danny Bange (handler),
Danny Bange and Kim Kadlec (owners)
3rd: HR Gabriel Maxwell "Gabe"—Rick
Anderson (handler and owner)
4th: Cypress Hall's Vader—Robert A.
Payne (handler and owner)

JAM (Judges' Award of Merit)
SHR Just Ducky's Miss Edgefield "Miss
E"—Carolyn Tillman (handler),

Stephen Tillman and Pam Kadlec (owners)

SHR Darby's Land Rush "Rush"— Chris Darby (handler and owner)

SHR No Pink Promise "Promise"— Dawn Crites (handler and owner)

Lulu's Captain Nemo—Jule Parkman (handler), Butch Shivers (owner)

Chairman's Cup for highest scoring novice dog with a handler age sixteen or less: Carolyn Tillman with Just Ducky's Miss Edgefield "Miss E"

Puppy

1st: Just Ducky's Just A Home Wrecker "Wrecker"—John Huddleston (handler and owner)

2nd: Buckeye's Jock of the Low Veld "Jock"—Chris Meurett (handler), Stephen Howell (owner)

3rd: Pocotaligo's Smokeless Powder— Jule Parkman (handler), Kim Parkman (owner)

4th: Buckeye's Justabigfish "Sauger"— Danny Bange (handler), Pam Kadlec and Elise Irwin (owners)

JAM (Judges' Award of Merit)

Just Ducky's Justalilrascal "Rascal"— Chris Meurett (handler), Mark Mulrain (owner)

Rock'n Creek Vivian Cole "Vivy"— Gary Edmonds (handler and owner)

Pocotaligo's Juke—Jule Parkman (handler), Sandra Johnson and Kim Parkman (owners)

Hurricane Charley Radar—Dan Stone (handler and owner)

Roustabout

1st: Amy's Pocotaligo Ellie—James Braswell (handler), Amy Braswell and Kim Parkman (owners)

2nd: Pocotaligo's Finest Brandy—James Braswell (handler), Jessica Braswell and Kim Parkman (owners)

Natural Abilities (passing)

Chesapeake Ginger III—Bob Haux (handler and owner)

Chesapeake Ginger IV—Bob Haux (handler and owner)

Double T Black River Gunnison—Ernie Tart (handler and owner)

Hokie Joe—Jim Glennon (handler and owner)

O Henry Boy—David Alford (handler and owner)

Pat's Maggie of Debordieu—Pat Dressler (handler and owner)

Gator's Boy Rudy—Larry Floyd (handler and owner)

Children's Handling Stake

Catherine Duvall with Dutch

Camile Sligh with Bear

Benjamin Duvall with Dutch

Andrew Garnett with Cracker

Brantley Tart with Gunner

2006

4th Annual Boykin Spaniel Society National Upland Field Trial

January 14–15

H. Cooper Black Jr. Memorial Field Trial and Recreation Area, Patrick, S.C.

Open

1st: Oyster Creek's Pistol Peat—Scott Culbreth

2nd: HRCH UH Pocotaligo's Amazing Grace—Blake Waggoner and Kim Parkman

3rd: UH HR Daisy Ray—Harriett Clark

4th: UH HR Kipper Ray—Harriett Clark

JAM (Judges' Award of Merit)

H and P's Naughty Girl Belle—Robin Spriggs

Intermediate

1st: Just Ducky's Just A Home Wrecker— John Huddleston

2nd: Oyster Creek's Pistol Peat—Scott Culbreth

3rd: Pocotaligo's No Pink Promise— Dawn Crites

4h: H and P's Naughty Girl Belle— Robin Spriggs

JAM (Judges' Award of Merit)
Moss Point's Elijah—Jack and Jan
Shannon

Novice
1st: Graham's Carolina Wrangler—
Sammy Graham
2nd: Unsinkable Molly Brown—
Mary Ann and Rich Mathias
3rd: Just Ducky's Just A Home
Wrecker—John Huddleston
4th: Just Ducky's First Edition—
Anne Livingston

JAM (Judges' Award of Merit)
Just Ducky's Nike Air Althea—Joe and
Cyndi Copeland
Story's Cocoa Break—Welch Livingston
Richland Reese's Piece of Work—
Danny Keith
Hatch—Jamie Newton

Gunners' Choice
Open: Oyster Creek's Pistol Peat—
Scott Culbreth
Intermediate: Pocotaligo's No Pink
Promise—Dawn Crites
Novice: Unsinkable Molly Brown—
Mary Ann and Rich Mathias

**26th Annual Boykin Spaniel Society
National Field Trial
March 30–April 2
Clinton House Hunting Plantation,
Clinton, S.C.**

Open (8 entries)
1st: GRHRCH Just Ducky's Justforkicks
"Mule"—Charles Jurney (handler),
Chris Meurett and Pam Kadlec
(owners)
2nd: HRCH Holland Ridge's Jeb Stuart
"Jeb"—Mark Lee (handler and owner)

Intermediate (27 entries)
1st: Chelsea's Woody Bear "Woody"—
John Inabinet (handler and owner)
2nd: HR Just A Home Wrecker
"Wrecker"—John Huddleston (handler
and owner)

3rd: Boulder Brook's "Brille"—
Bill Wright (handler and owner)
4th: HR Gabriel Maxwell "Gabe"—
Rick Anderson (handler and owner)

JAM (Judges' Award of Merit)
HR Buckeye's Kickn It Upa Notch
"T-Boy"—John Cafiero (handler and
owner)
HR Oyster Creek's Pistol Peat "Peat"—
Scott Culbreth (handler and owner)
Amy's Pocotaligo Ellie "Ellie"—James
Braswell (handler), Amy Braswell and
Kim Parkman (owners)
HR Silvestre Acadiana—Dr. James G.
Dickson (handler and owner)

Novice (56 entries)
1st: HR Just A Home Wrecker
"Wrecker"—John Huddleston (handler
and owner)
2nd: Just A Coosawatchie Run
"Hatch"—Jamie Newman (handler),
Jamie Newman and Pam Kadlec
(owners)
3rd: SHR Just Ducky's First Edition
"Edie"—Anne Livingston (handler and
owner)
4th: Pathfinder's Point Shako Jakeco
"Jake"—Scott Kinder (handler and
owner)

JAM (Judges' Award of Merit)
Hap Man Do—Amelia Skipper (handler), Dock and Amelia Skipper
(owners)
Gainer's Pride Blunder—Dan Stone
(handler), George Gainer (owner)
Reese's Piece of Work "Reese"—
Danny Keith (handler and owner)
Lulu's Sugar n Spice—Jule Parkman
(handler), Julius D. Shivers III (owner)
Chairman's Cup for highest scoring
novice dog with a handler age sixteen or
less: Marian Huggins and I'm Drake II

Puppy (27 entries)
1st: Pocotaligo's Shotgun Red—Greg
Hendrick (handler), Greg Hendrick and
Kim Parkman (owners)

2nd: Reese's Piece of Work "Reese"—
Danny Keith (handler and owner)
3rd: Just Ducky's Mercury Rising
"Heat"—Joe Copeland (handler), Joe
and Cyndi Copeland (owners)
4th: Just Ducky's Justadducks
"Woody"—Jerry Bozeman (handler),
Jerry Bozeman and Pam Kadlec (owners)

JAM (Judges' Award of Merit)
Just Ducky's Justabetterhunter
"Huney"—Chris Meurett (handler),
Pam Kadlec (owner)
Richland's Camden Legacy "Cam"—
Anne Livingston (handler and owner)
Nuf Ced Sweet Hazel—David Alford
(handler and owner)

Roustabout
1st: SHR Brandywine's Northern Dixie—
Phil Hinchman (handler and owner)
2nd: HR No Pink Promise—Dawn Crites
(handler and owner)
3rd: Lulu's Captain Nemo—Kim
Parkman (handler), J. Shivers (owner)
4th: Lily's Promise to Piper—Dawn
Crites (handler and owner)

2007

5th Annual Boykin Spaniel Society
National Upland Field Trial
January 13–14
H. Cooper Black Jr. Memorial Field Trial
and Recreation Area, Patrick, S.C.

Open (11 entries)
1st: HR UH Daisy Ray "Daisy"—
Harriett Clark (handler), Lee and
Harriett Clark (owners)
2nd: HR Just Ducky's Justadducks
"Woody"—Gene Putnam (handler),
Jerry Bozeman and Pam Kadlec (owners)
3rd: HR UH Oyster Creek's Pistol Peat
UOCH06 "Peat"—Scott Culbreth
(handler and owner)
4th: HR Hi-Brass Harley—Kim Parkman
(handler), Kevin Freeman (owner)

JAM (Judges' Award of Merit)
HRCH UH Pocotaligo's Amazing Grace
"Gracie"—Blake Waggoner (handler
and owner)

Intermediate (26 entries)
1st: Brandywine's Chocolate Covered
Cherry—Phil Hinchman (handler), Phil
and Karen Hinchman (owners)
2nd: HR UH Graham's Carolina
Wrangler UNCH06—Sammy Graham
(handler and owner)
3rd: HR Just Ducky's Justadducks
"Woody"—Gene Putnam (handler),
Jerry Bozeman and Pam Kadlec (owners)
4th: Gainer's Bride Blunder—Dan Stone
(handler), George Gainer (owner)

JAM (Judges' Award of Merit)
HR Just A Coosawhatchie "Hatch"—
Jamie Newman (handler and owner)
Richland Reese's Piece of Work
"Reese"—Danny Keith (handler and
owner)
Lulu's Captain Nemo—Kim Parkman
(handler), Butch Shivers (owner)
HR UH River's Turn Naughty Girl
Belle—Gene Putnam (handler),
Robin Spriggs (owner)

Novice (32 entries)
1st: Just Ducky's Mercury Rising
"Heat"— Joe Copeland (handler),
Cyndi Copeland (owner)
2nd: Brandywine's Browning Citori
Feather—Phil Hinchman (handler),
Phil and Karen Hinchman (owners)
3rd: Richland Reese's Piece of Work
"Reese"—Danny Keith (handler and
owner)
4th: Gainer's Pride Blunder—Dan Stone
(handler), George Gainer (owner)

JAM (Judges' Award of Merit)
Brandywine's 12 Gauge "Gauge"—
Matt Behe (handler and owner)
HR Brandywine's Mighty Duramax—
Phil Hinchman (handler), Phil and
Karen Hinchman (owners)

Gunners' Choice
Open: HR UH Graham's Carolina Wrangler UNCH06—Sammy Graham (handler and owner)
Intermediate: HR Brandywine's Mighty Duramax—Phil Hinchman (handler), Phil and Karen Hinchman (owners)

27th Annual Boykin Spaniel Society National Field Trial
March 30–April 1
Clinton House Plantation, Clinton, S.C.

Open (15 entries)
1st: HRCH UH Darby's Teal Boy—Chris Darby (handler and owner)
2nd: HRCH Pocotaligo's Amazing Grace—Blake Waggoner (handler and owner)
3rd: HRCH Caton's Rooty Toot Toot—Dan Caton (handler and owner)
4th: HR Hi-Brass Harley—Kim Parkman (handler), Kevin Freeman and Kim Parkman (owners)

JAM (Judges' Award of Merit)
HR UH Just Ducky's Justadducks "Woody"—Gene Putnam (handler), Jerry Bozeman (owner)
HRCH Holland Ridge's Jeb Stuart—Mark Lee (handler and owner)

Intermediate (28 entries)
1st: HR UH Pathfinders Point Shako Jakeco "Jake"—Scott Kinder (handler and owner)
2nd: Richland Reese's Piece of Work "Reese"—Danny Keith (handler and owner)
3rd: HR Just Ducky's Ubetyourbippy—Pam Kadlec (handler and owner)
4th: HR Justa Coosawhatchie Run "Hatch"—Jamie Newman (handler and owner)

JAM (Judges' Award of Merit)
HR Buckeye's Kickin It Upa Notch "T-boy"—John Cafiero (handler and owner)
HR Just Ducky's Just A Home Wrecker

"Wrecker"—John Huddleston (handler and owner)
HR UH Just Ducky's Justadducks "Woody"—Gene Putnam (handler), Jerry Bozeman (owner)
HR Silvestre Acadiana—James Dickson (handler and owner)

Novice (61 entries)
1st: Richland Reese's Piece of Work "Reese"—Danny Keith (handler and owner)
2nd: Mississippi Flash and Splash—Ralph Barbare (handler and owner)
3rd: HR Just Ducky's First Edition "Edie"—Anne Livingston (handler and owner)
4th: HR St. Thomas Chief—Dan Reel (handler and owner)

JAM (Judges' Award of Merit)
Just A Grand Illusion "Deke"—Lance Waggoner (handler and owner)
SHR A. J. Jumper—James Barbare (handler and owner)
Boulder Brook's Beebee—Bill Wright (handler and owner)
Lily's Promise to Piper—Dawn Crites (handler and owner)
Chairman's Cup for highest scoring novice dog with a handler age sixteen or less: Marian Huggins with I'm Drake II "Drake"

Puppy (25 entries)
1st: Jeff's True Luck Tucker—Jeff Matthews (handler and owner)
2nd: Rock'n Creek Lord of the Wings "Wings"—John Huddleston (handler and owner)
3rd: A.J.'s Big Boy—James Barbare (handler and owner)
4th: Brandywine's Special Reserve—Lance Waggoner (handler and owner)

JAM (Judges' Award of Merit)
Stickpond's Raz Ma Taz "Taz"—Dan Caton (handler and owner)
Richland Stonewall Jackson—Charles Herb (handler and owner)

Carolina Magic R.J.—Sheila Johnson (handler and owner) Bogey—Mary Ann Mathias (handler), Richard Garer (owner)

Roustabout
1st: Holston River's Sparky—John Rucker (handler and owner)
2nd: Justa Grand Illusion "Deke"— Lance Waggoner (handler and owner)
3rd: Mocha Sunrise Freeze—John Rucker (handler), Bob and Denise Freeze (owners)
4th: Holston River's Buster Brown— John Rucker (handler and owner)

Doubles Champions
UH SHR U-AG1 Pooshee's Dusa Lily Pad—Bill Crites (handler and owner)
Justa Grand Illusion "Deke"—Lance Waggoner (handler and owner)

2008

6th Annual Boykin Spaniel Society National Upland Field Trial
January 19–20
H. Cooper Black Jr. Memorial Field Trial and Recreation Area, Patrick, S.C.

Open (12 entries)
1st: HR Just A Home Wrecker UICH06—John Huddleston (handler and owner)
2nd: HR UH Just Ducky's Justadducks— Gene Putnam (handler), Jerry Bozeman (owner)
3rd: HR UH Hi-Brass Harley—Jule Parkman (handler), Kevin Freeman and Jule Parkman (owners)
4th: HRCH St. Thomas Chief—Dan Reel (handler and owner)

Intermediate (17 entries)
1st: HR UH Moss Point's Elijah— Jack Shannon (handler and owner)
2nd: Gainer's Pride Blunder—Dan Stone (handler), Jessica and George Gainer (owners)

3rd: Carolina Magic Chaser—Harriett Clark (handler and owner)
4th: HR UH Hi-Brass Harley—Jule Parkman (handler), Kevin Freeman and Kim Parkman (owners)

JAM (Judges' Award of Merit)
HR Brandywine's Mighty Duramax— Phil Hinchman (handler and owner)

Novice (35 entries)
1st: Charlie Espy—Brian Espy (handler and owner)
2nd: OTM Win One For The Gipper— John Huddleston (handler and owner)
3rd: HR Just Ducky's First Edition— Anne Livingston (handler and owner)
4th: Richland's Camden Legacy—Welch Livingston (handler), Anne Livingston (owner)

JAM (Judges' Award of Merit)
Lily's Promise to Piper—Dawn Crites (handler), Bill and Dawn Crites (owners)
River's Turn Son of Sam—Robin Spriggs (handler and owner)
Story's Cocoa Break—Welch Livingston (handler and owner)
OTM's No Last Call LC Mae—Kevin Kees (handler and owner)

Completions
HR AJ Jumper—James Barbare (handler and owner)
Lily—Ray Bloom (handler and owner)
Pocotaligo's Annie of Cedar Grove— Don Brown (handler), James Kinnear (owner),
Carolina Magic Ruby—Jayne Raymond (handler), Jayne Raymond and Sheila Johnson (owners)
Web's Lil Trapper Brown BD—Rich Mathias (handler and owner)
Hurricane Charley Radar—Dan Stone (handler and owner)

28th Annual Boykin Spaniel Society National Field Trial
March 28–30
Clinton House Plantation, Clinton, S.C.

Open (18 entries)
Judges: Jim Reichman and Paul Lemmond
1st: GRHRCH UH Just Ducky's Justforkicks "Mule"—Joe Dawson (handler), Chris Meurett and Pam Kadlec owners)
2nd: HRCH St. Thomas Chief "Chief"—Dan Reel (handler and owner)
3rd: HRCH Buckeye's Kickin It Upa Notch "T-boy"—John Cafiero (handler and owner)
4th: HRCH Holland Ridge Jeb Stuart "Jeb"—Mark Lee (handler and owner)

JAM (Judges' Award of Merit)
HR UH Just Ducky's Justadducks "Woody"—Gene Putnam (handler), Jerry Bozeman (owner)
HR Richland Stonewall Jackson—Butch Herb (handler and owner)

Intermediate (35 entries)
Judges: Glenn Stelly and Michelle Love
1st: Stickpond's Raz Ma Taz "Taz"—Dan Caton (handler and owner)
2nd: HR UH Fist Full of Dollars "Cash"—Kim Parkman (handler), Chad Funderburk (owner)
3rd: Brandywine's Special Reserve "Belle"—Lance Waggoner (handler and owner)
4th: HR Brandywine's Mighty Duramax "Max"—Phil Hinchman (handler), Phil and Karen Hinchman (owners)

JAM (Judges' Award of Merit)
HR Richland Stonewall Jackson—Butch Herb (handler and owner)
HR Just Ducky's Justagentleman "Jack"—Pam Kadlec (handler), Joel Eisler (owner)
HR Just Ducky's Justasaltydog "Skip"—Pam Kadlec (handler), Neely Page (owner)

HR Just Ducky's Justforchuckles "Chuck"—Dan Caton (handler and owner)

Completions
NYSSA—Robert McDole (handler and owner)
Pocotaligo's Shotgun Red "Red"—Greg Hendrick (handler), Greg Hendrick and Kim Parkman (owners)
HR Just Ducky's First Edition "Edie"—Anne Livingston (handler and owner)

Novice (54 entries)
Judges: Tom McKenzie and Chris Darby
1st: Pocotaligo's Shotgun Red "Red"—Greg Hendrick (handler), Greg Hendrick and Kim Parkman (owners)
2nd: Carolina Magic Chaser "Ace"—Harriett Clark (handler), Lee and Harriett Clark (owners)
3rd: SHR Island Creek Buck "Buck"—Sarah Harris (handler and owner)
4th: Jeff's True Luck Tucker—Jeff Matthews (handler and owner)

JAM (Judges' Award of Merit)
Shadow Bend Gabe's Gabrielle "Bree"—Rick Anderson (handler and owner)
Amanda of Pocotaligo—DeVon Ruth (handler and owner)
Story's Cocoa Break "Cocoa"—Welch Livingston (handler and owner)
Rock'n Creek Lord of the Wings "Wings"—John Huddleston (handler and owner)

Completions
Hokie Jo "JoJo"—Jim Glennon (handler and owner)
Lily Belle Bloom "Lily"—Ray Bloom (handler and owner)
Nuf Ced Lucca the Jester "Lucca"—Andrew Musashe (handler and owner)
Brandywine's Special Reserve "Belle"—Lance Waggoner (handler and owner)
I'm Drake II—Marian Huggins (handler and owner)
Jessie's Annie Page "Page"—Destry Burch (handler and owner)

Minstrelboy Clan Chieftain "Chief"—
Michael Elliot (handler and owner)
OTM's Win One For the Gipper—
John Huddleston (handler and owner)
Hurricane Charley Radar—Dan Stone
(handler and owner)
Brandywine's Browning Citori Feather—
Phil Hinchman (handler), Phil and
Karen Hinchman (owners)
Charlie Espy—Brian Espy (handler and
owner)
Brandywine's Duramizer Chip "Chip"—
Lance Waggoner (handler), Phil and
Karen Hinchman (owners)
Brandywine's Till the Next Time Tillie
"Tillie"—Phil Hinchman (handler), Phil
and Karen Hinchman (owners)
Boulder Brook's Bee Bee—Bill Wright
(handler and owner)
Brandywine's Rich'n Smooth Amberbock
—Matt Behe (handler and owner)
SHR Salem Farm's Just Rocknroll
"Rock"—Robert Duce (handler and
owner)
Queen Hollie Noel—Judge Bill Cade
(handler and owner)
Chairman's Cup for highest scoring
novice dog with a handler age sixteen or
less: Sarah Harris (age 8) with SHR
Island Creek Buck "Buck"

Puppy (39 entries)
Judges: Mike Witt and John Love
1st: Brandywine's Rich'n Smooth
Amberbock—Matt Behe (handler and
owner)
2nd: Lily Belle Bloom "Lily"—
Ray Bloom (handler and owner)
3rd: Just Ducky's Sports Page "Sport"—
Carolyn A. Tillman (handler), John C.
Logan (owner)
4th: Jackson's AceintheHole "Ace"—
Jeff Huggins (handler), Teddy Williams
(owner)

JAM (Judges' Award of Merit)
Rocky River's Holy Henna "Henna"—
Cheryl Behe (handler and owner)

Brandywine's Till the Next Time Tillie
"Tillie"—Phil Hinchman (handler),
Phil and Karen Hinchman (owners)
Shadow Bend Madison "Madi"—
Rick Anderson (handler and owner)

Completions
Hodges Special Force "Rambo"—
Marie Hodge (handler and owner)
SHR Salem Farm's Just Rocknroll
"Rock"—Robert Duce (handler and
owner)
Jessie's Annie Page "Page"—Destry
Burch (handler and owner)
Brandywine's Duramizer Chip "Chip"—
Lance Waggoner (handler), Phil and
Karen Hinchman (owners)
Bryan's Santee Delta Sunrise "Delta"—
Trey Bryan (handler and owner)
Just Ducky's Justreadallaboutit
"Extra"—Justin Morgan (handler),
Pam Kadlec (owner)
Just Ducky's Justafeatherduster
"Dusty"—James Barbare (handler),
Pam Kadlec (owner)
Just Red "Red"—Justin Morgan
(handler), Steve Beecham (owner)

2009

**7th Annual Boykin Spaniel Society
National Upland Field Trial**
January 17–18
**H. Cooper Black Jr. Memorial Field Trial
and Recreation Area, Patrick, S.C.**

Novice (42 entries)
Judges: Deb Schoene and Bruce Kephart
Novice Gunners' Choice: Emma's Buck
Creek Sadie
Upland Novice Champion: Brandywine's
Duramizer Chip—Phil and Karen
Hinchman
2nd: OTM's Win One For The Gipper—
John Huddleston
3rd: OTM's No Last Call LC Mae—
Kevin Kees
4th: Pocotaligo's Annie of Cedar Grove—
James Kinnear

JAM (Judges' Award of Merit)
Rock'n Creek Lord of the Wings—
John Huddleston
Justalildog'lldoya—Pam Kadlec
Rocky's Georgia Peach—Frank Semken
Mr. Winchester—Adam Littlefield

Completions
Larry's Copper Penny—Larry Lynch
Webs Best Sweet Gypsy Rose—
Mary Ann Mathias
Maggie Rose—Danny Keith
Curious Missy—Clint Evert
Just Ducky's Justhavalittle Faith—
James Barbare
Brandywine's Front Page News—
Phil Hinchman
Emma's Buck Creek Sadie—Todd Deal
Story's Cocoa Break—Welch Livingston
Shadow Bend Gabe's Gabrielle—
Rick Anderson
Chief—Mike Elliott
Pocotaligo's Texas Willie—
Daniel Hendrick
Harley Maurer—Chris Maurer

Intermediate (22 entries)
Judges: Cathy Lewis and Mike Witt
Intermediate Gunners' Choice:
Richland Reese's Piece of Work
1st: Amie's OTM Maggie Rose—
Danny Keith
2nd: Richland Stonewall Jackson—
Butch and Jane Herb
3rd: Pocotaligo's Shotgun Red—
Greg Hendrick and Kim Parkman
4th: Bogey—Richard Gardner

JAM (Judges' Award of Merit)
Richland Reese's Piece of Work—Danny
Keith
Carolina Magic Chaser—Harriett Clark

Open (19 entries)
Judges: Cathy Lewis and Mike Witt
Open Gunners' Choice: Brandywine's
Chocolate Covered Cherry
1st: Graham's Carolina Wrangler—
Sammy Graham

2nd: Just A Home Wrecker—
John Huddleston
3rd: Pocotaligo's Shotgun Red—
Greg Hendrick and Kim Parkman
4th: St. Thomas Chief—Dan Reel

JAM (Judges' Award of Merit)
Amanda of Pocotaligo—DeVon Ruth
Just Ducky's Justadducks—Jerry Bozeman
and Pam Kadlec

Crazy Quail Competition (a new organized event to showcase dog and owner's ability to work as a team)
1st: Ray Bloom and Lily
2nd: Rick Anderson and Bree
3rd: Bill Crites and Story
4th: Kevin Kees and Mae

**29th Annual Boykin Spaniel Society
National Field Trial**
March 26–29
Clinton House Plantation, Clinton, SC

Chairman's Cup: Sarah Harris

Open (17 entries)
*Judges: Michelle Love and Tom
McKenzie*
Open Champion: GRHCH UH Just
Ducky's Justforkicks "Mule"—Joe
Dawson (handler), Chris Meurett and
Pam Kadlec (owners)
2nd: HRCH Buckeye's Kickin It Upa
Notch "T-Boy"—Joe Cafiero (owner
and handler)
3rd: HRCH UH St. Thomas Chief—Dan
Reel (owner and handler)
4th: HRCH UH Pathfinders Point Shako
Jakeco—Scott Kinder (owner and
handler)

JAM (Judges' Award of Merit)
HR Just A Grand Illusion "Deke"—
Lance Waggoner (owner and handler)
HRCH Stickpond's Raz Ma Taz "Taz"—
Dan Caton (owner and handler)
HRCH Brandywine's Special Reserve
"Belle"—Lance Waggoner (owner and
handler)

HRCH Richland Stonewall Jackson— Butch Herb (owner and handler)

Novice (67 entries)
Judges: Davis Byrd and Paul Lemmond
Novice Champion: SHR Just Ducky's Justaplaceoutwest "Tana"—Sarah Harris (owner and handler)
2nd: Rock'n Creek Lord of the Wings "Wings"—John Huddleston (owner and handler)
3rd: Mr. Winchester "Chester"— Adam Littlefield (owner and handler)
4th: Maggie Rose—Danny Keith (handler), Amy Keith (owner)

JAM (Judges' Award of Merit)
Bryan's Santee Delta Sunrise "Delta"— Trey Bryan (owner and handler)
Rocky River's Holy Henna "Henna"— Cheryl Behe (owner and handler)
Brandywine's RS Amberbock "Amber"— Phil Behe (owner and handler)
Nuf Ced Lucca the Jester "Lucca"— Andrew Musashe (owner and handler)

Completions
Hap Man Do "Hap"—Amelia Skipper (handler), Dock and Amelia Skipper (owners)
Shadow Bend Madison "Madi"— Rick Anderson (owner and handler)
Hurricane Charley Radar—Dan Stone (owner and handler)
Whatawreck Tess "Tess"—Andy McGinnis (owner and handler)
OTM's Wrecker's License to Carry "Kara"—John Huddleston (handler), John and Kelly Huddleston (owners)
Brandywine's Duramizer Chip "Chip"— Lance Waggoner (handler), Phil and Karen Hinchman (owners)
Hodge's Special Force "Rambo"— Marie Hodge (owner and handler)
OTM's No Last Call LC Mae—Kevin Kees (owner and handler)
Minstrelboy Clan Chieftain "Chief"— Mike Elliott (owner and handler)

Intermediate (22 entries)
Judges: Jean Reichman and Danny Sanders
Intermediate Champion: HR UH Brandywine's Chocolate Covered Cherry "Cherry"—Phil Hinchman (handler), Phil and Karen Hinchman (owners)
2nd: HR UH Brandywine's Browning Citori Feather —Phil Hinchman (handler), Phil and Karen Hinchman (owners)
3rd: HR UH Pocotaligo's Shotgun Red "Red"—Greg Hendrick (owner and handler)
4th: HR Jeff's True Luck Tucker— Jeff Matthews (owner and handler)

JAM (Judges' Award of Merit
Nick Kinder—Jack Kinder (owner and handler)

Puppy (36 entries)
Judges: Bobby Jones and Billy Moxley
Puppy Champion: Pocotaligo's First Shot—Jule Parkman (handler), Cory Buchanan (owner)
2nd: Pocotaligo's Ritz Carlton "Ritz"— Trey Bryan (handler), Sandra T. Johnson (owner)
3rd: Toney's River Doc "Doc"—Eddie Toney (handler), Beth Toney (owner)
4th: Pocotaligo's Cash Advance "Vance"—Chad Funderburk (owner and handler)

JAM (Judges' Award of Merit)
Just Ducky's Scotch'n Soda "Grouse"— Justin Morgan (handler), Pam Kadlec (owner)
Brandywine's Special Cut "T-Bone"— Lance Waggoner (owner and handler)
OTM's Wrecker's License to Carry—John Huddleston (handler), John and Kelly Huddleston (owners)
Vader's Babe's Reese "Reese"—Ron Foster (owner and handler)

Completions
True Luck's Justarayofsunshine
"Shine"—Jeff Matthews (owner and
handler)
Hank—Russell Scott (handler), Sheila
Johnston (owner)
Brandywine's Majestic Water Lily—Rod
Payne (handler), Rod and Jess Payne
(owners)

Roustabout Singles
1st: Lily's Promise to Piper "Piper"—
Bill Crites (handler)
2nd: Brandywine's RS Amberbock
"Amber"—Matt Behe (owner and
handler)
3rd: Mr. Winchester "Chester"—Adam
Littlefield (owner and handler)
4th: Lily and Piper's Never Ending Story
"Story"—Bill Crites (handler), Dawn
Crites (owner)

Doubles Roustabout
1st: Brandywine's RS Amberbock
"Amber —Matt Behe (owner and
handler)
Mr. Winchester "Chester"—Adam
Littlefield (owner and handler)
2nd: Emma's Buck Creek Sadie
"Sadie"—Todd Deal (owner and
handler)
HRCH UH St. Thomas Chief—Dan Reel
(owner and handler)
3rd: Amazing Grace's Blind Faith
"Faith"—Blake Waggoner (owner and
handler)
Lily's and Piper's Never Ending Story
"Story"—Bill Crites (handler), Dawn
Crites (owner)

Carolina Boykin Spaniel Retriever Club
Awards and Titles, 1983–2008

1983

First Gun Dog Trial
August 15
Home of Gene and Ann Griffith,
Lake Murray, S.C.

Open Gun Dog (29 entries)
1st: Banjo—Ned Beard, Camden, S.C.
2nd: JC's Meggie—Robert Caulder, Camden, S.C.
3rd: Beth—Robert Caulder, Camden, S.C.
4th: Cocoa—Brownie Campbell, Dillon, S.C.

JAM (Judges' Award of Merit)
Grizzly—Chris Bishop, Florence, S.C.
Moxie—Chris Bishop, Florence, S.C.
Buck—Clay Hasty, Camden, S.C.
Dette—Dock Skipper, Newberry, S.C.
Dumpy—Brent Shirley—Camden, S.C.
Brown Sugar—Van Richardson, Heath Springs, S.C.
Smokey—William Coleman, Blair, S.C.

Puppy Gun Dog
1st: Maggie—Russell Fox, Batesburg, S.C.
2nd: Woody—Tom Lord, Columbia, S.C.
3rd: JC's Elizabeth—Janice Caulder, Camden, S.C.

4th: JC's Dove Bandit—Robert Caulder, Camden, S.C.

Dog of Year Awards

1983–84
Gun Dog: Banjo—Ned Beard, Camden, S.C.
Novice: Boykin—Joni Bishop, Florence, S.C.
Puppy: Fiddle—Ned and Meta Beard, Camden, S.C.

1984–85
Gun Dog: JC's Meggie—Robert Caulder, Camden, S.C.
Novice: Wade Hampton—Grady Phillips, White Oak, S.C.
Puppy: Bootsie Boo—Lewis Smoak, Florence, S.C.

1985–86
Gun Dog: Banjo—Ned Beard, Camden, S.C.
Intermediate: General Beauregard—Randall May, High Point, N.C.
Novice: General Beauregard—Randall May, High Point, N.C.
Puppy: A.C.—Joni Bishop, Florence, S.C.

1986–87

Gun Dog: Banjo—Ned Beard, Camden, S.C.
Intermediate: Coffee—Kim Parkman, Sumter, S.C.
Novice: Firestone—Charles Jurney, Mooresville, N.C.
Puppy: Drum—Ned Beard, Camden, S.C.

1987–88

Gun Dog: Coffee—Kim Parkman, Sumter, S.C.
Intermediate: Firestone—Charles Jurney, Mooresville, N.C.
Novice (tie): Socks—Marvin Blount, Greenville, N.C.; Rascal—Edward Eatmon, Kingstree, S.C.
Puppy: Bailey—Jule and Kim Parkman, Sumter, S.C.

1988–89

Gun Dog: Coffee—Kim Parkman, Sumter, S.C.
Intermediate: Buster—Bobby Lowery, Sumter, S.C.
Novice: Sumter—Steve Edwards, Darlington, S.C.
Puppy: Pat—Kim Parkman, Sumter, S.C.

1989–90

Gun Dog: Coffee—Kim Parkman, Sumter, S.C.
Intermediate: Rascal—Edward Eatmon, Kingstree, S.C.
Novice: Brandy—Bob King, Charleston, S.C.
Puppy: Bandit—Bobby Lowery, Sumter, S.C.

1990–91

Gun Dog: Firestone—Charles Jurney, Mooresville, N.C.
Intermediate: Dixie Blair—Bubba Pope, Columbia, S.C.
Novice: Clark—Nancy Updegrave, Awendaw, S.C.
Puppy: Decoy—Donnie Watts, Lexington, S.C.

1991–92

Gun Dog: Bailey—Jule and Kim Parkman, Sumter, S.C.
Intermediate: Angus—Ed Moore, Roanoke Rapids, N.C.
Novice: Woody—Roy Thompson, Vance, S.C.
Puppy: Cody—David Carmichael, Florence, S.C.

1992–93

Gun Dog: Coffee—Kim Parkman, Sumter S.C.
Intermediate: Woody—Roy Thompson, Vance, S.C.
Novice: Denver—Ricky Rainey, Waynesboro, Ga.
Puppy: Rick—Kim Parkman, Sumter S.C.

1993–94

Gun Dog: Dixie Blair—Bubba Pope, Columbia, S.C.
Intermediate: B.J.—Rogers Moody, Fayetteville, N.C.
Novice (tie): Decoy—Pat Smith, Leesville, S.C.; Quincy—Marian Williams
Puppy: Lady Winchester—Ackron Alexander

1994–95

Gun Dog: Dixie Blair—Bubba Pope, Columbia, S.C.
Intermediate: Malcolm—Joni Bishop, Gresham, S.C.
Novice: Cracker—Becky Burney, St. Augustine, Fla.
Puppy: Brownie—Kim Parkman, Sumter, S.C.

1995–96

Gun Dog: Dixie Blair—Bubba Pope, Columbia, S.C.
Intermediate: Mick—Curtis Hodge, Sumter, S.C.
Novice: Sydney—Jake Rasor, Cross Hill, S.C.
Puppy: Rush—Jim and Millie Latimer, Leesville, S.C.

1996–97
Gun Dog: Bailey—Jule and Kim Parkman, Sumter, S.C.
Intermediate: Sydney—Jake Rasor, Cross Hill, S.C.
Novice: Miggie McGirt—Charles Graham III
Puppy: Bird Boy—Jim and Millie Latimer

1997–98
Gun Dog: Mr. Mick—Curtis Hodge
Intermediate: Miggie McGirt—Charles Graham III
Novice (tie): Widgeon of Pocotaligo—Lynn Wallace; Pocotaligo's Wednesday—Kim Parkman
Puppy: Brandy—Pat Burton

1998–99
Gun Dog: Mr. Mick—Curtis Hodge
Intermediate: Boyd—Chesley Hall
Novice: Sammy—Pam Kadlec
Puppy: Harley—Kevin Freeman

1999–2000
Gun Dog: Sydney—Jake Rasor
Intermediate: Sammy—Pam Kadlec
Novice: Drake—Eddie Hughes
Puppy: Fancy—Mac McClary

2000–2001
Gun Dog: Curlee Gurlee—Pam Kadlec
Intermediate: Philly—Kim Parkman
Novice: Stoney—Harry Smutzer
Puppy: Chica—David Hull

2001–2
Gun Dog: Sam—Gene Putnam
Intermediate: Mojo—Ronnie Dawkins
Novice: Ellie—Amy Braswell
Puppy (tie): Marley—Wade Collins; Jeb—Mark Lee

2002–3
Gun Dog: Sam—Gene Putnam
Intermediate: Daisy—Harriett Clark
Novice: Jeb—Mark Lee
Puppy: Izzy—Millie Latimer

2003–4
Gun Dog: Sam—Gene Putnam
Intermediate: Teal—Chris Darby

Novice (tie): Cocoa—Russell Scott; Peat—Scott Culbreth
Puppy: BG—Lindwood Jernigan

2004–5
Gun Dog: Sam—Gene Putnam
Intermediate: Grace—Blake Waggoner
Novice: Promise—Dawn Crites
Puppy: Vivy—Gary Edmonds

2005–6
Gun Dog: Jeb—Mark Lee
Intermediate: Peat—Scott Culbreth
Novice: Hatch—Jamie Newman
Puppy: Hatch—Jamie Newman

2006–7
Gun Dog (tie): Grace—Blake Waggoner; Teal—Chris Darby
Intermediate: Hatch—Jamie Newman
Novice: Red—Greg Hendrick
Puppy: Big Boy—James Barbare

2007–8
Puppy: Rambo—Marie Hodge
Runner Up: Annie—James Kinnear and Don Brown
Novice: Ace—Harriett Clark
Runner Up: Amanda—DeVon Ruth
Intermediate: Chief—Dan Reel
Runner Up: Buck—Sarah Harris and Russ Harris
Open: Chief—Dan Reel
Runner Up (tie): Grace—Blake and Shelby Waggoner; Jake—Scott Kinder

Champion Hunter Titles

1988
Banjo—Ned Beard, Camden, S.C.
Firestone—Charles Jurney, Mooresville, S.C.
Coffee—Kim Parkman, Sumter, S.C.
B.J.—Chris Bishop—Florence, S.C.

1989
Brambles—Edward Eatmon, Kingstree, S.C.
Wade Hampton—Grady Phillips, White Oak, S.C.

Buster—John Trenary, Moncks
  Corner, S.C.

1990
Rascal—Edward Eatmon, Kingstree, S.C.
Buster—Bobby Lowery, Sumter, S.C.

1992
Blair—Bubba Pope, Columbia, S.C.
Bud—Keith Cain, Jenkinsville, S.C.

1994
Pocotaligo's Bailey—Jule and Kim
  Parkman, Sumter, S.C.

1995
Hubba Bubba—Richard Coe,
  Summerville, S.C.

2003
Sam—Gene Putnam
Curlee Gurlee—Pam Kadlec

2004
Philly—Kim Parkman
Daisy—Harriett Clark

2005
Jeb—Mark Lee

2007
Teal—Chris Darby
Toot—Dan Caton

2008
Grace—Blake Waggoner

Boykin Spaniel Placements in Hunting Retriever Club Field Tests, 1998–2007

In Boykin spaniel retriever trials programs and lists abbreviations such as SHR HR HRCH and UH often precede individual dog names. These abbreviations indicate the dog's level of retrieving skills based on tests conducted by the international Hunting Retriever Club Inc., often called just HRC. The Hunting Retriever Club's hunt-test program for all gun dog breeds has become a big part of training and field trialing the Boykin.

In the HRC hunt tests a retriever such as a Boykin spaniel may participate in five ability-based (not age-based) categories to earn five titles: Started Hunting Retriever (SHR), Hunting Retriever (HR), Hunting Retriever Champion (HRCH), Grand Hunting Retriever Champion (GRHRCH), and Upland Hunter (UH). Unlike field trials these "tests" are not competitive first-, second-, third-, and fourth-place events. Each dog is judged on a pass-or-fail basis against a hunting standard. HRC field tests are true hunting scenarios where the handler fires the gun. Each judge is a qualified HRC member whose own dog has been trained for and passed the level he or she is judging. The organization maintains a friendly, wholesome family atmosphere.

The HRC is affiliated with the United Kennel Club, Inc. (UKC), which carries the HRC registry. Titles earned are used as a prefix to the dog's registered name on its pedigree. Since its beginning in 1984, the HRC has grown to 132 clubs with more than eighty-five hundred members. HRC clubs hold more than 350 licensed Hunt Tests each year with an average of 73 retrievers and 182 people participating in each event.

A March 6, 2008, computer search of Hunting Retriever Club records identified all Boykin spaniels that had earned titles in Hunting Retriever Club tests to that date. Those qualifying dogs are listed below with an explanation of each category.

Started Hunting Retriever (SHR)

The list below contains all Boykin spaniels that have earned a Started Hunting Retriever title from 1998 through 2007.

10/24/1998—Pocotaligo's Camo
03/06/1999—Pocotaligo's Sprig
03/26/2000—Harlequin of Pocotaligo
11/04/2000—Savannah Roses Martha Duke
02/25/2001—Dawkins Pocotaligo Mojo
03/17/2001—H and P's Little Stoney
03/17/2001—Kathy's Gabriel
05/19/2001—Boulder Brook's Bonbon
05/20/2001—Warren's 1st Scout
03/16/2002—Scape 'Ore Li'l Scarlett
09/29/2002—Amy's Pocotaligo Ellie
11/24/2002—Darby's Chocolate Lady
02/02/2003—Just Ducky's Justacrooner
02/23/2003—Pooshee's Dusa Lily Pad
03/29/2003—Breanna's Gracious Gracey
05/18/2003—Creek Boat Snappin Turtle
06/21/2003—Creek Boat Gunner
09/21/2003—Hap Man Do
11/08/2003—Tugtown Molly
02/21/2004—Chelsea by the Sea
02/21/2004—Jakes Tugtown Edisto
03/13/2004—Carolina Magic Drake
03/13/2004—Windshadow's Jeb Stuart
03/14/2004—Creek Boat Hunter
03/21/2004—Hollow Creek's Decoy II
03/28/2004—P.K. Charlie Brown
05/22/2004—Just Ducky's Justaluckybet
05/22/2004—Wares' Pocotaligo Boomer
05/23/2004—Waccamaw River's Sally Brown
09/19/2004—Shelby's Little Lulu
09/19/2004—Ware's Pocotaligo Banjo
09/26/2004—Lulu's Sugar n Spice
10/02/2004—Augustus Mars Gus
10/03/2004—Just Ducky's Front Page News
11/06/2004—Creekboat Sailor
02/13/2005—Lulu's Captain Nemo
03/12/2005—Darby's Land Rush
05/01/2005—Black's New Millennium

05/14/2005—Buster Brown
09/03/2005—Salem Farm Reelfoot
09/11/2005—Maggie's Northern Ruby
09/18/2005—Pocotaligo's Juke
09/25/2005—Bette's Carolina
09/25/2005—Hollow Creek's Victoria
10/02/2005—Barry Lynn's Stella Marie
10/08/2005—Addisons Big Riggs
10/16/2005—Brandywine's Northern Dixie
11/13/2005—Carolina Magic Hoss
11/13/2005—Tugtown Bellini Belle
11/13/2005—Tugtown Palmetto Rose
02/19/2006—Mississippi Flash & Splash
04/09/2006—Blue Bayou Beaux
05/14/2006—Story's Cocoa Break
05/14/2006—Web's Besst Sweet Gypsy Rose
09/10/2006—J and L's Lucky Nellie Mae
09/17/2006—Brandywine's Big Brown Bear
09/23/2006—Brandywine's Hokey Smokes Okey
09/24/2006—Nick Kinder
10/01/2006—Maggie's Just Been There
10/07/2006—Just Ducky's Justagentleman
10/08/2006—Pocotaligo's Shotgun Red
11/11/2006—Web's Lil Trapper Brown BD
11/12/2006—Just Ducky's Justanibble
02/17/2007—Emma's Buck Creek Sadie
04/29/2007—Just Ducky's Justasaltydog
05/05/2007—J&L's Sweet Caroline
05/12/2007—Peyton Davis O'Neal
07/15/2007—J and L's Super Chewbaka 2nd
08/26/2007—Mostyn
09/09/2007—Island Creek Buck
09/29/2007—Rock'n Creek Lord of the Wings
10/13/2007—Pocotaligo's Texas Willie
10/14/2007—Brandywine's Special Reserve
10/21/2007—Amanda of Pocotaligo
10/21/2007—Dixie Ridge's Johnny Rebel
11/10/2007—Boyd's Jake BJ
11/10/2007—Just Have a Little Faith
12/01/2007—Just Ducky's Justaslamdunk

Hunting Retriever (HR)

The list below contains all Boykin spaniels that have earned a Hunting Retriever title from 1989 through 2007.

10/08/1989—Joe's Alabama Bear
09/08/1990—Garza's Chip
10/07/1990—Beau Jiminy
11/10/1990—S. Comforts Chantilly Lace
03/18/1995—Rainey's Denver
05/06/1995—Buster Junior
11/18/1995—Mr. Mick
03/16/1996—Catherine's Dolly
10/19/1996—Catherine's Little Brownie
11/08/1997—Miggie McGirt
11/09/1997—Pistol Pete Fetchum
03/15/1998—White Sands Buck
09/27/1998—Sydney of Woodbine
02/27/1999—Vecchione's Barthalamew
02/28/1999—Unsinkable Molly Brown
03/14/1999—Just Ducky's Justasample
10/10/1999—Widgeon of Pocotaligo
11/14/1999—P.K. Maxwell Smart
04/15/2000—Cooper
10/07/2000—Riptide's Colonial Run
11/05/2000—Pocotaligo's Philly
02/24/2001—Just Ducky's Tourbillion
03/31/2001—Daisy Ray
10/06/2001—Hi-Brass Harley
04/07/2002—Pocotaligo's Tasmanian Jake
04/27/2002—Dovewood's Major
11/02/2002—Kipper Ray
02/23/2003—Beal's Jig
05/10/2003—Penny's Wooden Nickle
09/20/2003—Edisto Rebel Colonel
12/06/2003—Woody's Cocoa-GI
03/13/2004—Just Ducky's Justdoit
05/15/2004—Harrelson Boy's Henry
05/23/2004—Just Ducky's Justmyluck
09/04/2004—Gabriel Maxwell of Buckhead
12/04/2004—Just Ducky's Ubetyourbippy
03/05/2005—Salem Farm's Just Hot Ash
03/20/2005—H and P's Naughty Girl Belle
04/10/2005—Just Ducky's Justagigalo
05/07/2005—Lily's No Pink Promise
09/18/2005—Pocotaligo's Finest Brandy
10/08/2005—Just Ducky's Nike Air Althea

10/08/2005—Just Ducky's Miss Edgefield
03/12/2006—Just Ducky's Just A Home Wrecker
05/07/2006—Graham's Carolina Wrangler
05/07/2006—Just Ducky's First Edition
05/20/2006—Moss Point Elijah
09/16/2006—Brandywine's Mighty Duramax
09/17/2006—Brandywine's Chocolate Covered Cherry
09/24/2006—Just a Coosawhatchie Run
10/07/2006—Fist Full of Dollars
10/08/2006—Pathfinders Point Shako Jakeco
10/15/2006—Justaintwhistlindixie
10/15/2006—Unsinkable Molly Brown
11/11/2006—Just Ducky's Justadducks
11/11/2006—Just Ducky's Justforchuckles
08/25/2007—Bogey (only 10.5 months old)
08/26/2007—Ceasarcreek Crown Charlie
09/08/2007—Silvestre Atchafalaya
09/29/2007—Richland Stonewall Jackson
10/13/2007—Brandywine's 12 Gauge
10/20/2007—A J Jumper
11/04/2007—Sir Murphee Maurer
11/04/2007—Winston Ducky Dela Chasse

Hunting Retriever Champion (HRCH)

09/29/1990—Clark's Sam
05/28/1995—Pocotaligo's Coffee
09/14/1996—Pocotaligo's Bailey
03/01/1997—Irene's Fancy Girl
03/28/1998—King's Curlee Gurlee
03/11/2001—Holy Moses
11/03/2002—Fancy's Mighty Sampson
09/12/2004—Darby's Teal Boy
02/12/2005—Just Ducky's Bookmark
03/13/2005—Holland Ridge Jeb Stuart
04/09/2005—Caton's Rooty Toot Toot
05/22/2005—Pocotaligo's Amazing Grace
08/26/2007—Duke of Earl
09/23/2007—Silvestre Acadiana
10/14/2007—Radde & Kim's Mud
11/11/2007—Buckeye's Kickin It Upa Notch
12/02/2007—St. Thomas Chief
02/10/2008—Oyster Creek's Pistol Peat

Grand Hunting Retriever Champion (GRHRCH)

Currently there are 350 GRHRCH titleholders, the vast majority of which (more than 300) are Labrador retrievers. On October 23, 2004, Just Ducky's Justforkicks "Mule," owned by Chris Meurett of Mount Pleasant, North Carolina, and Pamela O. Kadlec of Edgefield, South Carolina, became the first (and so far the only) Boykin spaniel to earn the Grand Hunting Retriever Champion title. He has also earned his Upland Hunter title and is the only HRC 2000 Point Club member of any spaniel breed to date.

Upland Hunter (UH)

The Upland test was added to the HRC/UKC hunting program in 1996.

11/07/1998—Pocotaligo's Bailey
11/07/1998—Sydney of Woodbine
03/06/1999—Miggie McGirt
03/07/1999—Widgeon of Pocotaligo
04/01/2001—Jack's Roux
04/01/2001—Vecchione's Barthalamew
04/01/2001—Zee
11/04/2001—Pocotaligo's Philly
01/27/2002—Fancy's Mighty Samson
01/27/2002—King's Curlee Gurlee
01/27/2002—Kipper Ray
03/16/2002—Daisy
01/26/2003—Darby's Teal Boy

03/08/2003—Pooshee's Dusa Lily Pad
05/18/2003—Beal's Jig
09/21/2003—Woody's Cocoa-GI
11/23/2003—Just Ducky's Justforkicks
05/23/2004—Oyster Creek's Pistol Peat
11/07/2004—Just Ducky's Justmyluck
03/19/2005—Caton's Rooty Toot Toot
05/01/2005—Pocotaligo's Amazing Grace
09/17/2005—H and P's Naughty Girl Belle
09/23/2006—Hi-Brass Harley
09/30/2006—Unsinkable Molly Brown
12/03/2006—Graham's Carolina Wrangler
01/07/2007—Fist Full of Dollars
01/07/2007—Lulu's Captain Nemo
01/07/2007—Pocotaligo's Juke
02/17/2007—Moss Point's Elijah
02/17/2007—Pathfinders Point Shako Jakeco
02/25/2007—Just Ducky's Justaddducks
03/18/2007—Brandywine's Chocolate Covered Cherry
03/24/2007—J and L's Sweet Caroline
06/03/2007—Radde & Kim's Mud
06/17/2007—Duke of Earl
12/01/2007—Bogey
01/06/2008—Pocotaligo's Shotgun Red
01/06/2008—St. Thomas Chief
02/09/2008—Brandywine's Mighty Duramax
02/23/2008—Brandywine's Browning Citori Feather
02/23/2008—J and L's Lucky Nellie Mae

Other Boykin Spaniels of Special Merit

Palmetto Retriever Club Awards Given to Boykin Spaniels

1985–86 Puppy of Year: Bootsie Boo— Lewis Smoak, Florence, S.C.

1991–92 Senior Hunter: Dixie Blair— Bubba Pope, Columbia, S.C.

North American Hunting Retriever Association (NAHRA) Master Hunter Titles Given to Boykin Spaniels

MHR Firestone—Charles Jurney (handler and owner), Mooresville, N.C.

MHR HR CH Pocotaligo's Coffee— Kim S. Parkman (handler), Kim and Jule Parkman (owners), Sumter, S.C.

Boykin spaniels have also earned NAHRA Working Retriever titles.

BIBLIOGRAPHY

Able, Gene. "Boykins Hold Trials." *State* (Columbia, S.C.), June 1, 1980, 10-G. Report on the Boykin Spaniel Society's first field trial.

American College of Veterinary Ophthalmologists, Genetics Committee. *Ocular Disorders Proven or Suspected to be Hereditary in Dogs.* Baton Rouge: American College of Veterinary Ophthalmologists, 1999.

Angle, Joanna, host-producer. "Boykin," *Palmetto Places.* SCETV, September 14, 1996 (program no. 155-0154). Program on Boykin, South Carolina, including three or four minutes on Boykin spaniels.

Associated Press. "Boykin Spaniel as State Dog Has Opposition." *Columbia Record,* February 25, 1985. Report stating that 58 of 124 House members have sponsored a bill naming the Boykin spaniel as the state dog.

Babb, Bill. "S.C.'s Boykin Spaniels a Breed Apart." *Augusta Chronicle,* May 31, 1998, B10. Article about the first edition of *The Boykin Spaniel: South Carolina's Dog.*

Barron, Clarenden W. *Carolina Sportsman: Official Publication of the Sportsmen's Association of South Carolina* 1 (January 1920). L. W. "Whit" Boykin was among this organization's founders and its first vice president, serving as temporary chairman of the first meeting, held on October 15, 1919, at the Jefferson Hotel in Columbia. The group urged the passage and enforcement of better conservation laws.

Barton, Jack. "Boykin Spaniels in Peru," letter to the editor, *South Carolina Wildlife* 22 (January–February 1976): 43. A letter from a correspondent in Nicaragua.

Bellune, Jerry. "Celebrating the South Carolina State Dog." *Lexington County Chronicle,* August 13, 1998, 8. Article about the first edition of *The Boykin Spaniel: South Carolina's Dog.*

Bennett, Charles. "Boykin Spaniels: S. Carolina's State Dog." *State* (Columbia, S.C.), December 21, 1997, C19. Article about the first edition of *The Boykin Spaniel: South Carolina's Dog,* including an interview with Mike Creel.

Benton, Bill. Interview with Lynn Kelley and Mike Creel, *Bill Benton Show.* WSCQ-Columbia, S.C., April 7, 1998. Discussion of the first edition of *The Boykin Spaniel: South Carolina's Dog.*

Berman, Pat. "Boykin Wonder-Spaniel Speeds from Underdog to Top Dog." *State* (Columbia, S.C.), April 18, 1997, D1, D3. This announcement of the next day's National Hunting Test and the twentieth anniversary of Boykin Spaniel Society includes a discussion with Boykin spaniel masters about the breed's history and merits. Featured in photographs by Eric Seals are Kim Parkman and Alice Boykin with Irene's Fancy Girl, Sydney of Woodbine, Pocotaligo's Bailey, Pocotaligo's Beretta, Pocotaligo's Pony, and Pocotaligo's Wednesday.

Boykin, Henry D., II. *Looking Back at the Boykin Hunting Club*. Camden. S.C.: Privately printed, 1984.

Boykin, L. Whit. *Winter Homes In South Carolina*. Advertising brochure. Columbia, S.C., circa 1925–32.

Boykin Spaniel Society. *Boykin Spaniel Society Newsletter* (Camden, S.C.), 1977– .

Braswell, Tommy. "Man's Best Friend—Well-trained Retriever No Accident." *Charleston News and Courier*, September 13, 1981, B15. Interview with trainer Calvin Baynard of Manning and a photograph of Boykin spaniel Skeet leaping into water.

"Breed of the Month: The Boykin Spaniel Great as a Retriever." *New York World-Telegram and Sun*, August 25, 1961. A story retelling the Spartanburg-origin account and quoting at length from the Boykin spaniel entry in Henry Davis's *Modern Dog Encyclopedia*.

Brunson, Charlotte Boykin Salmond. *Kershaw County Cousins*. Columbia, S.C.: R. L. Bryan, 1978.

Burger, Ken. "It's a Dog's Life among the Wildlife." *Charleston News and Courier*, February 20, 1994. An account of Chris Bishop's Boykin retrieving demonstration at the Southeastern Wildlife Exposition.

Clark, Anne Rogers, and Andrew H. Bruce, eds. *The International Encyclopedia of Dogs*. London: Mirabel Books, n.d. The entry on the Boykin spaniel (p. 433) includes photograph of Mike Creel's dog Booger.

Collins, Elizabeth. "A Puppy Buyer's Guide." *Boykin Spaniel Society Newsletter* 19 (October 1, 1995): 1–2, 4.

Cooper, Ashley [pseud.]. "As Ashley Cooper Sees It." *Aiken (S.C.) Standard*, November 26, 1981. A humorous discussion about the Boykin spaniel's prospects for becoming state dog and about Charlestonian Ben Moïse's Boykin spaniel Belle.

Corley, E. A. *Hip Dysplasia*. Columbia, Mo.: Orthopedic Foundation for Animals, 1993.

Cornelison, Jimmy. "The Last Word in Hunting Dogs." *Greenville News*, May 18, 1984, C1. An article recounting the history of the Boykin spaniel and the personal experiences of David Parr, his wife, Margaret, and his son David Jr. of Newberry, South Carolina, with their dogs. Featured are Ted Ramsaur's color photographs of the Parrs' Boykins, Scarlet and Cheney, in action.

Creel, Mike. "Boykin spaniel." In *The South Carolina Encyclopedia*, edited by Walter Edgar, 93. Columbia: University of South Carolina Press, 2006. Includes a South Carolina Department of Natural Resources photograph by Robert Clark.

———. "Boykin Spaniel Day Opens Dove Season." Press release, Columbia, S.C. Wildlife and Marine Resources Department, August 27, 1984. Includes photographs of Gov. Dick Riley with Boykin spaniel Sarge, owned by Butch and Judy Pendarvis of Edgefield, and with the Boykin spaniel print by Burton E. Moore Jr.

———. "Boykin's Popularity on the Rise in South Carolina." *Resource* (S.C. Wildlife and Marine Resources Department), January 1977, 8.

———. "The Dog That Doesn't Rock The Boat." *Outdoor Life* 166 (October 1980): 76–78, 139–40. Includes photographs by Art Carter.

———. "The Dog That Fits." *Turkey Call* 19 (September–October, 1992): 28–31. Includes a Boykin spaniel portrait by Prescott Baines of Lexington, South Carolina.

———. "The Last Section Boat Raised from the Dead" *Resource* (S.C. Wildlife and Marine Resources Department), September 1977, 1–5. Revised as "Uncle Toot's Convertible." *South Carolina Wildlife* 28 (January–February 1981): 43–47. Article on the origin, construction, and use of section boats with photographs and diagrams of the last section boat discovered at the farm of Mrs. Julian E. Sanders Jr. These boats were used extensively on the Wateree River in the early 1900s by hunting parties in which Boykin spaniels participated. Harry Hampton credited the Boykin family with developing these boats.

———. Photograph. *1996–97 Rules & Regulation for Hunting, Freshwater and Saltwater Fishing in South Carolina.* Columbia: S.C. Department of Natural Resources, 1996. Some 450,000 copies were printed and distributed with a photograph of Chris and Joni Bishop's Boykin spaniel Clark on the cover.

———. Photograph for February 1987. *Sportsman's Calendar, 1986–87.* Columbia: South Carolina Wildlife, 1986. Photograph of Ryan Jordan of Florence, South Carolina, with twelve-week-old Ryan's Swamp Fox.

———. "The Retriever That Won't Rock the Boat." *Waterfowl and Wetlands Magazine* 7 (Summer 1993): 22–28. Includes photographs by Marion Bull. The cover of this issue features Jim Killen's Carolina Heritage duck-stamp print of the Boykin spaniel.

———. "The Spaniels of Boykin." *South Carolina Wildlife* 22 (September–October 1975): 44–49. Republished in *Carolina's Hunting Heritage,* edited by John Culler, 54–63. Columbia: South Carolina Wildlife, 1978. The cover photograph by Art Carter for the September–October issue of *South Carolina Wildlife* shows a Boykin spaniel charging through corn stubble. *Carolina's Hunting Heritage* includes the full article but not the cover photograph.

———. "Triumph over Kennel-shyness." *Family Circle,* 192 (September 18, 1979): R6, appendix 162+.

———. "Triumph over Kennelshyness: A Difficult Undertaking." *Resource* (S.C. Wildlife and Marine Resources Department), February 1977, 9.

Crites, Bill. *Piper Anne Crabby Pants's First Big Adventure,* forthcoming 2009. A children's story about Boykin spaniel manners, with illustrations by Julia Horner; available from the author in late 2009 at www.LilypadBoykins.com.

Culler, John M. Editorial. *Outdoor Life* 166 (September 1980). Witty editorial mentioning current and upcoming articles on Boykin spaniels.

————. "The Retriever from Hell." In *Purple Heaven and Other Stories*, 32–38. Camden, S.C.: John Culler & Sons, 1995. Short story about an avenging Boykin spaniel.

Dabblemont, Larry. "The Boykin Spaniel: Super Dog?" *Gun Dog*, September–October 1981, 26–29.

Davis, Henry P., ed. *The Modern Dog Encyclopedia*. 2nd ed. Harrisburg, Pa.: Stackpole, 1956. The Boykin spaniel entry (pp. 468–69) includes a photograph of Sir Bolivar, a Boykin owned by Mrs. M. L. Smythe of Palm Beach, Florida.

Davis, John. "Best Friends." *South Carolina Wildlife* 33 (September–October 1986): 24–29. Includes Mike Creel's photograph of Ryan Jordan of Florence, South Carolina, with twelve-week-old Ryan's Swamp Fox.

"Dixie Blair Tops in Boykin Contest." *Charleston Post and Courier*, May 7, 1995, B13. Results of the 1995 Boykin Spaniel Society National Hunting Test, held near Society Hill, South Carolina.

Duffey, Dave. "The Boykin Spaniel: Brown, Busy and Bright." *Gun Dog*, August–September 1993, 70–74.

Educational poster of South Carolina wildlife symbols. Harry Hampton Memorial Wildlife Fund (1988). Includes a Boykin spaniel with other state wildlife symbols. Printed to promote the March 18–20, 1988, Palmetto Sportsmen's Classic show in Columbia, South Carolina.

Evans, Robbie. "Boykin Spaniels—Gist Finds Pleasure in His Dogs." *Sumter Item*, November. 20, 1994, B11. An article profiling Nat Gist of Sumter, South Carolina, and his experiences with Boykin spaniels since 1975. Featured are photographs by Bruz Crowson of Gist with his dogs Charlie, Cricket (a winner at the first Boykin Society trial in 1980), and two pups.

Ervin, Louise. "A Breed Apart—Boykin Spaniel Earning Reputation for Hunting." *Anderson Independent-Mail* (June 14, 1984). An article recounting the origin of Boykin spaniels and experiences of Honea Path Boykin owner Frank Friddle Jr. with his dogs Behron and Peanut. A photograph by Patricia Griggs shows Peanut retrieving.

Flamholtz, Cathy J. *A Celebration of Rare Breeds*. Ft. Payne, Ala.: QTR Publications, 1986. The Boykin spaniel entry (pp. 45–47), by Lee West of Wisacky, South Carolina, includes West's photographs of Tom Lord's Boykin spaniels Greywood Woody and Poppy.

Foster, Jack. "The Boykin Spaniel." *Esquire*, July 1943.

Gaddis, Mike. "Dogs That Do It All." *North Carolina Wildlife*, March 1989, 4–9. Includes photographs of Gaddis's Boykin spaniel Jody on the cover and inside with Brittany spaniels.

Garrison, Ed. "Spaniels Becoming Celebrities." *Camden Independent*, March 22, 1978, A11. An article on the new Boykin Spaniel Society, the breed's history, efforts to make the Boykin spaniel the state dog, and Camden mayor James L. Anderson's Boykin spaniel, Charley II.

Gregg, Louise. "Smartest Dog?" *Wichita Falls Times,* September 13, 1979, D1. An article praising the breed and focusing on late Boykin Spaniel Society board member Bill Hale and his dog Beck.

Griffen, Jeff. *The Hunting Dogs of America.* Garden City, N.Y.: Doubleday, 1964. The entry on the Boykin spaniel (pp. 100–102) includes a photograph by Evelyn Shafer of two Boykin spaniels on a beach.

Hampton, Harry R. E. "The Boykin Spaniel." Woods and Waters column. *State* (Columbia, S.C.), November 1, 1964, C8. An account of John McClain's column in the October 31 issue of the *New York Journal American,* discussing the breed origins and the feats of Northam Griggs's Boykin spaniel King, which saved a disabled sea gull at a beach in Southampton, New York.

———. "The Boykin Spaniel" and "Meeting the Boykins." In *Woods and Waters and Some Asides,* 130–31, 138–44. Columbia, S.C.: State Printing, 1979. Two columns from Hampton's Woods and Waters column in the *State* newspaper from the 1950s.

Hartnett, Thomas F. "Memories of His Dog Muffin." *Quail Unlimited,* July–August 1993.

Haynie, Rachel. "The First Boykin Spaniels: The Story of Dumpo and Singo." *Columbia (S.C.) Star,* December 3, 2004, 2. Review of the first children's book featuring the Boykin spaniel.

Huckabee, Gigi Mabry. "Owner's Choice." *South Carolina Wildlife* 33 (November–December 1986): 44–49. An article about Boykin spaniels with photographs by Robert Clark and Michael Foster.

Idoux, Frances. "The Boykin Spaniel: High-Spirited State Dog." *Pee Dee Magazine,* November–December 1997, 18–23. This article includes photographs by Benton Henry and interviews with Boykin owners and trainers Joe Watkins of Florence, Kim Parkman of Sumter, and Ricky Williams of Conway.

Iwabu, Takaaki. Photograph of "Chad and Morgan Hunter from Charleston with their Boykin Spaniel Watch as Floats Pass during Boykin's Christmas Parade." *State* (Columbia, S.C.), December 20, 1999, B1.

Jenkins, Austin. "Retriever Fever." *South Carolina Wildlife* 54 (September–October 2007): 16–21. This article discussing the Boykin spaniel and several retriever breeds includes photographs of Boykins by Pam Kadlec.

Jones, Phillip. Photograph for December 1996. *Sportsman's Calendar, 1996–97.* Columbia: South Carolina Wildlife, 1996. Photograph featuring Kim Parkman's Boykin spaniel Pocotaligo's Colt under a Christmas tree.

———. Photograph for November 1984. *Sportsman's Calendar, 1984–85.* Columbia: South Carolina Wildlife, 1984. Photograph featuring George Brown Campbell's Boykin spaniel Cocoa.

Kadlec, Pamela O. *Retriever Training for Spaniels.* Edgefield, S.C.: Just Ducky Publishing, 2002.

Kelley, Lynn. *The First Boykin Spaniels: The Story of Dumpy and Singo.* Columbia, S.C.: Berke Books, 2004. The first children's book about the Boykin spaniel, illustrated in color by Lisa Gardiner. The book is available in independent bookstores in South Carolina or by writing Boykin Children's Book, P.O. Box 862, Columbia, S.C. 29202.

Kelley, Lynn, and Mike Creel. "The Boykin Spaniel—Book Excerpts." *Orangeburg Times and Democrat,* November 26, 1998, C1. Full-page of excerpts from the first edition of *The Boykin Spaniel* with the cover photograph from the book.

Kern, David F. "Spaniels Lobby for State Dog." *State* (Columbia, S.C.), February 28, 1985, C1. An article about the visit of four Boykin spaniels (Fiddle, Banjo, Lucky, and Edisto Dutchman)—and Boykin Spaniel Society members Nat Gist, John Chappell, and Ned and Meta Beard—to the South Carolina House of Representatives Agriculture and Natural Resources Committee meeting.

Knight, Jaime. "Good Companions: State Dog Has Close Ties to Williamsburg County." *Kingstree News,* July 22, 1998, B1. An article including interviews with Boykin spaniel masters Mike Creel, Edward Eatmon, Plexie Baker, Rena and Ron McClure, and Mable O'Bryan.

"L. Whit Boykin Dies Saturday: Well Known Sportsman Has Heart Attack." *State* (Columbia, S.C.), June 5, 1932, A1. A lengthy front-page obituary summarizing the life of L. W. "Whit" Boykin Sr.

Lanford, Jill Jones. "At Home with the Boykin." *Spartanburg Herald-Journal,* March 22, 1992, C1. An article about Margii Roldan's Boykins and the origins of breed. Includes photographs by Gerry Pate of Roldan's dog Waverly and pups.

Lanier, Al. "Some Imaginative Bills Failed." *State* (Columbia, S.C.), July 31, 1978, B5. An article by the Associated Press capital correspondent reporting with "regret" the Boykin bill's death in House committee. Lanier wrote "What probably killed it was somebody's suggestion that South Carolina also ought to have a state nut."

Laurie, Pete. "Boykin Spaniel Painting Hit of Wildlife Exposition." *Southeast Farm Press,* March 7, 1984, 72. An article recounting public reaction to and purchases of the new Boykin spaniel art print by Burton Moore Jr. and the auctioning of the original painting for $10,000 to the owner of the dog that posed for the artist. "But the star of the show was a little ragamuffin dog with a questionable heritage that has wormed its way into the hearts of a good many South Carolinians."

Leonardi, Rick. "Gun Pups." *South Carolina Wildlife* 40 (September–October 1993): 16–24. Includes a photograph by Ted Borg of Kim Parkman's Boykin spaniel Pocotaligo Coffee in front of a haystack.

Long, Anna. "Couple Seek to Make Boykin the State Dog." *Batesburg-Leesville Twin City News,* August 30, 1984. An article on the breed's history and Russell and Amy Fox of Leesville's support for making the Boykin state dog.

"Mason-Dixon Top Dog In Field Competition." *Kingstree News,* February 12, 1986, 8. An article reporting the results of a February 1 Carolina Boykin Retriever Club field event at Indian Hut Tree Farm, where Mason Dixon, owned by Jerry Bennett of Quinby, won the gun-dog competition.

McClure, Bill. "Boy Oh Boykin." *American Hunter,* July 1999, 5. This illustrated article centered on D. B. Parr and his Boykin Ida also contains information about the history of the breed and mentions of the Boykin Spaniel Society.

McDonald, Bill. "State Dogs Find a Friend." *State* (Columbia, S.C.), February 16, 1998, B1, B10. Article about the founding of the Boykin Spaniel Rescue in 1997 by Christy Whitlock and Bill Bennett.

McKoy, Peter. "About Boykin Spaniel Society," letter to the editor. *South Carolina Wildlife* 25 (March–April 1978): 42. Progress report on the recently created Boykin Spaniel Society.

———. "Breeding Your Boykin." *Boykin Spaniel Society Newsletter* 7 (January 1, 1983): 2.

———. "Thoughts on Breeding Practices." *Boykin Spaniel Society Newsletter* 6 (October 1, 1982): 2.

Mize, Jim. "The Perils of Naming Your Pup." *South Carolina Wildlife* 42 (November–December 1995): 14–15. Includes Phillip Jones's photograph of Kim Parkman's Pocotaligo's Colt under a Christmas tree.

Moïse, Ben McC. "On Patrol: Tales of a South Carolina Game Warden's Most Trusted Partner." *Garden & Gun,* July–August 2008, 118. Moïse's story of his Boykin spaniel Belle.

Montgomery, Rachel. *Camden Heritage: Yesterday and Today.* Camden, S.C.: Guardian of Camden, 1971.

Moore, Thomas A. Letter to the editor. *Spartanburg Herald,* April 1, 1992. Letter adding some important missing details to a March 22, 1992, *Herald* article about Boykin spaniels.

Mower, Joan. "Boykin Spaniel Bill Fails to Make It out of Committee. *State* (Columbia, S.C.), May 24, 1978. This United Press International article was widely circulated in the state's print and electronic media.

———. "Brown-Eyed Spaniels Fail to Sway Panel." *Columbia Record,* May 24, 1978, B1. A UPI report of W. A. "Anc" Boykin's visit to the House Agricultural and Natural Resources Committee, which he urged to adopt the Senate-passed Boykin bill. He brought three "yellow-eyed" dogs (Cheob, Ralph, and Barney) to the cramped committee room. Debate was adjourned before action was taken. The story features a photograph of a Boykin with the state flag, taken by Darrell H. Hoemann of the *Record* staff.

Mueller, Larry. "True Hunting Buddies." *Outdoor Life* 207 (May 2001): 34–35. Mueller's hunting-dog column about Boykin spaniels features an interview with breeder Patricia Watts of Leesville, South Carolina.

Nichol, Howard T. "Boykins, Pheasants and South Dakota." *Spaniels in the Field,* Spring 1986. Reprinted in *Boykin Spaniel Society Newsletter* 20 (October 1, 1996).

Niedringhaus, Lindsay. "Man's (and Woman's) Best Friend: South Carolina's Boykin Spaniel." *Columbia Metropolitan* 19 (June 2008): 36–39.

Parker, E. "Many People Interested in History of Spaniel," letter to the editor. *State* (Columbia, S.C.), June 9, 1978, A16. A Camden resident wrote this letter after attending a May 23 meeting of the Senate Agriculture Committee, which was debating making the Boykin spaniel the state dog. Parker's message was that, like him, "Many people who belong to the Boykin Society do not own one of the dogs, but are interested in its history."

Rainey, Steve. "Boykin Field Trials Offer Exciting Day." *Lexington Dispatch-News,* February 20, 1985. A story about a day of field trialing with Cal Watkins, his father, Bill, and their dog Dux Back at Gresham, South Carolina, with the Carolina Boykin Spaniel Retriever Club.

Reynolds, Henry. "Boykin Spaniels Were Impressive on Mississippi Dove Hunts." *Memphis Commercial Appeal,* September 16, 1979, D9. An article praising performance of Jim and Mary Kinnear's dogs and discussing the history of Boykins in Memphis, the breed's origin, and the Boykin Spaniel Society.

Richbourg, Eppie. "Little Spaniel Sports Special Qualities." *Charleston News and Courier,* November 6, 1983, E1. A feature article on the origin and history of the Boykin spaniel and the experiences of Boykin spaniel breeder George Brown Campbell, a physical-education teacher from Dillon, South Carolina.

Riddick, Sheila. "The Boykin Spaniel Subject of New Book." *Camden Chronicle-Independent,* January 30, 1998, B2. A review of the 1997 edition of *The Boykin Spaniel* with information on the dog's origins and Camden connections.

Rine, Josephine Z. *The World of Dogs.* Garden City, N.Y.: Doubleday, 1965. Boykin entry on p. 193.

Robertson, Pat. "Better than Good Enough, Moore's Boykin Spaniel Brings Rave Reviews." *State* (Columbia, S.C.), February 15, 1984, D15. Article about artist Burton Moore's Boykin spaniel painting, which was the centerpiece of fund-raising efforts for the Harry Hampton Memorial Wildlife Fund.

———. "Books About Dogs Perfect For Hunters." *State* (Columbia, S.C.), December 13, 1998, C13. A review of three books that calls the 1997 edition of *The Boykin Spaniel* "the definitive book on South Carolina's State Dog."

———. "Boy Finds Success in Training Boykins." *State* (Columbia, S.C.), June 11, 2000, C11. Profile of fifteen-year-old outdoorsman James Bedenbaugh of Prosperity, South Carolina, who trains and handles Boykin spaniels from the Rocky Ridges line.

———. "Boykin Spaniel Day." *State* (Columbia, S.C.), August 22, 1984, D6. Story about Gov. Richard Riley's declaring opening day of dove-hunting season as Boykin Spaniel Day. A photograph features the governor with Boykin spaniel Sarge and an art print of a Boykin by Burton Moore.

———. "Boykins Are Here to Stay." *Columbia Record,* May 29, 1980, D6. Column about the history of the breed and the Boykin Spaniel Society, its first field trial, and the desirability of making the Boykin the State Dog.

———. "A Dog with 'Personality.'" *State* (Columbia, S.C.), April 12, 1998, C17. Article on the first edition of *The Boykin Spaniel: South Carolina's Dog.*

———. "Dove Dogs of the South." *Outdoor Life,* South Edition, September 1980.

———. "First in the Field." *South Carolina Wildlife* 30 (September–October 1983): 22–29. This issue features Phillip Jones's photographs of Cocoa, owned by George Brown Campbell of Dillon, South Carolina, on the front cover and Coach Campbell's Flea Baggins, Cocoa's grandson, on the back cover.

———. "Hubba Bubba Headed for an Early Retirement." *State* (Columbia, S.C.), May 5, 1996, C14. Report on winners of the National Boykin Spaniel Society hunting test with a profile of the 1996 open champion, Hubba Bubba, and his owner-trainer, Richard Coe of Summerville, South Carolina. After this win Hubba Bubba was retired from competition and breeding because of chronic hip dysplasia.

———. "It's Now Time to Make the Boykin State Dog." *State* (Columbia, S.C.), May 13, 1984, D14. An article offering arguments for making the Boykin state dog; includes a photograph of Mike Creel's first Boykin, Booger.

———. "Minnesota Man Making Imprint on Duck Stamp." *State* (Columbia, S.C.), February 11, 1988, B1. An article reporting that Jim Killen has become first two-time winner of the South Carolina's duck-stamp contest, this time with a painting of a Boykin spaniel holding a wigeon.

———. "Mr. Mick Is Boykin Spaniel National Test Winner." *State* (Columbia, S.C.), April 26, 1998, C13. Report on the entire results of the 1998 Boykin Spaniel Society National Hunting Test with all four classes. Mr. Mick, owned and handled by Curtis Hodge of Sumter, South Carolina, won first place in open.

———. "Pocotaligo's Coffee Gets Better With Age." *State* (Columbia, S.C.), July 9, 1995, C10. A profile of eleven-year old Coffee, owned by Kim Parkman of Sumter. At that time Coffee was only Boykin spaniel to hold both a Hunting Retriever Champion title from United Kennel Club and Master Hunting Retriever title from North American Hunting Retriever Association.

———. "Pocotaligo's Coffee Named Nation's Top Boykin Spaniel." *State* (Columbia, S.C.), May 18, 1988, C6. A report on the 1988 National Boykin Spaniel Retriever Trial results with a photograph of the 1988 overall open champion, Pocotaligo's Coffee.

———. "Pope's Dixie Blair Claims Consecutive National Titles." *State* (Columbia, S.C.), May 3, 1995, C6. Report of the 1995 National Field Test results with a profile of the 1995 open champion, Dixie Blair, owned by Bubba Pope of Columbia, South Carolina.

———. "Pope's Dixie Blair Developing into Legend among Retrievers." *State* (Columbia, S.C.), May, 15, 1994, C10. A report on the 1994 National Field Test results with a profile on the 1994 open champion, Dixie Blair.

———. "St. Matthews Dog Wins Second National Test." *State* (Columbia, S.C.), April 18, 1999, C16. Report on the second open win for King's Curlee Gurlee, owned by Pam Kadlec of Starke, Florida, in the 1999 Boykin Spaniel National Hunting Test.

———. "Sumter Dog Wins Boykin Field Trial." *Columbia Record*, May 29, 1980, D6. A full account of the first Boykin Spaniel Society field trial with a photograph of Nat Gist of Sumter and his dog Charlie Brown.

———. "Taxidermist's Payment Becomes Open Champ." *State* (Columbia, S.C.), May 4, 1997, C12. Report on the 1997 Boykin Spaniel Society National

Hunting Test winners with a profile of the 1997 open champion, King's Curlee Gurlee.

———. "Texas Dog Overall Champ in Boykin Spaniel Trials." *State* (Columbia, S.C.), May 22, 1985, E6. Results of the annual Boykin field trial at which Boykin's Thunder, owned by Cue D. Boykin of Austin, Texas, was the overall open champion.

———. "Turkey Dogs—No Joke," in *Carolina's Hunting Heritage*, edited by John Culler, 51–52. Columbia: South Carolina Wildlife, 1978.

Seifert, William Eugene "Bud." "Boykin Breed Originated in Spartanburg." *Spartanburg Journal*, October 31, 1969, 9. Article in a series about pets.

Siddons, Anne Rivers. *Sweetwater Creek*. New York: HarperCollins, 2005. The first novel in which a principal character is a Boykin spaniel, a dog named Elvis.

South Carolina Wildlife. "Boykin Spaniel: Official State Dog." *South Carolina Wildlife* 32 (July–August 1985): 61.

———. "First-Place Duck Stamp." *South Carolina Wildlife* 35 (May–June 1988): 60.

S.C. Wildlife and Marine Resources Department. "Boykin Spaniel Day Opens Dove Season." Press release no. 84-220, August 27, 1984. Announcement that on August 17 Gov. Dick Riley signed a proclamation designating September 1, 1984, as South Carolina's first official Boykin Spaniel Day. Two photographs were released, one with Boykin spaniel Sarge on the governor's desk with a group of people and a second with Governor Riley standing beside Sarge, who is seated in the governor's chair.

———. "Hampton Fund Offers Boykin Spaniel Print." Press release no. 84-54, February 27, 1984. Announcement of a fund-raising project for the Harry Hampton Memorial Wildlife, sales of the print *South Carolina's Own*, by Burton E. Moore Jr., and auctioning of the original for $10,000 on February 17 at the Southeastern Wildlife Exposition.

"S.C. Wildlife Features Native Boykin Spaniel." *Carolina Outdoors* (Columbia, S.C.), October 17, 1975, 6. A story discussing stories in the September–October 1975 issue of *South Carolina Wildlife*, including Mike Creel's article on the Boykin spaniel.

State editorial writers. "The State's Dog." *State* (Columbia, S.C.), March 10, 1985, B2. Editorial stating "State Rep. Robert Sheheen, D-Camden, Chairman of House Judiciary Committee, has used his considerable influence to promote a law declaring the retriever as the state's official canine. The Boykin spaniel doesn't have much to worry about a future dog fight in the Legislature over his official status since he is one of a kind. But what happens when the official state dog comes across the official state wild game bird, the wild turkey."

Sternberg, Dick. *Upland Game Birds*. Minnetonka, Minn.: CyDecosse, 1995. The brief section on the Boykin spaniel includes a photograph of Mike Creel's Booger on a boat dock at Wood Creek Lake, near Pontiac, South Carolina.

Strung, Norman. "Chief and the Pistol." *Field and Stream*, May 1982. A story about how Strung's Labrador retriever, Chief, learned to accept Pistol, Strung's new Boykin spaniel.

Surratt, W. Clark. "An Official State Dog???" *State* (Columbia, S.C.), February 10, 1978, B1. Report on the state-dog bill introduced February 9, 1978, by Sen. Arnold Goodstein of Charleston, which passed the Senate but not the House.

Sweet, Ethel Wylly, Robert M. Smith Jr., and Henry D. Boykin II. *Camden: Homes and Heritage*. Camden, S.C.: Kershaw County Historical Society, 1978.

Ullman, Hans J. *Spaniels: Everything about Breeding Care, Nutrition and Diseases*. Woodbury, N.Y.: Barrons Educational Series, 1982. The Boykin spaniel is called the "Boylien [*sic*] spaniel" in the American water spaniel section.

Walkowicz, Chris, and Bonnie Wilcox. *Successful Dog Breeding: The Complete Handbook of Canine Midwifery*. New York: Prentice Hall, 1985.

Wenzell, Ron. "A Breed Apart." *State* (Columbia, S.C.), January 31, 1985, B1. A lengthy article tracing the history of the Boykin spaniel and the Boykin Spaniel Society. Includes color photographs by Maxie Roberts of Boykins afield with owners Janice Caulder and Ned Beard.

Wheeler, Nancy. "South Carolina's Native Son." *Carolina Game & Fish*, March 1995, 12–13.

Wilcox, Bonnie, and Chris Walkowicz. *Atlas of Dog Breeds of the World*. Neptune, N.J.: T.F.H., 1989. Boykin entry on p. 224.

Wolters, Richard. "America's Third Dog." *Connoisseur* 218 (October 1988) 154–61. The author refers to the Boykin spaniel as the third retriever breed with American origins, behind the Chesapeake Bay retriever and American water spaniel

———. *Duck Dogs—All About the Retrievers*. New York: Dutton, 1990. In a seventeen-page chapter titled "Another Spaniel, the Boykin" the author repeats much of the Boykin spaniel's origin story from the 1975 South Carolina Wildlife article, referring to the story as a tall tale or "cartwheel."

INDEX

Page numbers in italics indicate illustrations.

ABOUT THE AUTHORS

South Carolina native **MIKE CREEL** is a retired public affairs specialist for the state's Department of Natural Resources and a longtime writer and photographer for *South Carolina Wildlife* magazine. Creel is a graduate of the University of South Carolina School of Journalism and recipient of the 1997 Harry R. E. Hampton "Woods and Waters" Conservation Memorial Award for journalism, given by the South Carolina Wildlife Federation. He is a self-taught authority on native plant propagation and discovered a new native azalea species in 1999.

LYNN KELLEY was a professor of political science in Missouri and a dean at three different institutions of higher education in Kentucky and Pennsylvania before moving to South Carolina in 1991. He served as a division associate director with the state's Commission on Higher Education until his retirement in 2009, when he was presented with the State of South Carolina's Order of the Silver Crescent for his distinguished service. Kelley is also the author of a children's book, *The First Boykin Spaniels: The Story of Dumpy and Singo.*